Cultures of Resistance

Critical Issues in Crime and Society

Raymond J. Michalowski and Luis A. Fernandez, Series Editors

Critical Issues in Crime and Society is oriented toward critical analysis of contemporary problems in crime and justice. The series is open to a broad range of topics including specific types of crime, wrongful behavior by economically or politically powerful actors, controversies over justice system practices, and issues related to the intersection of identity, crime, and justice. It is committed to offering thoughtful works that will be accessible to scholars and professional criminologists, general readers, and students.

For a list of titles in the series, see the last page of the book.

Cultures of Resistance

Collective Action and Rationality in the Anti-Terror Age

HEIDI REYNOLDS-STENSON

Rutgers University Press
New Brunswick, Camden, and Newark, New Jersey, and London

Library of Congress Cataloging-in-Publication Data

Names: Reynolds-Stenson, Heidi, author.
Title: Cultures of resistance : collective action and rationality in the anti-terror age / Heidi Reynolds-Stenson.
Description: New Brunswick : Rutgers University Press, [2022] | Series: Critical Issues in Crime and Society | Includes bibliographical references and index.
Identifiers: LCCN 2021039401 | ISBN 9781978823730 (Paperback : acid-free paper) | ISBN 9781978823747 (Hardback : acid-free paper) | ISBN 9781978823754 (ePub) | ISBN 9781978823761 (mobi) | ISBN 9781978823778 (PDF)
Subjects: LCSH: Political persecution. | State-sponsored terrorism. | Social movements. | Radicalization. | Group identity.
Classification: LCC JC571 .R4878 2022 | DDC 323/.044—dc23/eng/20220211
LC record available at https://lccn.loc.gov/2021039401

A British Cataloging-in-Publication record for this book is available from the British Library.

www.rutgersuniversitypress.org

Manufactured in the United States of America

To my mom, Anne, who taught me the power
of both protest and the written word.

To my mom, Anne, who taught me the power
of both protest and the written word.

Contents

Cultures of Resistance

1

Repression, Mobilization, and the Cultural Construction of Rationality

A million Chinese civilians, mostly students, gathered in Tiananmen Square in Beijing to demand democratization in late spring of 1989, triggered in part by the death of a popular reform-minded former Communist Party leader. For weeks, they marched and rallied. They held vigils and hunger strikes and teach-ins. But, on June 4, over 200,000 soldiers arrived to put an end to the demonstrations. The students were told they had an hour to disperse, but within minutes, tanks began running over demonstrators, many of whom were sitting with arms linked, while soldiers opened fire on the crowd. Some demonstrators tried to escape but were unable to do so. Others fought back, burning tanks and overturning military trucks. Captured in a now-iconic photo, a lone man stood in front of a line of tanks as they headed for Tiananmen Square. When it was all over, thousands were dead (Lusher 2017). The result of this brutal repression was the effective killing of the pro-democracy student movement in China. Even mourning the dead, or speaking publicly about the events of June 4, was forbidden. Today, the anniversary of the massacre is still marked each year by such heavy-handed online censorship that many in China refer to it ironically as "Internet Maintenance Day" (Thien 2017).

The massacre at Tiananmen Square is a case in which state repression of a popular movement "worked." The movement was crushed, and dissent was largely silenced. Nearly two decades earlier, at an anti-war demonstration at Kent State University in the United States, military personnel also opened fire on a crowd of student demonstrators, but with very different results. The killing of four students, and injuring of nine others, led to national outrage and galvanized the student and anti-war movements. In response, students struck on campuses across the country, causing hundreds of colleges and universities to shut down (Roberts 2010). The next weekend, 100,000 people gathered in Washington, D.C., to protest the deployment of U.S. troops to Cambodia. The incident at Kent State fueled the anti-war movement, helped increase radicalism on college campuses across the country, prompted members of the Weathermen to bomb National Guard headquarters days later (Berger 2006), and marked the beginning of the end for the increasingly unpopular Nixon administration (Haldeman and Dimona 1978).

Mixed Effects of Repression

These two contrasting examples illustrate what decades of social movement research has concluded: that repression may harm or even kill movements for change, but, in some cases, it backfires and actually breathes new life into a movement. Repression refers to efforts by the state or other actors to thwart or contain social movements. It is not always as visible or as lethal as the military firing on a crowd of students; it can also include riot police using tear gas or other "less lethal" weapons on protesters, tax codes that restrict social movement organizations, covert surveillance of activists, or mobs of citizens attacking protesters, as segregationists did during the civil rights movement (Earl 2003). But the point is that the historical record suggests that repression can have wildly disparate effects on mobilization. In some cases, like the brutal crackdown on the pro-democracy student movement in China, repression has a chilling effect on dissent and deters future protest. In other cases, like the Kent State shootings, repression can fuel mobilization, embolden activists, and shift public sympathy in favor of a movement.

Social movement scholars have amassed much evidence of both a positive and a negative relationship between repression and mobilization, and theories have been developed to explain both effects (for reviews of this debate, see Davenport 2007; Earl and Soule 2010; Earl 2011a). Some scholars argue that repression should generally deter mobilization, because it increases the costs of participation (Tilly 1978). Lending credence to this theory, many studies find that repression can be effective at discouraging participation or otherwise quelling protest (Fantasia 1988; Muller and Weede 1990; White 1993; Churchill 1994; Earl 2005; Davenport 2010; Earl and Beyer 2014). For example, Ward Churchill (1994) describes how the federal counterinsurgency campaign against the American Indian Movement (AIM) following the Alcatraz Occupation (1969–1971) culminated in the brutal repression of a protest on the Pine Ridge

Reservation in 1973. The incident left two activists dead (and one U.S. marshal paralyzed), and over 500 AIM activists, including the entirety of the leadership of the organization, in jail. With the leadership embroiled in lengthy trials and the majority of fundraising and organizing capacity directed toward bailing out and defending the arrested activists, the movement, which had seemed so strong—and so promising to many—coming out of the Alcatraz Occupation, was effectively dead by the late 1970s.

Others argue that repression leads to more intense mobilization because it reinforces boundaries between activists and opponents (drawing on classic works by Simmel 1955; Coser 1956), confirms activists' sense that the state or other targets are in need of reform or revolution, or provokes emotions, such as outrage, which may motivate further mobilization (e.g., White 1989). In fact, many studies have found evidence of repression backfiring—escalating mobilization or galvanizing commitment (Hirsch 1990; Khawaja 1993; Loveman 1998; Wood 2001; Einwohner 2003; Almeida 2003, 2008; Jenkins and Schock 2004; Francisco 2004, 2005; Zwerman and Steinhoff 2005; Ondetti 2006; Ortiz 2007; Odabaş and Reynolds-Stenson 2017; Adam-Troïan, Çelebi, and Mahfud 2020). For example, Khawaja's (1993) study on resistance in the Palestinian West Bank from 1976 to 1985 found that, with few exceptions, repressive incidents were followed by an increase in the rate of mobilization. In a more recent example, Odabaş and Reynolds-Stenson (2017) demonstrate, through analysis of survey data from participants in the Gezi Park protests in Istanbul, Turkey, in 2013, how a harsh police response to a small occupation in the park, publicized through social media, inspired scores of new protesters to join, transforming an initially small sit-in protest into a massive nationwide movement.

In short, extant research suggests that repression has the potential to both deter and backfire. In fact, one recent article summarized research in this area by saying, "After 40 years, we still know very little about how state repression influences political dissent. In fact, to date, every possible relationship, including no influence, has been found" (Sullivan, Loyle, and Davenport 2012, 1). The task for researchers has become teasing out under what circumstances, and in what form, repression has one effect rather than the other.

To this end, various contingent factors moderating the impact of repression on mobilization have been identified, such as the form (Barkan 1984; Koopmans 1997), timing (Rasler 1996; Sullivan, Loyle, and Davenport 2012), consistency (Lichbach 1987), or perceived legitimacy of the repression (Opp and Roehl 1990; Hess and Martin 2006). For example, Barkan (1984) demonstrates that legalistic forms of repression, such as the arrest and trial of activists, were effective at deterring mobilization in the civil rights movement, whereas violent repression was not. And Sullivan, Loyle, and Davenport (2012) demonstrate how the effect of repression can depend on recent trends in mobilization. Using newspaper data on conflict between the British state and Irish nationalists in Northern Ireland from 1968 to 1974, a period known as the "Troubles," the authors show that when mobilization is waning, repression can breathe new life into a movement, but when mobilization is on an upswing, repression has a chilling effect.

Others have argued that the relationship between repression and mobilization is not linear. In other words, they argue that repression's effect depends on the level or intensity of repression (e.g., Muller 1985). Various nonlinear relationships have been hypothesized, including a normal U-curve (Shadmehr 2014), inverted U-curve (Khawaja 1993), normal lying S-curve (Neidhardt 1989), and inverted lying S-curve (Francisco 1995).

With a few exceptions, most work on contingent repression effects focuses on the state side of the state–movement relationship, working to reconcile conflicting evidence on repression effects through examining exactly what the state does to movements, when it does it, and with what intensity or consistency. This approach assumes that the specifics of the repressive actions hold the key to explaining variation in consequences, and by implication that, if properly specified, repressive actions should have consistent effects across individual activists and across different organizations and movements. The idea that some individuals, organizations, or movements may be affected very differently by objectively similar repressive actions has been much less explored.

In one notable exception, Opp and Roehl (1990) found, using a panel study of antinuclear activists, that repression can embolden activists when it is seen as illegitimate and uncalled for (e.g., when the protest was peaceful and legal) and, furthermore, that this radicalization effect was stronger for those who are integrated into networks encouraging protest. And Linden and Klandermans (2006) demonstrate, through interviews with extreme-right activists in the Netherlands, that how individual activists perceive state repression, as well as "soft" repression such as social stigma, depends in part on how they came to the movement in the first place. Those who sought out or were attracted to the movement early on tended to see repression and stigma as a badge of honor, while those who had become involved primarily because someone they knew was involved, or who otherwise "fell into" it in a less intentional way, struggled more when they experienced state repression and social stigma.

What these two studies highlight, and what I argue we need more research on, is the subjective experience of repression. Taking care to specify exactly what we mean by "repression" in a given case (e.g., exactly what is being done to dissidents, when, and by whom) is an important step toward untangling the mass of conflicting evidence on the relationship between repression and mobilization. But this will only get us so far if we do not also attend to the other side of the relationship and try to understand how different individuals, groups, and movements absorb and respond differently to objectively similar acts of repression. I will argue that paying attention to how rationality is culturally constructed within protest groups, and how this in turn shapes the subjective experience of repression, provides a new avenue for making sense of the conflicting evidence on repression effects. But doing so requires bridging a long-standing divide in social movement theory and research: that between rational choice–based models of collective action and those that attend to the cultural and emotional dynamics of protest.

Toward a Synthesized Theory of Collection Action

In 1996, John Lofland described the study of social movements as "a special case of the study of contention among deeply conflicting realities" (p. 3). This conception of the field calls our attention to the fact that social movements are, at their heart, battles over meaning and values—over defining what is and what ought to be. Yet, from reading much of the scholarship on social movements since the early 1970s, one would not know this. The "rational turn" that transformed social movement studies beginning in the 1960s and 1970s (Olson 1965; Oberschall 1973; McCarthy and Zald 1977; Opp 1989; Tarrow 1994; Lichbach 1998) has stimulated many important advances, but these advances have mostly been confined to the relatively narrow set of questions that it guides scholars to ask—questions about the resources, structures, and organizations that provide the material base for mobilization. This paradigm shift was critical to moving the subfield forward, but, as many before me have argued, something was also lost along the way. Research became largely focused on how people mobilize, almost giving the impression that we stopped wondering why they do. Efforts to correct for this myopia have largely amounted to the assertion that factors like ideology, identity, and emotions "matter too," with little dialogue between these "cultural" and "rational" approaches to understanding collective action.

After outlining both the "rational turn" and the "cultural turn" that have occurred in social movement studies in recent decades, and their respective limitations, I argue that what is needed is a synthesized theory of collective action—in other words, a theory of why and how people come to participate in collective action and protest (Opp 2009; Jasper 2010). As I will describe, even social movement theories that are generally focused on the meso level of social movement organizations (SMOs) and movements, or the macro level of states and societies, tend to come with implicit (or sometimes explicit) individual-level mechanisms and assumptions about why and how individuals come to act together. I argue that not only should we work to make these underlying assumptions of social movement theories more explicit, but that we must also overcome the divide between "rational" and "cultural" theories of collective action and move toward a more integrated theory, one that does not assume rationality and culture are antithetical, and instead appreciates the ways that individual rationality is constructed, mediated, and obscured by collective practices and meanings. I begin to develop this approach in this chapter and demonstrate it throughout the book by examining how the dynamics of repression—one of the most frequently cited costs of participation in collective action—are fundamentally altered by the practices and meanings that activist milieus make available to the individuals embedded in them. More generally, I demonstrate how social movement actors' rationality is fundamentally shaped by the protest cultures in which they participate.

The "Rational Turn" in the Study of Social Movements

Until the 1960s, most academic theorizing and research on social movements explained the phenomenon as a spontaneous collective response to the strain or relative deprivation experienced by those at the margins of a rapidly changing society (Blumer 1939). In general, there was an assumption, if not an outright assertion, that protest was irrational, counterproductive, and something to be prevented whenever possible (Buechler 2004). In a particularly extreme example of this line of thinking, Le Bon (1960 [1895]) argued that some crowds had a psychology of their own, distinct from the sum of the psyches of the individuals who form them. Individuality and independent thought vanish, creating a groupthink that is irrational, impulsive, highly emotional, and suggestible. As he put it, "by the mere fact that he forms part of an organized crowd, a man descends several rungs in the ladder of civilization" (p. 33). Decades later, Eric Hoffer described those involved in social movements as "desperate fanatics" driven by frustration. Hoffer's "true believers" seek to lose themselves in, and give themselves over to, a cause because they otherwise lack a sense of identity or meaning. He argued this behavior was inherently irrational because "self-sacrifice is an unreasonable act" that is avoided by normal people with fulfilling lives (1951, 79).

The rising tide of protest in the United States and Western Europe in the 1960s caused sociologists and other scholars to revise some of their negative assumptions about protest and consider the possibility that protest might constitute a legitimate, strategic—and sometimes even effective—political expression (Tarrow 1994). Many scholars took to heart Michael Schwartz's assertion that "people who join protest organizations are at least as rational as those who study them" (1976, 135). A theory of protest as rational behavior developed, borrowing heavily from theories and conversations happening within economics, specifically rational actor theory (RAT). Central to RAT, the utility maximization hypothesis holds that individuals seek to satisfy their desires or needs while taking into account the constraints imposed upon them.

Rational choice models of human behavior have a long history in the social sciences, with several variants, but here I am concerned specifically with how they have been applied to explain participation in collective action and protest. Scholars in this tradition examine how a seemingly irrational behavior is made rational. Most famously, Olson (1965) argued that because collective action, by definition, seeks a public good—meaning that even those who do not participate can enjoy the benefits—a rational actor would choose to "free ride," to reap the benefits while avoiding the costs of participation. To overcome this "collective action problem," participants must receive "selective incentives," benefits that come only through participation and tip the cost-benefit calculus in favor of action. Olson (1965) primarily emphasized material selective incentives—for example (in the context of social movements), the direct benefits one receives from being a member of a labor union or an advocacy organization like the American Association of Retired Persons.

Oberschall (1973) and McCarthy and Zald (1977) applied Olson's logic to social movements, while Lichbach (1998) later detailed a variety of ways that social movements can overcome the free-rider problem and facilitate collective action. In contrast to Le Bon's unthinking hooligans and Hoffer's gullible fanatics, these new approaches "depicted shrewd entrepreneurs, rational actors coolly calculating the costs and benefits of participation, and people mobilized by incentives rather than by passionate anger or righteous indignation" (Goodwin, Jasper, and Polletta 2000, 70–71). While this approach has been critiqued and modified since, the assumption that individuals will only participate in collective action when it is made rational to do so, and that making collective action rational requires resources and organizations, remains fundamental to modern social movement studies. Arguably still the two most dominant theoretical approaches to understanding social movements, resource mobilization and political process/opportunity theory are both built upon these rational choice assumptions of human behavior. Whereas resource mobilization focuses on how costs and benefits are shaped by the resources and organizational infrastructure available for mobilization (Jenkins and Perrow 1977; McCarthy and Zald 1977, 2002; Morris 1981), political process/opportunity theory focuses on how costs and benefits are shaped by the expansion and contraction of opportunities in the external political environment (Tilly 1978; Kitschelt 1986; McAdam 1999; Meyer 2004).

Taking Stock of What Was Lost in the Rational Turn

Almost as soon as it gained popularity among social movement scholars, RAT came under fire. In 1977, Fireman and Gamson warned: "Beware of economists bearing gifts. Their models are catching the fancy of a number of sociologists interested in social movements. . . . But the economists' models carry their own set of blinders" (p. 1). Criticisms leveled against RAT by social movement scholars tend to fall under three main interrelated arguments: (1) its reductionism and attempt at a universal theory of action fails to capture the complexity and range of human motivation and forms of collective action (Fireman and Gamson 1977; Ferree 1992; Stryker, Owens, and White 2000; Crossley 2002); (2) it is unable to explain why actors seek the ends that they do, or how preferences or values are formed and reinforced (Taylor 1988; Jagger 1989; Crossley 2002; Jasper 2010); and (3) efforts to correct for these shortcomings by incorporating cultural and emotional factors into RAT as "soft incentives" render it tautological (Fireman and Gamson 1977; Knoke 1988; Jasper 2010). My aim is not to duplicate these existing discussions of the limitations of the rational choice framework as it is applied to social movements, but to focus, on a broad level, on what was lost in this rational turn and how this relates to the question of repression's effects on movements.

In the shift to focusing on the material, strategic, and rational foundations of protest, the idea that people could be driven to act by their deeply held beliefs or strongly felt emotions, rather than by narrow self-interest, was often lost. Along with it, the idea that groups could have a powerful influence on how individuals think and feel—a fact that had been used by collective behaviorists as proof of the wickedness of crowds—was rejected. But this rejection, in fact, betrayed a point of agreement between rational choice theorists and collective behaviorists over the inherent undesirability of such influence. Collective behaviorists argued that individuals, when they become part of a group, are willing to act in ways that they would be unwilling to do on their own. At the risk of ruffling feathers, I would argue that they were actually quite right about this. In fact, this entire book can be read as an illustration of this fact. Their mistake was not in thinking that groups have a powerful effect on how individuals think, feel, and act, but in thinking that this was, in all instances, a bad thing. To challenge accepted authority and divest from dominant ways of thinking and living, one almost always needs others with whom to do this.

The protest cultures that emerge in social movement communities and organizations provide individuals with a critically needed alternative source for support, interpretations, and identity that can replace, or at least compete with, those available in the dominant culture. Just because individuals could not, or would not, often make such a break in thinking and acting "on their own" does not mean it is irrational, or inherently undesirable. Nor is this unique to social movements. Concerns about the "mob mentality" of protest groups seem to be based on the false assumption that outside such groups—in mainstream society—individuals are not similarly swayed by those around them. But, whether in the context of social movements or not, humans are social creatures and we construct our ways of living and thinking together. This co-creation is explicit and laid bare in protest cultures and countercultures, but is no less present (even if much more taken for granted) in the broader society.

Therefore, the social movement actor emerged from the "rational turn" redeemed, but only by being stripped of her full range of possible motivations and of her capacity to be moved by others, by being remade as a calculating, autonomous individual. This paradigm shift did not leave much (if any) room for ideologies, identities, and emotions to drive social movement actors' behavior, but it also caused us to lose sight of the fundamentally sociological fact that individuals' ideologies, identities, and emotions are forged through interaction with others, and, more generally, led us to underestimate the power that groups can have over individuals.

The "Cultural Turn" in the Study of Social Movements

Social movement studies has experienced a "cultural turn" in recent decades, mirroring that in American sociology in general (Friedland and Mohr 2004). Especially beginning in the 1990s, social movement scholars started discussing the importance of concepts like "collective identity" (Taylor and Whittier 1992), "consciousness raising" (Hirsch 1990; Reger 2004), and "narrative" (Polletta 1998). Not only scholars with a more cultural bent, but even those rooted in more structural traditions, were influenced by this turn. McAdam, the father of political process theory, began to argue that "cognitive liberation," the belief that a situation is both unjust and changeable, is necessary for movement emergence (in addition to the structural opportunities that were the focus of his theory) because, as he aptly pointed out, "mediating between opportunity and action are people and the subjective meanings they attach to their situations" (McAdam 1999, 48).

There was a growing awareness that how social movement actors thought and talked about what they were doing, among themselves and with their opponents and the broader public (often through the media), was a worthwhile subject of study in its own right. In addition to the material base that had become the focus of the field, many argued that there was also a symbolic dimension of mobilization that was no less important. They pointed out that the blind spots created by the existing paradigm not only led us to miss important aspects of movements (Eyerman and Jamison 1991; Snow and Oliver 1994), but to privilege some kinds of movements (e.g., those making reformist material claims against the state) over others (e.g., those striving to change individuals' attitudes or lifestyles or create more far-reaching and radical social change; Goodwin and Jasper 1999; Snow 2004b; Armstrong and Bernstein 2007).

Framing theorists, in many ways, can be credited with opening the door for this "cultural turn" and for bringing grievances, ideology, and culture back into the study of social movements (Snow et al. 1986; Snow and Benford 1992; Snow 2004a). What this perspective offered that the collective behaviorists before them did not was a focus on the factors that "politicize discontent" (Buechler 2011, 143). Resource mobilization and political process/opportunity theorists started from the observation that grievances are ubiquitous while social movements are not, and explained this disconnect in terms of varying levels of resources and opportunities that are needed for social movement emergence. But framing theorists problematized the assumption that grievances, perceived as such, can be taken for granted. They argued that whether issues or situations are perceived as political in the first place depends on the interpretive frame through which the issue at hand is viewed. Frames take the experiences and observations of everyday life and construct them into a more cohesive story of "what's going on" by drawing attention to some details and not others (Snow 2004a). We all use frames every day to make sense of the world, but frames in the context of social movements construct a particular kind of story—one in which the situation or issue becomes defined not only as unjust but as correctable. The effective telling of this story is necessary if grievances, or potential grievances, are to lead to action. In other words, framing theory promised a way to understand how McAdam's (1999) "cognitive liberation" is achieved.

In addition to developing a shared sense of the problem to be solved, and those at fault to be targeted, movements must also develop a shared sense of themselves as a collective. Therefore, the development and elaboration of the concept of "collective identity" followed soon after and can be seen as the next major step in the cultural turn. Scholars have argued that collective identity, that sense of "we-ness" that often underlies collective action for social change, is both a precondition and a product of mobilization (Klandermans 2004). In response to the recognition of identity as an important factor in mobilization, some began to focus on how such an identity is constructed and how individual identities become aligned with collective identities in ways that inspire and sustain movement participation (Taylor and Whittier 1992; Snow and McAdam 1997; Hunt and Benford 2004).

A Subfield Divided

These works have provided an important corrective to research in the resource mobilization and political opportunity/process traditions that emphasized the structural and material conditions facilitating and constraining mobilization and carried with them narrow conceptions of rationality inherited from rational actor theory. But, because this line of research has not generally been explicitly reconciled with RAT-inspired approaches to social movements, this has led to a subfield that remains theoretically divided. Melucci has argued that "the study of social movements has always been divided by the dualistic legacy of structural analysis as a precondition for collective action and the analysis of individual motivations. These parallel, and sometimes intertwined, sets of explanations never fill the gap between behavior and meaning, between 'objective' conditions and 'subjective' motives and orientations" (1995, 42). He is not alone in this assessment of the subfield (see Polletta 1997, 1999; Goldberg 2003). This sense of a divided subfield comes from the fact that this new cultural work has generally not been integrated with the existing paradigm, but has rather developed alongside it, explored as a kind of "residual category" (Polletta and Jasper 2001, 285). When culture has been integrated with more structural RAT-based theories, rather than truly bringing the two approaches together, cultural factors have been fit into the rational choice framework. They have been incorporated only by being framed in the logic and language of rational choice, leaving the rational choice paradigm fundamentally unchanged. To work toward a more complete theory of collective action, I argue that we must acknowledge the thoroughly cultural nature of rationality—the collective construction not only of costs and benefits, but of the ends actors seek, and of the identities that obscure, constrain, and at times preclude individual "choice."

Doing so requires a clear definition of "culture" and a theory of how (or if) it guides action. Sociologists of culture have explicitly or implicitly defined culture in a variety of ways, perhaps giving the sense that there is no consensus on what is meant by the term even among those who study it. Varying definitions reflect differences in the degree of agency actors are presumed to have in relation to culture, the degree of coherence or underlying logic to cultural systems, and the degree to which culture is understood as something located within us, in the objects we create, or in the practices in which we participate. I will use a simple yet inclusive definition of culture: a set of available meanings generated through and generative of practice. When a connection between culture and action is explicitly stated or (more often) implied in social movement research, it is often based on the assumption that culture influences action primarily through values, a notion that is heavily contested by sociologists of culture (Swidler 1986, 1995). As I will argue and demonstrate in later chapters, defining the ends or values that actors seek is only one way, and maybe neither the most powerful nor the most common way, that culture influences action, and practice theories of culture can help social movement scholars to develop more sophisticated models of culture in (collective) action.

Collective Action, Collective Rationality

Most research on repression still assumes a RAT model of human behavior and has arguably been less influenced by the cultural turn than other areas of social movement research. Within this rational choice framework, repression has been viewed as one of the key factors that can raise the costs of engaging in protest and therefore, all else being equal, is expected to hamper dissent. In fact, for Tilly (1978), this was integral to the definition of repression, which he defined broadly as actions that increase the cost of protest. Repression can be costly to individuals, organizations, and movements in multiple ways. Most obviously, when states engage in repression, the risk of physical harm to protesters is greater. Like the students who died in Tiananmen Square or at Kent State, some even pay the ultimate cost for their political convictions. Individuals and organizations can also experience legal consequences, which can take a great deal of money and time to resolve. The time, energy, and resources that organizations and movements put toward fighting criminal charges and otherwise responding to repression by the state can take their focus away from their original cause or struggle. And individuals are sometimes left with criminal records that follow them through their lives and can hinder employment and other opportunities. Therefore, it is no wonder that repression is viewed, through the rational choice lens, as a cost and as something that helps explain why some individuals choose not to participate in protest, why some organizations collapse, and why some movements fail.

Rational choice explanations have also been developed to account for cases where repression backfires or fails to deter (for example, Opp and Roehl's [1990] study of antinuclear activists discussed previously or White's [1989] study of the IRA). While these studies provide some helpful insights, the rational choice perspective has been much more helpful in explaining those cases in which repression deters rather than those in which it backfires. To really make sense of the heterogeneous effects of repression, we need a broader conception of rationality, one that attends to its collectively constructed nature.

As I will illustrate in subsequent chapters, rationality in the context of protest is collectively constructed in at least three ways. First, groups[1] can shape individuals' experiences by preventing and preparing for costs, and especially by supporting those who bear the brunt of them. Second, groups can shape individuals' motivations by redefining the goals of protest and changing how individuals interpret repression. Finally, groups can shape individuals' identities by providing individuals with a sense of self that, in time, can lead them to take participation (and the repression that can result from it) for granted. Because not all groups exhibit these features to the same degree, and not all individuals are equally invested in and socialized into these groups, these mechanisms can help us make sense of the variety of ways that individuals and groups are impacted by repression.

Repression provides a unique case to develop a synthesized theory of collective action. By demonstrating how even in an area to which we tend to think of concepts such as costs and benefits as highly applicable, rational actor theory fails to adequately explain how activists respond, I hope to demonstrate the need to rethink the limits of the dominant RAT-based paradigm for understanding of collective action.

In the following chapters, I will demonstrate these mechanisms by which groups "set limits" on rationality (Friedland and Alford 1991), and more generally the way that individual rationality is culturally constructed within groups, and in doing so, work toward a more complete and nuanced theory of collective action. I will demonstrate how an approach that takes into account how individual rationality is collectively constructed, not only in the narrow ways rational choice scholars have aptly brought our attention to, but in deeper, more internalized ways as well, can help us better understand how collective action is made possible, both generally and in the face of repression specifically. Of course, some individuals undoubtedly come to activism with higher levels of motivation, conviction (Klandermans 1997; Weinstein 2006), or with certain personality traits, such as a greater tolerance for risk, compared with others who also become involved. As already discussed, Linden and Klandermans (2006) show that how one comes to join a movement impacts their ability to withstand the stigmatization and "soft" repression they encounter later. Still, throughout this book, I show how "individual" traits such as risk tolerance, motivation, and conviction (and, in turn, persistence in the face of repression) are also, to a large extent, collective achievements emergent from collective action and reinforced by the cultural milieus surrounding protest.

In chapter 2, I provide an overview of relevant history of the repression of dissent in the United States, with special attention to developments in the post-9/11 era that have created a climate of heightened concern about repression, especially covert repression, among activists and others concerned with the freedom to engage in dissent. This chapter provides critical background for understanding the mobilization context faced by the activists who are the focus of this study.

In chapter 3, I describe the divergent responses to repression among the activists I studied and examine one likely explanation for this variation that flows from rational actor theories of repression and mobilization: some experiences of repression are simply costlier than others, and this explains the variation in responses to these experiences. After demonstrating that repression type and severity do little to explain why some persist and others disengage, the next three chapters explore three ways in which protest cultures can shape the subjective experience of repression, therefore mediating its impact on participation.

In chapter 4, I focus on the practices activist groups develop to reduce the costs of repression for individuals, and therefore shape the experience of repression. More specifically, I examine the efforts made by activists to protect one another from repression, especially covert repression, by increasing security, anonymity, and privacy for those engaged in dissent. Furthermore, I examine how groups work to prepare individuals for the costs of repression, both mentally and physically, to thereby reduce its deterrent effects. Finally, I document the networks of support that develop and have often become institutionalized in activist circles to provide both material and nonmaterial support to repression targets, thus redistributing and sharing costs among the group. I then demonstrate that these cost-mitigation practices help explain individual persistence and disengagement following experiences of state repression.

In chapter 5, I go beyond the predictions of rational choice theory on how groups impact the cost-benefit ratio of individuals and demonstrate the way that socialization into protest cultures can also change the way that actors think about the ends of protest. In doing so, individuals' motivations toward protest and repression, not just the experiences and choices they face, are impacted. I find evidence that some individuals come to adopt alternative definitions of "success," come to see resistance as meaningful in itself, and interpret repression as proof of the significance of their cause. I further demonstrate how redefining the ends and meaning of protest and repression in these ways is associated with persistence in the wake of repressive experiences.

Finally, in chapter 6, I demonstrate that groups also make individuals less vulnerable to the potential deterrent powers of repression by cultivating in them personal identities that are intimately tied up with participation in activism. In time, participation can, for those with a salient activist identity, feel like less of a "choice" and become taken for granted to the extent that individuals can no longer imagine other courses of action. I demonstrate that a salient activist identity is associated with persistence following repression and then explore, through respondents' narratives, some of the factors that seem to contribute to, as well as detract from, the development of such an identity. Chapters 4 through 6 build on each other to contribute to a more expansive understanding of the collectively constructed nature of rationality as it relates to repression and its consequences for protest participation.

In chapter 7, I review the central arguments of the book and discuss how attending to the collective construction of rationality, as I have, can not only help to reconcile mixed findings on repression effects from previous studies, but also contributes to a more integrated and fuller understanding of individual participation in social movements and points to fruitful areas for future research.

2

A Brief History of the Policing of Dissent in the United States

To begin to understand how U.S. activists consider the risks of participating in protest, and how protest cultures shape these considerations, we must understand the context in which activists today are mobilizing. This includes not only the current political and legal context, but also the history of the repression of dissent in the United States. Just as generations of activists pass down institutional knowledge about how to mobilize (Taylor 1989), they also pass down narratives of state repression in previous eras. This collective memory, along with that of the successes of past movements, help activists to construct a sense of themselves as heirs to a legacy of resistance, and of their movements as a continuation of a long, and often difficult, struggle for change. To provide context for examining how activists think about the risks and rewards of protest, this chapter presents a brief history of state repression—both overt and covert—in the United States, with particular attention paid to developments in recent decades that figure most prominently in the collective memory and mobilizing context of activists today.

Early American Police and the Red Squads

It was primarily in response to a wave of labor unrest of the mid-1800s that the first full-time police forces emerged in American cities, replacing the more informal "night watch" system in the North and, after the Civil War, the slave patrols in the South (Walker 1977; Hahn and Jeffries 2003). Boston developed a police department in 1837, New York City did so in 1844, and, by 1880, all major U.S. cities had followed suit (Harring 1983). Curbing the growing tide of riots and strikes in American cities was the raison d'être of early police agencies, and a focus on fighting crime would not become part of the police mission for another half century (Walker 1977). These early police were given the broad mandate to "maintain order" and great latitude in doing so (Hahn and Jeffries 2003, 4). Police not only responded to events like the Tompkins Square Riot in 1874, the "Great Upheaval" (aka Great Railroad Strike) of 1877, and the Haymarket Riot of 1886 with great violence, but, in concert with private agencies like the Pinkerton Detective Agency, increasingly engaged in covert surveillance and infiltration of striking workers, socialists, anarchists, and other dissidents (Donner 1990). Police units devoted to this, sometimes referred to as "Red Squads," became institutionalized in the 1930s as the Great Depression threatened to radicalize another generation of American workers (Donner 1990). In 1938, the House Special Committee on Un-American Activity was created and the FBI was tasked with weeding out and suppressing political subversives, with local law enforcement funneling intelligence to them. While the Red Squads' work lessened with the end of the Great Depression and the decline of labor disputes across the 1940s and 1950s, the rise of the civil rights movement and then the anti-war movement quickly provided new targets (Donner 1990).

1956–1971: The COINTELPRO Era

On March 8, 1971, an unlikely crew of burglars—including two professors, a graduate student, and a social worker—broke into a Federal Bureau of Investigation (FBI) office in Media, Pennsylvania.[1] There had been multiple instances of overt state repression of the anti-war movement in the preceding years. Two years before the Kent State shooting, for example, anti-war demonstrators were met with extreme police violence and slapped with "conspiracy to riot" charges at the 1968 Democratic National Convention protests (Berger 2006). But many in the movement had begun to suspect that the FBI had also been engaging in more covert efforts to undermine the movement. One man, Bill Davidon, a "mild-mannered" physics professor and committed anti-war activist, knew that he wouldn't be able to get the American public to care about this issue on suspicion alone (Medsger 2014, 3). He needed hard proof and decided that the best way to get it was to break into an FBI office and take documents that would show the world the illegal and undemocratic ways that the FBI was repressing dissent. He slowly started to assemble a team of trusted activists. In the end, they numbered eight and they called themselves the Citizens' Commission to Investigate the FBI. They chose March 8 for the break-in because it was the night of a huge boxing match between two undefeated heavyweights—Muhammad Ali and Joe Frazier. They figured that the people living in the apartments that shared the building with the FBI office would be less likely to hear them breaking in with the fight blaring on their televisions. And, they reasoned, no FBI agent would choose to come to work after hours on such a big fight night. They were right. Despite a few setbacks, they forced their way into the office, stuffed suitcases full of documents, and escaped undetected. They spent the following days at a remote farmhouse, poring over the thousands of pages of documents they had taken. It didn't take long before they found definitive proof of what they had suspected. In fact, it was much worse than they had feared (Medsger 2014).

It turned out that, ironically, their crime—breaking in and stealing documents—was also a favorite tactic of the FBI. But that was only the beginning. The FBI, under the direction of J. Edgar Hoover, had been spying on and infiltrating social movement organizations for decades, motivated as much by stopping ideologies they labeled as threatening to the American way of life as by stopping crime. They had a tap on Martin Luther King's phone. Hoover had requested the wiretap after seeing the crowds that MLK had been able to turn out to his March on Washington (Gordon 2006). He was looking for proof that MLK was a communist but would settle for evidence that he was an adulterer, or for anything that could be used to discredit the popular civil rights leader.

The stolen documents showed that the FBI was deeply concerned about the possibility that MLK or another civil rights leader, like Stokely Carmichael, leader of the Student Nonviolent Coordinating Committee and later the Black Panther Party, would become a "black messiah" able to "unify and electrify" the black liberation movement. Hoover would stop at nothing to prevent that from happening. In a 1969 letter to the special agent in charge (SAC) in the FBI's San Francisco office, Hoover scolded the agent for not doing enough to disrupt the Black Panther Party's (BPP) children's breakfast program. The agent had previously declined to target this particular BPP activity, citing its value to the community. Hoover chastised the SAC, stating, "You have obviously missed the point," arguing that the breakfast program should be stopped precisely because it brought positive publicity to the Black Panther Party (Churchill and Vander Wall 2001, 144–145).

In other cases, it seemed as if the FBI was always one step ahead of the activists, quietly thwarting their efforts. When the Republic of New Afrika (RNA), a black separatist group, tried to buy a small plot of land in Mississippi, the FBI "interviewed" the landowner, persuading him that leasing the land to the group "would not be a wise endeavor." The RNA never knew why the deal mysteriously fell through at the last minute. When the Students for a Democratic Society (SDS) distributed flyers about an upcoming rally, the FBI distributed flyers announcing it had been canceled. When the Black Panther Party sent out its newspaper, the FBI would do what it could to make sure it never made it to its destinations (Churchill and Vander Wall 2001).

They started false rumors that wives were cheating on husbands and husbands on their wives, sometimes leading to the dissolution of marriages (Churchill and Vander Wall 1988). They sent an anonymous letter to a faculty tenure committee, posing as a "concerned" alum, slandering a philosophy professor at Arizona State University because he was a vocal opponent of the Vietnam War and helped sponsor the SDS chapter on campus. His contract was terminated, and he was unable to secure another job in academia (Blackstock 1988). FBI agents watched as individuals' lives were ruined, all in the name of weakening radical political groups. Sometimes the rumors they started had even more dire consequences. Once, the FBI sent a letter to the Black Panthers, posing as another black power group called United Slaves (US). The letter said that US was aware of BPP plans to kill the leader of US and, in retaliation, US members were making plans to ambush BPP leaders soon. All of this was a fabrication of the FBI; neither group had any plans to hurt or kill leaders of the other group. The point was to sow distrust and division between the two groups that had been working together (Churchill and Vander Wall 2001, 92). And it worked: tension between the two groups rose until members of United Slaves assassinated two Black Panthers on January 17, 1969 (Berger 2006).

All of this, and more, was part of a secret, often illegal FBI program called COINTELPRO, short for "COunterINTELligence PROgram." COINTELPRO was started in 1956, with the mission to, in Hoover's own words, "expose, disrupt, misdirect, discredit, or otherwise neutralize" the activities of social movement organizations and individuals labeled as "extremists" (Churchill and Vander Wall 2001, 92; Cunningham 2004). The program was first established to fight communism, but soon expanded to target radical civil rights groups like the Black Panther Party, New Left groups like Students for a Democratic Society, and white hate groups like the Ku Klux Klan. As the name of the program suggests, what the FBI was engaging in was not simply "intelligence"—it was "counterintelligence." The FBI used surveillance, infiltration, and other covert methods not simply to gather information about potential criminal activity, but to disrupt and intimidate. They tried to hurt groups' public image through sending anonymous letters to newspapers, planting infiltrators to make statements that made groups appear more extreme, and disseminating anonymous pamphlets against targeted groups. They worked to disrupt internal organization and cohesion by starting rumors that members were FBI agents (sometimes referred to as "badjacketing" or "snitchjacketing"; Boykoff 2006), sending falsified letters from ex-members defaming leaders, planting infiltrators to promote schisms, and making anonymous harassing phone calls.

Similar methods were used to cause conflict between groups working in coalition with one another, to destroy or otherwise reduce resources of activist groups, or to make it harder for individuals and groups to participate in protest (for example, sending anonymous letters to students' parents notifying them of their political involvement; Churchill and Vander Wall 1988, 2001; Cunningham 2004).

Much of this work was done through undercover agents or informants embedded in activist groups. In 1966, at the height of an FBI investigation into the activities of the Ku Klux Klan (KKK), at least 6 percent of the total membership of the organization, or about 300 individuals, were actually undercover FBI agents (Cunningham 2004). It is important to note that while the FBI did sometimes, as in the case of the KKK, target right-wing groups, this was the exception to the rule. In fact, 98 percent of the files exposed in the COINTELPRO break-in were related to leftist groups (Cunningham 2004, 11). But the disparity is even more apparent when examining the differences between how the FBI approached right-wing "extremists" compared with left-wing "extremists." For example, while the New Left was targeted because of their ideology, white hate groups were of concern because of their use of violence. The goal of the FBI in targeting New Left groups was to disrupt the groups' capacity to mobilize, while the goal with respect to white hate groups was merely to reduce the violence and destruction they caused (Cunningham 2003, 2004).

The Citizens' Commission sent the stolen documents to the press, and the *Washington Post* ran the story. The response was resounding. The FBI officially ended the COINTELPRO program, and for the first time in U.S. history, the Senate set up a committee to investigate the FBI (named the Church Committee after its chair, Senator Frank Church). Many Americans lost faith in the once-venerated FBI, and in their government more generally. Legislation was eventually passed banning some COINTELRPO practices as unconstitutional (Medsger 2014), and Attorney General Edward Levi established stricter procedural guidelines for law enforcement investigations (Fernandez 2008). But a great deal of damage had already been done. Many credit COINTELPRO with effectively killing some organizations, like the Black Panther Party, and driving others—like the Weathermen who split off from the Students for a Democratic Society—to violence (Cunningham 2004; Berger 2006).

1972–1999: An Uneasy Peace

Around the same time that the Church Committee was pushing the FBI to clean up the tactics it had been using behind closed doors, there was also a major shift happening in how police were addressing public protest in the streets. Throughout the 1950s and 1960s, police engaged in an approach to protest policing that McCarthy and McPhail have termed "escalated force" (1999). Under this model of protest policing, there was little or no tolerance for disruption. Large numbers of law enforcement officers were deployed to protests, in hopes that the show of force would be enough to disperse the crowd. If this did not work, police would use force of increasing severity, including using batons, police dogs, fire hoses, and chemical weapons like tear gas, until the crowd would finally disperse. Iconic photos from the civil rights movement, like those of dogs attacking young demonstrators in Birmingham, Alabama, reflect this aggressive approach in dealing with public displays of dissent.

As protests grew larger, more frequent, and more organized throughout the 1960s, there was a growing recognition among some leaders in law enforcement that this approach was not effective at containing protest and, often, fanned the flames of dissent and escalated already tense protest situations (Gupta 2017). Four different presidential commissions scrutinizing police response to unrest in the nation's cities and campuses also created pressure for change (McCarthy and McPhail 1998; Gupta 2017). But, perhaps just as importantly, police were at the time engaged in the "second wave" of police professionalism and, amid all the criticism of how they had been handling protest during the 1960s, they saw an opportunity to remake themselves in the image of professional public servants (Earl and Reynolds-Stenson 2018). A new approach to protest policing emerged, described by McCarthy and McPhail (1999) as "negotiated management." This new approach was pioneered by law enforcement in Washington, D.C., where protests were especially frequent and had become a major focus of police resources. From there, it diffused, through professional associations and other means, to police departments throughout the United States (McCarthy, McPhail, and Crist 1999).

Central to this approach was the seemingly counterintuitive idea that the best way to reduce disruption was to allow it—at least to a certain point. This new protest policing model tolerated temporary, low-level disruption of public order, and ceded to social movements a platform (albeit a regulated one) to air their grievances, in hopes of preventing more serious disturbances. The idea was not to suppress protest, but to manage it by controlling the time, manner, and place that it occurred. Communication with protest leaders was key to this and helped to make protests more predictable for police. The spread of a permitting system, whereby protest groups request permission to hold a demonstration, established a line of communication between police and protest leaders, created mutual expectations and agreements prior to events, and often conscripted protest leaders as partners (with law enforcement) in keeping the peace. In some cases, protest leaders organized "marshals"—protesters tasked with making sure the protest stayed within the lines of the permit as negotiated between police and protest leaders (Gupta 2017).

After this shift in protest policing in the early 1970s, there was a marked decrease in police violence at protests (Noakes and Gillham 2006; Soule and Davenport 2009; Gillham, Edwards, and Noakes 2013; Maguire 2015). In fact, Soule and Davenport (2009) find that police violence occurred about half as often in the 1970s and 1980s as it did in the 1960s. However, how much this can be credited to police changing their tactics, as opposed to shifts happening within protest, namely the professionalization of social movement organizations and the routinization of protest, or simply to the decline of the protest cycle, is a subject of debate (McCarthy and McPhail 1998; Soule and Davenport 2009; Reynolds-Stenson and Earl 2021; Elliot et al. 2022).

And many have argued that, rather than facilitating protesters' rights, as law enforcement often claims, applying for permits and negotiating with police gives police the upper hand and defangs protest (Mitchell and Stacheli 2005; Fernandez 2008; King 2017) by taking away its most potent tool for change—disruption (Piven and Cloward 1977). Negotiated management helped police to proactively head off threats to the status quo and more effectively maintain public order, all while appearing as protectors and facilitators of protesters' First Amendment rights (King 2017).

It is also important to note that the rise of negotiated management did not preclude the use of violence to quell protest, but instead (usually) reserved it for situations in which protesters did not cooperate with police efforts at preemptively managing demonstrations (King 2017). In fact, during this same period that negotiated management dominated protest policing, law enforcement's capacity for violence was growing, as policing generally (and protest policing in particular) became increasing militarized (Kraska and Kappeler 1997; Kraska and Paulsen 1997; Balko 2013; Wood 2014). Under this model, when violence is used against protesters, the overarching "soft" negotiated management approach lends greater legitimacy to this violence, as law enforcement and others are able to claim that protesters could have avoided these consequences if only they had followed the new "rules" of protest (Williams 2014). As King (2017) argues, under negotiated management, "the use of violence was never rescinded but restrained, reserved for instances when the subtler repression of negotiation failed. If that discipline of negotiated management were to fail, riot police would be waiting to hand out forceful reminders about the appropriate comportment of dissent" (p. 33).

Just as negotiated management did not end state violence at protests, the Church Committee also did not fully reform the more unsavory covert tactics of the FBI. One notable case of this is the FBI campaign against the Central American Solidarity and Sanctuary movements during the Reagan administration (Churchill and Vander Wall 1988; Gelbspan 1991). The Sanctuary movement was church-based and committed to strict nonviolence, but the FBI actively worked to spread rumors that it was a terrorist-controlled movement created to smuggle Latin American terrorists into the United States. Hundreds of mysterious break-ins at offices, churches, and private homes of people involved in the Sanctuary movement between 1984 and 1988, in which nothing of value was stolen, caused many to speculate that the FBI had resumed some of its COINTELPRO-era tactics (Churchill and Vander Wall 1988). In fact, the procedural guidelines established in the wake of COINTELPRO had been loosened by Attorney General William French Smith in 1983 (Fernandez 2008). Unconstitutional covert tactics against social movements by the FBI likely neither started in 1956 nor ended in 1971 (the years that COINTELPRO was in operation). Rather, the U.S. government has likely resorted to such methods throughout our history, especially in periods of political instability (Cunningham 2004). We simply know the most about the covert repression under COINTELPRO because of the break-in and leak by the Citizens' Commission.

From the early 1970s until the late 1990s, between the Church Committee's banning of some covert tactics by the FBI and the adoption of negotiated management as the dominant protest policing protocol, a sort of truce formed between law enforcement and social movements in the United States. But it was an uneasy peace, punctuated by occasional overt repression when social movements failed—or refused—to play by the new rules, and marked by a lingering suspicion, among many activists, of continued covert repression. As will be discussed in the next section, this truce arguably came to an end in 1999. A new wave of unrest was rising, and social movements were innovating their tactics and organizational forms. And law enforcement agencies were taking notice.

1999–Present: Anarchists, Terrorists, and Other Boogeymen

If the wealth of research aimed at explaining repression—its distribution across protests, movements, and regimes and its rise and fall across time—has led to consensus on anything, it is that state repression is a function of threat (for a review, see Davenport 2007), a threat to political elites and the status quo but also to police as the enforcers of public order (Earl and Soule 2006). The rising tide of protest at the close of the millennium, especially as part of the global justice movement, combined with the September 11 terrorist attacks of 2001 to create a climate of renewed threat and instability in the United States. The increase in state repression that has followed should not be a surprise to students of repression, or of history. The fear of "communists" of the 1940s and 1950s and of "radicals" of the 1960s and early 1970s gave way to a focus on fighting "terrorists" (at home as well as abroad) and "anarchists" (sometimes by conflating the two). The political construction of these new threats propelled an escalation of state repression—both overt and covert—and marked the end of the "uneasy peace" that had prevailed over the last quarter of the twentieth century. Massive amounts of state resources were redirected to "counterterrorism" efforts and to the monitoring and control of protest movements. And, as the legal definition of "terrorism" was increasingly broadened, the line between the two began to blur.

The "Battle in Seattle" and the End of Negotiated Management

Tactics of repression and tactics of resistance emerge in interaction with one another, through repeated confrontation between the state and movements (McAdam 1983; Barkan 1984; Koopmans 1997; McCarthy and McPhail 1999; Hardt and Negri 2004). This has never been as clear as in the case of the World Trade Organization (WTO) protests in Seattle in 1999. These protests marked a key turning point in this dance between police and protesters, leading to a renegotiation of police–protester relations and the innovation of tactics on both sides (Noakes and Gillham 2007).

The WTO protests drew a wide variety of groups opposed to neoliberal trade and development—including labor unions, environmental groups, human rights organizations, and anarchists (Gupta 2017). These protesters employed a diversity of tactics, some preplanned in coordination with police and some not. Some of these groups were decentralized and horizontally structured. They made decisions through consensus and coordinated actions through small affinity groups. Such features of this new wave of mobilization, often reflecting an explicit commitment to prefigurative politics (Leach 2013), made it difficult for police to predict what protesters were planning or to coordinate with "leaders" (as there often were none), making negotiated management difficult to achieve (Gupta 2017). The protests caught law enforcement by surprise, delayed the opening of the WTO meetings (Burgess and Pearlstein 1999), and resulted in millions of dollars of property damage (Gupta 2017).

Law enforcement agencies around the country viewed this as a failure of the negotiated management model and vowed to not let the same thing happen again (Gupta 2017). And, only six months later, at the 2000 Republican National Convention (RNC) in Philadelphia, they had a chance to prove it (Hermes 2015). A new federal designation created in 1998—the "National Special Security Event" (NSSE)—was applied to the 2000 RNC, giving police greater power to control the protests and paving the way for an increased role for federal law enforcement. These protests also saw the debut of a police tactic that would come to mark many of the major political convention and economic summit protests in years to come: preemptive raids and arrests. Days before the convention started, police surrounded and raided a warehouse where protesters were making protest signs and large puppets (sometimes used to add theatrical flair and media-catching visuals to protest marches) in preparation for the upcoming demonstrations. Police forcefully arrested all seventy-nine people in the warehouse, based on a "tip" that there were weapons inside. No weapons were found. The police destroyed the puppets and signs the activists had spent weeks creating, along with tens of thousands of dollars in protesters' personal property. Not only did the arrested protesters not get to use the props they had created, they didn't get to participate in the protests at all. They were not released until several days later, after the convention was over. All charges against them were eventually dropped (Hermes 2015).

These and other new tactics of repression used at the 2000 RNC were honed and added to over the next few years, forming what was referred to by activists as the "Miami Model" because it was unveiled at the 2003 Free Trade Area of the Americas (FTAA) protest in Miami, Florida. Since the "Battle of Seattle," police departments across the country had engaged in a massive retraining project to meet the threat posed by this new brand of protest. And they were growing their capacity for force with increased transfers of equipment from the military (Gillham and Noakes 2007). The Miami-Dade Police Department, with the help of forty other federal, state, and local law enforcement agencies, met demonstrators with overwhelming force, at a level and scale, and with a degree of coordination, that had not previously been seen. Police trained for the FTAA protests for six months, in a training effort that the Miami-Dade Police Department boasted was "unprecedented" (Fernandez 2008, 98). Thousands of riot cops surrounded the demonstrators, while armored vehicles patrolled the streets and helicopters flew overhead. Police tear gassed and shot into crowds with rubber bullets indiscriminately, and at one point chased protesters for twenty blocks—grabbing and arresting anyone they could get their hands on (Starr and Fernandez 2009). Many likened the scene to a "war zone" (Fernandez 2008). The police assumed everyone on the street was a protester, and therefore treated them as a criminal, because the city had effectively been shut down and all avenues for dissent had been effectively blocked in preparation for the FTAA meetings (Fernandez 2008). Permits requested by organizations were denied (Starr and Fernandez 2009). A city ordinance was passed a week before the protests that defined a gathering of three or more people as an "illegal assembly" (Fernandez 2008). The city ordinance also banned anything that could conceivably be used as a projectile or weapon, giving police authority to stop any protester to search them for banned objects (Fernandez 2008). All they recovered were gas masks (used by protesters to protect themselves against chemical weapons like tear gas; Starr and Fernandez 2009). The city ordinance was rescinded a few months after the protest, before it could be legally challenged. It likely wouldn't have held up to legal scrutiny, but, just as the hundreds of arrests at the protest failed to secure a single conviction, this didn't matter. Regardless of whether the ordinance or the arrests were lawful, they were effective tools in clearing the streets and suppressing dissent during the event.

The Miami Model caught on and was developed into what scholars now refer to as "strategic incapacitation," a new model of protest policing that has largely displaced negotiated management (Gillham and Noakes 2007). Strategic incapacitation is characterized, among other things, by extensive and real-time surveillance, information sharing across law enforcement agencies, and extensive and proactive control of public space (Gillham and Noakes 2007). Under this model, police go to great lengths to spatially contain protesters, with "hard zones," "soft zones," "free speech zones," and "free press zones." Force is more readily used, when necessary, when these efforts at containment fail. And, in the move away from negotiated management, police have turned to surveillance to collect information that would previously have been shared with police in pre-event negotiations (Gillham, Edwards, and Noakes 2013). In its lack of tolerance for disruption, strategic incapacitation harkens back to escalated force (Vitale 2007). In its proactivity, it resembles negotiated management (Gillham and Noakes 2007). But, like zero tolerance and "broken windows" policing outside the context of protest, it proactively nips potential problems in the bud, not by under-enforcing the law as was the case under negotiated management, but by over-enforcing it (Noakes and Gillham 2006). Passavant (2021) goes further, arguing that twenty-first century protest policing also increasingly features intentional degradation and intimidation of protesters, signs of what he describes as a "post-democratic, postlegitimation protest policing regime" (p. 69).

As new approaches to protest policing are developed, they never completely eclipse the old, but instead contribute to a more diverse repertoire of social control (Reynolds-Stenson and Earl 2020) and allow for a more selective and variegated police response, as demonstrated by the way that strategic incapacitation combines elements of older models. The result is what Vitale (2007) has referred to as a "two-pronged" approach to protest policing. He argues that, by the 2004 RNC protests, there were two distinct sets of police tactics in use: "soft hat" tactics of channeling and micromanaging protest and the more overtly coercive "hard hat" tactics associated with the Miami Model.

Scholars have documented how strategic incapacitation has continued to prevail in recent years, including in the policing of the Occupy movement in New York City (Gillham, Edwards, and Noakes 2013) and Oakland (King 2017). And, just as was the case with negotiated management (McCarthy, McPhail, and Crist 1999), this U.S.-grown approach to protest policing has diffused to other countries as well (King and Waddington 2006; della Porta and Reiter 2006; Starr, Fernandez, and Scholl 2011).

Counterterrorism and the Rise of the Surveillance State

The shift toward strategic incapacitation might have been triggered by the WTO protests in Seattle, but it was accelerated by the post-9/11 focus on security and terrorism (Gillham 2011). And some the most significant changes were playing out not on the streets at large protests, but behind closed doors. In the wake of the terrorist attacks of September 11, heightened concerns about national security and domestic terrorism led to a series of legislation, like the PATRIOT Act in 2001, the Homeland Security Act of 2002, the Intelligence Reform and Terrorism Prevention Act of 2004, and the Animal Enterprise Terrorism Act of 2006, that, together, relaxed privacy protections, legally redefined some acts of protest as "terrorism" that carried much stricter penalties, and allotted billions of dollars to build new infrastructure and create new jobs focused on tracking potential domestic terrorism threats. While Arab Americans and Muslims bore the brunt of increased state surveillance immediately after 9/11 (Santoro and Azab 2015), the state response to the terrorist attacks has fundamentally changed the dynamics of dissent for all Americans.

Frank Donner, writing in 1990, warned that "terrorists" were already becoming the new favorite menace, and that this was facilitating the "re-politicization of police," just as "communists" had done in the past. "If the past is a guide," he wrote, "'terrorist' may well be converted into an all-purpose taint or stigma against an expandable body of targets" (p. 367). He predicted a new phase of surveillance—one that, due to less public support, would be more secretive and rely more heavily on private sector proxies and on new, less traceable, technologies. The next decade and a half, unfortunately, proved him right (Boghosian 2013).

Passed in the month following the 9/11 attacks, the PATRIOT Act expanded investigative and prosecutorial powers of the state in many ways, including by expanding the definition of terrorism to include domestic terrorism, and by defining terrorist groups broadly, as any group involved in an illegal act that endangers human life (Chang 2002). This could even include actions that endanger the lives of protesters themselves and is broad enough to include activities of several well-known organizations, such as Greenpeace (American Civil Liberties Union 2002).

In fact, in 2005, FBI Deputy Assistant Director John Lewis labeled animal rights and environmental activists as the "Number One" domestic terrorist threat in the United States, paving the way for the prosecution and long-term imprisonment of several activists from these movements and leaving the organizations and communities they were a part of in shock (Grigoriadis 2011; Potter 2011). Lewis's statement to Congress in 2005 sounded eerily similar to the language Hoover had used about radical groups in the 1960s. "Together with our partners, we are working to detect, disrupt, and dismantle the animal rights and environmental extremist movements that are involved in criminal activity," he boasted (Esquivel 2013, 317). In what many would call the "Green Scare" (harkening back to the "Red Scare" of the 1940s and 1950s), the state has worked to quell this "number one domestic terrorism threat" using tools both new and old—including conspiracy charges, grand jury investigations, and terrorism enhancements to sentencing made possible through the PATRIOT Act, the Animal Enterprise and Terrorism Act, and other new laws (Potter 2011).

The Animal Enterprise and Terrorism Act (AETA) specifically targeted animal rights activism and redefined "terrorism" so broadly that it included acts of peaceful civil disobedience like physically blocking the entrance of an "animal enterprise" (which includes factory farms, laboratories that test on animals, fur farms, rodeos, circuses, etc.). The law made it an act of "terrorism" to do anything that causes a loss of profits for such businesses (even if that loss of profits is caused by peaceful free speech and assembly; Boghosian 2013). The act specifically excludes boycotts, but virtually anything else that could interfere with the profits of animal enterprises can be prosecuted under the law (18 U.S.C. § 43 [2006]). This includes rescuing or assisting in the rescue of animals, but also filming conditions at factory farms or slaughterhouses to expose animal welfare violations. And many states have tried (some successfully) to pass even more punitive "Ag-Gag" laws that penalize whistleblowers, investigators, and journalists who leak footage or information that is damaging to the reputation of companies in this industry (Potter 2011). AETA, and these state-level Ag-Gag laws, classify acts of disruptive civil disobedience and investigative journalism directed at the animal industry as "terrorism," carrying up to twenty years in prison (U.S. Code 18), whereas these same acts targeting different types of businesses or other entities would be considered much lesser crimes.

AETA was not a new law, but rather a stricter revision of the Animal Enterprise Protection Act (AEPA), in place since 1992. AEPA was used in 2004 to indict a group of U.S. activists who ran a website as part of an international campaign to shut down Huntingdon Life Sciences, Europe's largest contract animal-testing laboratory. Six activists, and the organization itself (Stop Huntingdon Animal Cruelty or SHAC), were charged under AEPA as "terrorists." They were not accused of personally engaging in any illegal activity, but rather of advocating on their website for the use of both legal and illegal tactics to shut down Huntingdon (but, importantly, they specifically advocated against any action that would cause harm to human or nonhuman animal life). Despite the fact that they only engaged in protected First Amendment activity, they were convicted and sentenced to four to six years in prison each (Center for Constitutional Rights 2011).

AETA, once passed, made it even easier to prosecute cases like this, and carried with it stricter penalties (up to twenty years in prison). The newly strengthened AETA was first used in 2009 to prosecute four people arrested by the Joint Terrorism Task Force in California for writing on sidewalks with chalk, leafletting, and googling people involved in animal research. They faced ten years in prison each, until the case was eventually dismissed (Boghosian 2013). Ag-Gag laws have been struck down as unconstitutional in some states, for example in Utah in 2017 (Center for Constitutional Rights 2017). AETA has also been legally challenged (in *Blum v. Holder* in 2011), but so far has been upheld (Center for Constitutional Rights 2013).

The years since 9/11 have not just been a period of stricter laws penalizing dissent. They have also been a time of great expansion in the U.S. government's technological and legal capacity for surveillance in the name of fighting "terrorism." The procedural guidelines that had been established after COINTELRPO, and partially rolled back in 1983, were made even more permissive, this time by Attorney General John Ashcroft in 2002 (Fernandez 2008). In the intervening years, federal agencies have been granted power to wiretap the phones of U.S. citizens if they are believed to be communicating with terrorists outside the United States (but, in practice, the use of warrantless wiretaps has been much broader; Risen and Lichtblau 2005; Macaskill and Dance 2013) and to detain American citizens labeled as "terrorists" indefinitely, without charge (Turley 2012). And, since 2006, the FBI has had the power to use individuals' cell phones as "roving bugs," meaning they can remotely switch on the microphone and use it to eavesdrop on nearby conversations, without the target's knowledge. The phone's power can even be switched on remotely, leading many activists to conclude that turning their phones off is not enough and to instead leave their phones at home or take their batteries out to avoid this form of surveillance (although this level of precaution may be becoming less common in activist circles; Esquivel 2013).

Around the country, seventy-seven "fusion centers" were established between 2003 and 2007, which was made possible by the PATRIOT Act of 2001, the Homeland Security Act of 2002, and the Intelligence Reform and Terrorism Prevention Act of 2004. These centers facilitate intelligence sharing between local law enforcement entities and federal agencies such as the FBI, the Department of Homeland Security, the U.S. Secret Service, and U.S. Immigration and Customs Enforcement for the purpose of monitoring potential domestic terrorism threats (Hodai 2013). While motivated by concerns about "terrorism," this apparatus of the state has, in practice, often been used to monitor U.S. activists (Monahan and Palmer 2009). Fusion centers have been very controversial, with many (including members of the U.S. Senate) raising concerns about their ineffectiveness, potential for mission creep, and violation of civil liberties (Monahan and Palmer 2009; Smith 2012). In an almost comical example of mission creep, the Tennessee Fusion Center actually flagged the Tennessee American Civil Liberties Union (ACLU) as participating in "terrorism events and other suspicious activity" after the Tennessee ACLU made a statement that public schools shouldn't "celebrate Christmas as a religious holiday" (Rittgers 2011).

With law enforcement emboldened by expanded investigative powers and heightened concerns with "terrorism," physical infiltration of activist groups by undercover officers and informants also have become more frequent. Infiltration of activist groups is now so common that many activists assume all meetings are infiltrated and that surveillance is pervasive, fundamentally altering the dynamics of mobilization and the daily practices of social movement organizations (Starr et al. 2008). Between 2004 and 2006, the FBI conducted a nationwide investigation called "Operation Backfire" that resulted in the indictment of several activists for allegedly committing arson and other acts of "eco-terrorism" against power lines, meat packing plants, a ski resort, and a car dealership, among other targets (Bond Graham 2015). In all, eighteen people were indicted as part of Operation Backfire, made possible through the testimony of an informant. Two are still at large, fifteen were sent to prison (some for as long as fifteen years), and one killed himself while awaiting trial (Williams 2013). Many argued that the label of "terrorism," and the inordinately long prison sentences that come along with it, were inappropriate for these crimes, which resulted in property damage but no loss of life (Woodhouse 2012).

Around this same time, an FBI informant known to activists as "Anna" persuaded an anarchist activist named Eric McDavid, through flirtation and promises of a sexual relationship, to agree to help her, along with two others, bomb several "unspecified targets" in Northern California. No bombings (or even specific plans) transpired, but Eric and two others were arrested for conspiring (with the informant) to commit the bombings. Federal prosecutors illegally withheld 2,500 pages worth of evidence that eventually exonerated McDavid, but not until after he had already spent nine years in prison (Aaronson and Galloway 2015; Pilkington 2015). "Anna" was paid $65,000 (Esquivel 2013, 317) over three years to travel the United States gathering intelligence for the FBI while posing as an anarchist activist (Tucker 2013). McDavid and his two codefendants were only one of twelve separate cases in which "Anna" acted as an informant. All twelve cases targeted individuals the FBI considered to be "anarchists" (Garvin 2006). A few years later, another FBI informant, Brandon Darby, encouraged two young men, Bradley Crowder and David McKay, to make Molotov cocktails at the 2008 RNC, leading to their incarceration for two and four years, respectively (Moynihan 2009). In both cases, many argued that the informants acted as agents provocateurs and entrapped the defendants by persuading them to consider acts that they would not have otherwise considered. And in both, the state was initially interested in these targets in part because they identified as or were presumed to be "anarchists." In fact, the word "anarchist" appears fifteen times in the twenty-six-page criminal complaint filed against McDavid (Tucker 2013, 295). In addition to nebulously defined "terrorists," "anarchists" seem to be playing the role of the political boogeyman that Hoover's "communists" and "radicals" once did. In advance of National Special Security Events, reports circulated to police now often warn of possible "anarchist attacks" (Boghosian 2013).

This recent history reminds us that the line between activism and terrorism is blurry, contested, and moves over time. Furthermore, where this line is drawn is often as much about activists' ideology as their tactics. Over time, environmental "monkey wrenching," for example, came to be redefined as "terrorism," despite the fact that human life was never targeted or harmed in any of these actions, and despite the fact that violent actions taken by right-wing activists (like white supremacists and anti-abortion activists) during the same period were not similarly branded in this way (Potter 2011). While many of the most high-profile cases of infiltration and of "terrorism" prosecutions targeted environmental and animal rights activists, these instances and others less well known sent shock waves through various movements and circles of activists throughout the United States (Starr et al. 2008).

Recent Developments

The surveillance infrastructure created, and the laws passed in the several years following September 11, largely remain with us, twenty years later. When another wave of protest began to rise in 2010, law enforcement was ready and armed with ever-advancing technology. Facial recognition technology has raised concerns about mass surveillance of citizens, including protesters (Singer 2014), and recent advances in this technology will soon make it possible to even identify individuals whose face is obscured, meaning that protesters who attempt to remain anonymous at demonstrations by partially covering their face may soon be unable to do so (Matsakis 2017).

Furthermore, this surveillance is increasingly coming not only from the state, but also from private companies. The company constructing the Dakota Access Pipeline, Energy Transfer Partners, contracted a private security firm called TigerSwan to monitor and police anti-DAPL protesters. TigerSwan, which had been previously contracted by the U.S. military to provide private security in Iraq, compared protesters to insurgent "jihadist fighters" and used, in coordination with local, state, and federal law enforcement, "sweeping and invasive" surveillance tactics on the protesters (Brown, Parrish, and Speri 2017). This kind of joint state–private surveillance is becoming increasingly common, according to former FBI Special Agent Michael German, in part because one of the primary goals of the nation's fusion centers is the protection of "critical infrastructure." Fully 85 percent of the national "critical infrastructure" (which includes pipelines) is owned by private corporations, meaning that the state and private corporations share a common interest in tracking and preventing threats to this infrastructure (Brown, Parrish, and Speri 2017).

In recent years, Freedom of Information Act requests and lawsuits demanding access to law enforcement records have revealed that federal and local law enforcement agencies have infiltrated anti-fracking protest groups (Fang and Horn 2016), infiltrated and monitored Occupy protesters around the country (Hodai 2013; Moynihan 2014), read the text messages and infiltrated the meetings of Black Lives Matter (BLM) activists in New York (Morrison 2017; Murdock 2017), monitored BLM protesters in California (Bond Graham 2015) as well as Minnesota (Fang 2015), infiltrated meetings of "Food Not Bombs" (an anti-war group that prepares and distributes free food in public parks; Brown 2016), surveilled anti–Dakota Access Pipeline activists (Levin 2017), and illegally monitored Keystone XL protesters (Lewis and Federman 2015). Even eighteen months after the FBI's investigation into the protests surrounding the Keystone XL pipeline was suspended due to several violations of internal rules, Keystone XL protesters were still being watch-listed and detained at airports and at U.S. borders because of their involvement in the protests (Federman 2015).

Finally, it is worth noting that, in the six years since the completion of the data collection for this book, forty-five states have drafted a total of 245 bills designed to increase penalties for protesting (International Center for Not-for-Profit Law 2022). The bills proposed increasing fines and jail time for protesters for obstructing traffic, tampering with or trespassing on "critical infrastructure" such as pipelines, or simply for picketing, wearing masks at protests, or refusing to leave an assembly declared by police to be unlawful. Three states introduced bills removing liability from drivers who hit and kill protesters. Other legislation proposed labeling protests as "economic terrorism," expanding what is legally classified as rioting, charging costs of policing to protesters and organizers, and allowing businesses to sue individuals who protest them (Yoder 2018). In Arizona, a bill proposed expanding antiracketeering laws to allow the seizure of protesters' assets if protests they participate in result in property damage (Farzan 2017). Of these bills, most have been defeated or have expired, but thirty-eight have been passed and forty-seven were still pending as of March 2022 (International Center for Not-for-Profit Law 2022).

Conclusion

Donner (1990) documents how, since the Haymarket Riot in 1886, U.S. law enforcement agencies have periodically engaged in "radical hunting." Through the decades, Donner argues, the specific missions and targets have shifted, but efforts to suppress radical movements have been a consistent feature of U.S. law enforcement and the "defense of the status quo a prime police mission" (1990, 364). Hoover himself, in a memorandum, bragged that COINTELPRO was just one instantiation of a broader counterintelligence mission: "the institution of a program such as COINTELPRO . . . in fact only encompasses everything that has been done in the past or will be done in the future" (Hoover 1964).

Today's "radical hunting" has been furthered by more advanced technologies, closer working relationships with private entities, legal changes and resources justified in terms of fighting "terrorism," heavily militarized police, and increasingly sophisticated models of policing, containing, and controlling public protests. As the following chapters will make clear, activists are often keenly aware of the historical and current legal and political context in which they mobilize. Key touchstones discussed in the brief history provided here—such as Red Squads, COINTELPRO, the Miami Model, and the Green Scare—were brought up, without prompting, again and again by the activists interviewed for this study. Given this history and context, how do activists consider the costs and risks of dissent? And how does personal experience of the repressive capacity of the state impact their willingness to continue to mobilize for causes they care about? And, perhaps most theoretically interesting, how are these considerations and decisions shaped by the groups of which they are a part?

3

Repression in the Eye of the Beholder

As discussed in chapter 1, scholars have amassed a great deal of conflicting evidence on whether repression tends to deter participation in social movements or to backfire and actually fuel protest. I argue that in order to unravel this puzzle, we must take seriously how activists themselves make sense of their experiences of state repression, both individually and collectively, and weigh the risks of continued involvement in protest. To do so, I studied activists and former activists in Arizona, a state with a broad and active social movement sector but also substantial repression of dissent, who were targeted for or in some way have experienced state repression. Individuals were recruited using a law enforcement watch list of activists from around the state (previously made public through a FOIA request) as a seed sample. Snowball sampling resulted in a sample of forty-five activists and former activists who had experienced state repression. To gain a better sense of the cultural landscapes from which these respondents draw and the social contexts in which they mobilize, I also analyzed activist pamphlets and writings suggested by my respondents and attended public protests which they participated in.[1]

These individuals reflected a variety of causes, organizations, as well as current and former levels and durations of political involvement. Despite this variation, what they shared was an experience of state repression, whether overt forms like police violence and arrest or covert forms like surveillance and infiltration. They served years in prison, had their heads slammed into street curbs and cell walls, and were pepper sprayed and shot with rubber bullets at protests. Others woke up to surveillance vans outside their homes for days on end, had their homes raided, were questioned by the FBI, had their mail consistently tampered with for years, and discovered that trusted friends had worn "bugs" at the behest of law enforcement.

As one might expect, these experiences (and even those far less extreme) caused some to back away from activism, deciding that despite the strength of their convictions, the costs were too high and risks to themselves and those they loved too great. Others refused to back down and continued to put themselves at risk of arrest, violence, and covert repression year after year. Ron,[2] a veteran environmental activist in his sixties, had been arrested over fifty times. Two others, who were also over fifty years old, had been arrested more than thirty times. Many people, even those who were still relatively young, had been arrested several times. And many others had multiple stories of police violence, surveillance, and infiltration.

In all, almost three-quarters of the activists who participated in the study maintained or increased their involvement over time, despite these experiences of state repression.[3] But the rest were effectively deterred by these experiences, to the point of disengaging from activism and avoiding situations, like street protests, that might put them at risk of further repression.[4] These differences in individual responses to repressive experiences are reflective of the conflicting evidence on repression effects from previous studies.

The first several sections of this chapter discuss these differing responses, establishing empirically the variation I observed. I then examine two possible explanations that previous findings and theory suggest might explain this variation. First, I examine whether some activists might simply have had different types of repressive experiences than others—in other words, that some types of repression are more likely to have a chilling effect than others. Second, I examine whether some activists, regardless of the type of repression they experienced, might have "gotten it worse" than others—that their repressive experiences were more severe or more costly—and that this explains why they disengaged while others persisted. Through analyzing these cases, I conclude that neither repression type nor repression severity can sufficiently explain these observed differences in individuals' responses to repression. This is why, in the chapters that follow, I work to unravel why some individuals respond so differently than others to objectively similar experiences of repression, and in doing so, illustrate the importance of activist networks and culture in shaping the subjective perception of these experiences and risks.

Radicalization and Persistence

In line with the previous studies showing that repression can sometimes backfire or be ineffective, most of those studied persisted despite personal experiences with repression. This was clear not only in how they described their trajectories over time and their current levels of involvement as participants and organizers in various movements, but was further corroborated by the fact that I continued to see most of them at protests in the months and years following my interviews with them. Some seemed to be at virtually every local protest, and many other activist meetings and gatherings, making it nearly a full-time (if unpaid) job.

I interviewed Debra shortly after she was arrested while counterprotesting with others at a campaign rally. The arrest was unexpected, and she was still quite shaken up by it when we talked. She was considering taking a break from activism for a while, telling me that now that she was in her late sixties, she couldn't bounce back from such experiences the way she used to. Despite these concerns, she began regularly attending protests again soon after. When protesters shut down a freeway exit ramp in response to a federal court jury finding a Border Patrol agent not guilty of second-degree murder after he shot and killed an unarmed Mexican teenager through the border wall, there she was—in the streets for the entire seven hours. She brought a cart with water and medical supplies, which she had started bringing to protests after a protest at which police pepper sprayed several people, including her and myself. Suzanne, another one of my interviewees, was at this same protest. She had been arrested dozens of times during the Occupy movement, and at this protest she was not only willing to risk arrest again, she volunteered for it. These women were not unique in expressing, through their discourse in their interviews as well as their subsequent actions, their continued willingness to risk repression.

Max not only continued to be an active organizer and participant after being arrested for providing humanitarian aid to migrants crossing through the desert, he was arrested again during the period of this study for attempting to block the deportation of a mother who had been in the United States for most of her life. Over a year after he told me about his own experiences with police violence and his dedication to supporting others who are injured at protests, I saw Bryan was still out working as a street medic—this time at a large protest at a campaign rally. At the same protest, Carl worked as a legal observer. When I had interviewed him months prior about his previous arrest at a protest, he told me that he had never personally experienced police violence at a protest, but that he would like to think that he wouldn't retreat if he were to be faced with it. And sure enough, even after he was tear gassed multiple times at this protest, he refused to leave so that he could record and bear witness to what the police were doing.

Many not only persisted despite instances of repression, but explicitly talked about these experiences as radicalizing, sometimes transformative, events that deepened their motivation to participate in collective action. A few specifically pointed to the experience of spending time in jail or prison, alongside others who were serving time for other kinds of criminal charges, as a radicalizing experience. Cory was a self-admitted "sheltered" white middle-class college student studying political science when he decided to check out the Occupy protests in his city, more out of curiosity than anything else. He had never been involved in protest before and the entire experience was transformative for him, from discussing political philosophy with people from very different walks of life and positions (on the left half) of the political spectrum, to being arrested in an attempt by police to clear the park on the first day that he joined the occupation. Jail was an especially illuminating experience for him, an opportunity to see what those with less privilege than he had experienced, and the way poor and working-class people become entangled in the dragnet of the criminal justice system. He explained that before this, "I'd never had to actually sit inside of a jail for eighteen hours and see what the rest of the country goes through because it's not something I go through . . . ever. It's not a world that I am shown very often, and so I think it was an incredibly eye-opening experience and it really changed my view of how the justice system works. And it doesn't. Once you're on the other side, inside the jail, you literally have no agency. You have no rights."

After he was released from the jail, he went directly back to the encampment and continued to be involved for weeks until the protests eventually died out, along with the other Occupy encampments across the country. He credited his arrest on that first day with fueling this newfound dedication to the cause. He explained, "I don't think I would've gone past the first day had I not been arrested. I think that really opened up my eyes to a bunch of different injustices that I didn't even know about. It just pissed me off, basically." He added, "All [the police] wanted to do was show a show of force, which they did. What they didn't understand is that we were getting a lot out of it too—that that experience itself was radicalizing us."

Angela, a nun who spent several months in prison for participating in an antinuclear civil disobedience action, echoed a similar sentiment. She told me: "The time I grew the most was when I went to the women's . . . prison. And I feel very, very proud that I not only went through that experience, but that I met, I now know, some wonderful people that I never would have known—people in my life that I would have never met. They made me aware of so much." At one point, she was transferred on a prison plane to another prison across the country, along with several other inmates. She was surprised to find out that almost none of the other inmates had ever been on an airplane before, and many were terrified. To her, the idea that these women were flying on a plane for the first time in their lives and were doing so under these circumstances—their feet and hands shackled together, and their waists shackled to one another for the entire cross-country flight so that it became a sizable feat of collective action every time one of them needed to use the restroom—was a tragedy, and a reminder of the profoundly limited opportunities they had had in their lives. She was struck by how young and poor her fellow inmates were, and by the fact that so many of them were serving time for nonviolent drug crimes, and, years later, she still can't forget them. Her time in prison, despite the discomfort, humiliation, and fallout with her family that she experienced as a result, ultimately served to deepen her commitment to social justice and strengthen her critique of inequality and injustice. This is consistent with Nepsted's (2014) finding that incarceration often served to confirm and strengthen the ideological commitments of other religious, antinuclear activists like Angela.

Not all who were jailed or served time in prison were radicalized, and this radicalization effect was not exclusive to those who were incarcerated in prison or spent time in local jails. On a more general level, for many I studied, confrontations with the state served to intensify their political commitments, or at the very least failed to deter them from continued participation.

Victor, a Latino and Native man in his forties who has been heavily involved in countercultural political and spiritual circles for years, recounted an experience in which the police unleashed violence on a small, spontaneous immigrant rights protest. He described being shocked and disturbed by the brutality of the police response to the peaceful protesters, many of whom were elderly, but when I asked him if this caused him to reconsider his involvement at all, he replied, laughing: "To be honest, no . . . but only because I'm weird. No, when I saw that happening, it strengthened my resolve."

But Victor's response might not be as "weird" as he thinks. Sean works for an environmental nonprofit, is the father of a young child, and has remained very active in movements on environmental and social issues for over a decade. He has been arrested "several" times and been hurt by police at protests on more than one occasion. At one protest, he was tear gassed, "drenched" in pepper gel (which is like pepper spray, but more concentrated, targeted, and stickier), and shot with paint balls (which police sometimes use to mark people for subsequent arrest), all within a matter of minutes. He described running through a sea of people who had also been affected by these "less lethal" weapons, feeling like his skin was "cooking" from the pepper gel and wanting to rip all his clothes off. "I mean, it's hard to explain, but I felt like I was dying." He vomited multiple times and jumped into a fountain in a vain attempt at relief (water does little for pepper spray, and even less for pepper gel) before finally finding street medics who were hosing off whole groups of people who had been sprayed, many of whom had stripped their clothes off, and providing rudimentary medical care to others who had been injured. "It felt like a war zone," he told me. Even talking about it years later, the emotional intensity of the experience was palpable. Another time, he was living at an environmental direct action camp when a man who was known to multiple people at the camp visited. Sean found out later, when the case went to court, that the man had been charged with arson, was facing decades in prison, and had come to the camp wearing a wire in hopes of getting information on others' illegal activities in exchange for a lighter sentence. The idea that someone had been wired at the camp with him clearly disturbed Sean, but when I asked whether this, or any of his other experiences with repression, made him question what he was doing or wonder if he was in over his head, he said, "Not really at the time. All of it felt, you know, exciting and like proof that there needed to be more of a fight."

Zach, who has maintained his resolve despite experiencing the full arsenal of state repression, told me that when he was federally indicted on charges of vandalizing a military recruitment center, "If it didn't embolden me, it would have destroyed me." Despite his fears about the very real possibility of going to prison, and despite finding out that an old friend was asked by law enforcement to wear a wire to gather evidence against him, he refused to be deterred—or to lose his sense of humor. He told me, "When I got my federal indictment from the FBI agent at my door, it said, 'United States of America vs. Me [real name redacted],' and I would joke like, 'That's funny, I always thought it was the other way around.'"

This radicalization effect extended to confrontations with the state outside of a protest context as well. Many had experience with arrest and police brutality in non-protest situations, and these experiences combined with their political arrests and other experiences of repression in shaping their beliefs about police, the state, and about themselves as political dissidents. For example, one man told me about a time the police violently broke up a house party he and his friends had put on. When I asked him if this experience made him or his friends think twice about risking police violence at protests, he told me,

> I mean, I think in many ways it just emboldened us. I don't think we shied away from it. I mean, we were geared at that time towards building a social insurrection. I believed then, as I believe now, that it's not going to come from a political sect. You know, it's people's friends. . . . And it's also, you know, creating a kind of a climate in which you and your friends experience that together, so that even if you're no longer hanging out with that person, you know, they're also a person with the same criticism in that situation, whereas most people maybe feel ashamed or like feel guilty about that—No. That confrontation was like righteous, you know. That was the extension of like my life project of struggle, that you're damned right we should stand up for ourselves to the f-cking cops.

Interestingly, it was not uncommon for others to talk about encounters with authorities in the context of their activism in the same breath as similar experiences in other contexts. Such an analytical distinction did not resonate with their understanding of their politics and reflected the way they saw their oppositional stance toward the world as inextricable from their sense of self.

Deterrence and Disengagement

While many were radicalized by or at the very least persisted despite such experiences, not everyone felt this way after paying high costs for their convictions. Emma, along with others, locked herself to a bulldozer using a bike U-lock around her neck, to stop a controversial construction project in her community. As she expected, the U-lock was eventually cut from her neck and she was arrested. But she didn't expect the experience to be as terrifying as it was or to be threatened by the officers. She also didn't expect the long legal ordeal that followed, which was still not completely resolved years later. This experience caused her to question her involvement, and she has since backed away from these more confrontational forms of protest. She explained, "I don't want to compromise my safety. And I enjoy my privacy, enjoy like my own life, and I also just don't want to compromise who I'm around either."

Gerald, who had spent years in prison on terrorism charges, told me with tears in his eyes that he wished he could still be involved, but just can't. His son died unexpectedly while he was incarcerated, his criminal record has made it difficult for him to find work, and his life has been forever changed. "I've already lost too much," he told me. Emily also found the weight of what she had lost to be too much to bear. In her early thirties at the time I spoke with her, she told me that she had given her entire twenties to activism, living on nothing and in constant fear of the state, as she saw friends go to prison or kill themselves to avoid it. Now she just wanted some peace and security. She even moved to a new town because she felt as if everyone in her old town knew that she was involved in the circle of people that had been swept up in a crackdown on so-called "ecoterrorists," and that in her words, she "embodied the past too much" in the eyes of others.

Brad had multiple arrests and experiences of police violence and then was interrogated by the FBI before deciding that he was in over his head and stopped engaging in political organizing. Jessica explained that, after she was violently arrested at a protest, she decided to take a break from activist work that she was, at that point, just starting to get involved in. She meant for it to be temporary: "I just knew I needed to take a break because I'd been traumatized. Like, I got home and my whole body was still burning from pepper spray. And my friend found some powdered condensed milk and gave me like a bath by dabbing my whole body with milk and like comforting me like a child while I cried for hours and hours. You know, I knew that my job was like to get my mental health together. . . . I just thought I needed to keep my head down, just stay out of trouble." But this temporary break turned into her "dropping out," as she put it. When she became a mother, and around the same time found out that that arrest had landed her on a law enforcement watch list, this solidified her desire to avoid arrest or other costs that might be associated with participating in protest. She explained her current situation: "I have been a single mom, mostly, for two years, and my son's not even two, he's a baby, so I feel exhausted. I can't go. I'm on an anti-terrorist watch list. And, you know, for whatever reason, some of these cops know who I am. And it makes me sad that I'm not able to participate and support and show solidarity."

She hadn't attended a protest since her arrest until one day when she heard through a text tree about a spontaneous protest that had formed around a Border Patrol vehicle. A migrant, whose asylum case was pending, was pulled over, along with two women who were volunteers with a local refugee/immigrant hospitality house, while returning from the hospital where his son had just been born. The volunteers had laid their bodies under the Border Patrol vehicle, refusing to let them take the young father away, and began texting everyone they knew to show up in solidarity. I was with Jessica when she got the text. She was visibly excited and said this was the first time in two years that she had been invited to something like this and could actually go. She asked me to come with her. As we drove, she began to express more apprehension, saying she needed to be extra careful. For one, her son was with us. But even if he weren't, she could not risk getting arrested because of him. When we arrived, about a hundred people were surrounding the vehicle, chanting "We are people, we are not illegal." After only about fifteen minutes, at the first sign that the police and Border Patrol intended to disperse the crowd, Jessica wanted to leave immediately. As we walked back to her car, she apologized, "Sorry, I am just super not willing to take risks. . . . They're awesome, I totally support it, but I can't be here with my baby." As she strapped her son into the car seat, she explained, "Who knows? They might be like, 'Look, that lady with the baby is the one on that terrorist list.'"

Nick also talked about how concerns about repression, and questions about the efficacy of protest, caused him to take a step back from the kind of confrontational political activity he had been involved in: "At this point, it's not where I'm at because . . . maybe if the state was a f-cking pillow, and every time we went we f-cking crashed headfirst into softness and no consequences, I'd do it forever. But that's not it. It's the same response or a modified response from five years ago. Which was a modified response from five years before that. It's the same thing. And there are young people doing it tonight, in theory. And it's great, you know. Go for it, guys. . . . But I'm also not convinced that . . . the mass consciousness of the people is going to be lit aflame by this happening tonight."

It should be noted that repression was not the sole cause of disengagement from activism for any of those I spoke with. Instead, experiences of and concerns about repression combined with other factors to lead some to question their involvement and move away from participating in protest. As already mentioned, Jessica's temporary break from activism as she recovered from a traumatic arrest turned out to not be so temporary, in part because she became pregnant soon after. Becoming a parent made her reconsider the risks she was willing to take. Johnny also told me that becoming a parent caused him to move toward taking on support roles in movements rather than being on the "front lines" of protest because he was no longer willing to risk getting hurt. Four respondents talked about physical or mental health problems combining with concerns about further repression to cause them to take time away from activism. Another talked of recent financial problems that made him less able to focus on activism, at a time when he was already questioning his participation due to concerns about repression.

For some, it was simply getting older and thinking more seriously about the future, in combination with concerns about repression, that caused them to disengage. Nick, who had said he'd "do it forever" if it weren't for the repressive consequences, also told me,

> I think when I was younger, I had more enthusiasm for getting off an eight-hour shift and going to [a protest]. Whereas now I think of my time differently. You know, I'm like, "I think I'd rather go home and do some cleaning." It's just that like there's just a point like, you know, just the way our society is, it allows for this time for young people. I was using the time young people were supposed to use for collegiate stuff . . . to raise hell. And then, there's like a point, I think definitely, usually your thirties, where it becomes a lot harder to do that. . . . Just managing your life becomes a lot harder, especially when you get to an age when you're on the cusp of deciding like, well I really have to decide my next ten years. Like do I want a family?

Another man, also in his early thirties, echoed these sentiments: "I think when I was younger, I was more willing to sacrifice my own personal economic security or my professional life. Even my social environment was based on activism. . . . I think about myself sometimes, wondering, 'Have I given up, sold out, whatever you wanna call it?' In many ways, I'm confused about it because I feel like I want more security in my life now and certain comforts that I was willing to forgo in the past."

Others had similar narratives, despite the fact that they had remained involved. For them, getting older changed their decision making around repression risks somewhat, but did not deter them completely. For example, Keith explained,

> In my twenties and thirties, I had a very different view of my own mortality in relation to revolution. And I thought it was coming. And just didn't expect to be—I'm going to turn fifty this year. I never expected that, or to look like this, so I made some really bold life choices back then, because I was all in. And I'm still all in, it just looks different now. It comes from a different perspective. So yeah, I am meek and humble in comparison to what I was when I was younger, but I'm also smarter and safer.

It is important to note that everyone who had disengaged from social movement involvement also expressed that they had not let go of their fundamental political beliefs and values. Emily, who, as previously discussed, has shied away from activism after being questioned by the FBI and losing a close friend to suicide while he was awaiting trial on "ecoterrorism" charges, told me, "I don't think that my views have changed that much. . . . I don't think they've really changed. But maybe I'm not—maybe I don't embody them as much right now." Others who had disengaged said they hold more nuanced perspectives now, or are more informed, but that their fundamental worldview had not changed and that they still care about the same causes that motivated them to become involved in the first place. Interestingly, even those who had persisted often had a similar narrative about their views becoming less black and white over time, but not fundamentally changing. So, for those who disengaged, it was their behavior, rather than their ideology, that had shifted. It is also important to note, as will become clear in later chapters, that just because someone steps away from participation in social movements due to repression, or for any other reason, does not mean that they do not continue to be active in working for changes they believe in, but just that they no longer do so through protest or other types of noninstitutional, confrontational, political activity. As will be discussed in chapter 6, many still express their politics through their lifestyle, career, or parenting choices. This all suggests that scholars need to develop a clearer, and more complex, understanding of what constitutes disengagement from activism, and what factors contribute to it.

In sum, there is clearly a wide range of responses to repression among those I studied. For some, these experiences caused them to dig in their heels, step up their commitments, strengthen their convictions, or at the very least continue to participate as they had before this experience. But for a sizable minority, the weight of the risks they were taking with their safety, livelihood, and freedom proved to be too much to bear, and they backed away from political involvement, despite the fact that their political beliefs remained largely intact. Often, this disengagement was described as a result of dealing with the costs of repression, in combination with other factors such as changes in life circumstances or priorities.

Repression Type

One way researchers have suggested that the mixed findings on repression effects might be reconciled is by distinguishing between different types of repression, reasoning that these types may impact mobilization differently and help explain seemingly contradictory empirical evidence. Earl (2003) demonstrates that some types of repression have received much more attention from researchers than others. For example, there has been much more research on overt types (such as arrest and police violence) of repression compared with covert types (such as surveillance and infiltration; Earl 2003). Some scholars have begun to examine explanations for when, and against which organizations or individuals, states engage in covert repression (e.g., Cunningham 2004; Davenport 2005), but the question of how covert repression impacts mobilization is less understood (save Cunningham 2004; Cunningham and Noakes 2008; Starr et al 2008; Davenport 2014). Considering extensive evidence that the capacity for state surveillance of movements is increasing (Cunningham and Noakes 2008; Fernandez 2008; Starr et al. 2008; Starr and Fernandez 2009; Gillham 2011; Shantz 2012), understanding how activists manage covert repression, in addition to overt repression, is critical.

After considering how my subjects' divergent trajectories might be explained by the specific type(s) of repression they experienced, I also consider how they think about and weigh the possible risks of different types of repression in hypothetical situations, regardless of what they have already experienced and regardless of their own trajectory. This allows me an additional way to examine how repression type might help explain mixed effects of repression on individual involvement, and to examine possible differences between how activists respond to repression costs already incurred versus possible repression risks in the future.

Experiencing Different Types of Repression

Table 3.1 displays the types of repression experienced by the interviewees. The first thing that becomes immediately apparent from table 3.1 is that all four forms of repression were remarkably common among those interviewed.[5] Each of the four types of repression was experienced by the majority of the interviewees, with 89 percent having been arrested, 58 percent experiencing police violence, 76 percent being under surveillance (or having reason to suspect they were), and 60 percent having been part of a group that was infiltrated by an undercover officer or informant. In fact, only four of the forty-five

Table 3.1
Types of Repressive Experiences Among Respondents

	Arrest	Violence	Surveillance	Infiltration	Total
Number (Percent) of Respondents	40 (89%)	26 (58%)	34 (76%)	27 (60%)	45

NOTE: Row percentages do not sum to 100 because people often experienced multiple types of repression.

individuals interviewed had experience with only one of these types. The most common was having experienced three of the four, which was the case for twenty respondents. And eleven individuals actually had experience with all four major types of repression, having been dedicated activists for years and feeling the full force of the state upon them.

The fact that most people experienced multiple forms of repression makes sense if you consider that individuals often experience more than one type at the same time (e.g., they are violently arrested) and because, once they get on the radar of law enforcement, they are increasingly at risk of further repression (e.g., an arrest might land them on a watch list of people to be surveilled). Others simply were very active for many years and it seemed as if it was only a matter of time before they experienced the full spectrum of state repression. For example, Charles was heavily involved with the radical environmentalist group Earth First! for years and had multiple experiences with all four types of repression. He was arrested a few times, sometimes planned and sometimes not. Once, he and other protesters held a nonviolent protest aimed at stopping trucks from getting to a nuclear plant. "We were hit by a flying wedge of cops to get the truck through. I tried to protect my friends from being hit by a baton and was pushed into the ditch. I still have back problems." He also had several experiences with covert forms of repression. Two people he met during this time had been confirmed (at the trial of some of his friends) to be undercover officers trying to get information on group members' activities, and there were others he suspected of being infiltrators as well. He also found out during this trial that he had been under surveillance. He explained, "For a while, I had to live in the Earth First! office to keep it secure. We found out in the trial that they were watching me the whole time. They even had notes about the dates I brought there." This had significant consequences for his personal life. He explained, "It was risky to date because she could be a fed. Or she could get a file and I would not want to put her through that. So when I met someone I liked, I had to think seriously about whether it was worth these risks. So, strip clubs were my coping mechanism [laughs]. . . . Some are therapists in their own way." But, like many others who had experience with the full spectrum of political repression, he persisted. He told me, "None

Table 3.2
Persistence/Disengagement, by Types of Repressive Experiences

	Arrest	Violence	Surveillance	Infiltration	Total
Persisted	32 (80%)	18 (69%)	24 (71%)	21 (78%)	33 (73%)
Disengaged	8 (20%)	8 (31%)	10 (29%)	6 (22%)	12 (27%)
	40 (100%)	26 (100%)	34 (100%)	27 (100%)	45 (100%)

of this caused me to be less involved. That was not an option because of what I knew and believed. I couldn't turn back or walk away. In some ways it made me madder, more committed, stronger. I am not above doing something out of spite."

I expected that the form(s) of repression respondents had experienced would help make sense of some of the variation in participation outcomes I observed. Perhaps those who were arrested and had to deal with the legal system might be more likely to be deterred than those who were pepper sprayed at a protest, or covert types of repression such as infiltration or surveillance may have more of a chilling effect than more obvious, overt repression like arrest or violence from police. Table 3.2 displays the number and percentage of activists who persisted and disengaged among those who experienced each of these four types of repression. For example, 69 percent of the twenty-six respondents who experienced police violence at a protest or other movement-related interaction with law enforcement (e.g., in the course of interrogation) persisted, while 31 percent disengaged.

Chi square tests of independence revealed that there were no significant differences in persistence/disengagement between individuals who had experienced police violence, surveillance, or infiltration compared with those who had not had each of these experiences ($p = 0.467$, 0.464, and 0.409, respectively). The only significant difference was between those who had been arrested and those who had not (Pearson $\chi^2(1) = 8.1818$, $p = 0.004$), with the frequencies suggesting that arrests may actually help induce persistence for some. The stories that some respondents, like Cory and Angela, told about having their eyes opened by a personal experience with the justice system might help explain the unique backfire effect of arrest experiences. Also, respondents sometimes talked about arrest as something that was planned (as part of an act of civil disobedience) and that they deliberately volunteered for, whereas this level of intentional choice was much less common with other forms of repression. This is another reason why experiences with arrest might be especially likely to radicalize, or at least not deter, activists. But the fact that those who disengaged and those who persisted exhibit indistinguishable rates of the other major types of repression—police violence, surveillance, and infiltration—suggests that examining the type of repression experienced only gets us so far in understanding individuals' dramatically different reactions to repression.

Considering Different Types of Repression

McAdam (1986) distinguishes between cost and risk as two different axes along which protest activities vary. An act of protest may be high cost but low risk, or vice versa. Costs are relatively known, and McAdam defines them as "the expenditure of time, money and energy required of a person engaged in any particular form of activism" (p. 67). Risks, on the other hand, are relatively unknown and defined as "the anticipated dangers—whether legal, social, physical, financial, etc.—of engaging in a particular form of activity" (p. 67). Wiltfang and McAdam (1991) expand on this by arguing that costs are first and foremost what is already "given up, foregone, spent, lost, or 'negatively' experienced," while risks are expected, possible consequences in the future (p. 989).

Therefore, repression that has already been experienced might be best considered a cost, whereas the possibility of future repression might be best considered a risk. It is possible that the risk of different types of repression may have altogether different impacts on one's willingness to participate in protest than the cost of repression already experienced. That is why, in addition to examining how respondents' actual experiences with different types of repression were associated with persistence or disengagement, I also examine how they think about the potential risk posed by these different forms. All respondents were asked not only about how they processed and reacted to personal experiences of repression, but also about how they considered the risks of different types of repression, regardless of whether they had experienced them. Using questions about hypothetical situations (for example, whether or not they would leave a protest if police threatened to make arrests), I sought to understand how these different types of risks might carry more or less weight than others in shaping their participation. Earl (2005, 2011a, 2011b) has problematized the idea that different types of repression are necessarily commensurate, and more specifically the assumption of many scholars that arrest is a "softer" or less severe or costly form of repression than other types such as violence. Rather than fall into such assumptions, I asked respondents how they thought about the risks of various types of repression. How activists themselves rank different types of repression against one another has not been examined in previous research (Earl 2011a).

It may be the case that activists are more concerned about some types than others, regardless of what they have experienced, and that these concerns shape their participation. For example, Nick, who had disengaged, was most concerned about arrest, the one thing that he hadn't experienced. "An arrest, you know, you'll have to poop in front of somebody you don't know . . . there's levels of like humiliation involved with it that violence, even while violence can like obviously be traumatizing, whereas going into police custody. . . . I would much rather get hit with a club or hit by a cop or shoved. Easily over like cuffs. No control. . . . Yeah, violence. Any day. Any day of the week."

I found that, while some individuals make distinctions between different types of repression, there are no consistent patterns across activists about what kinds of repression risks they put more weight on than others. Like Nick, a few respondents explained that they were more concerned with arrest and legal consequences than with violence or physical injury. Kyle, who was at one point facing years in prison, told me that "False arrest and the fear of malicious prosecution is like way scarier to me than probably most physically violent things that I could imagine that would happen at a protest. Like, I would take that way before the other thing." These sentiments expressed by these activists fit with Barkan's (1984) finding that legalistic repression was more effective at deterring subsequent mobilization than was violent repression. But there was far from consensus on this. Rudiger said he was more worried about violence and had been more affected by the violence he witnessed against others at protests than by his own arrest at an anti-war protest, despite the fact that it was unexpected and, in his eyes, very unjustified. Emily also told me that she feared violence above all else. She explained that her fear of incarceration, harassment, and surveillance was rooted in the fact that these types of repression can ultimately lead to violence from the state. But others talked about being more concerned about infiltration, because of the sense of betrayal involved in this kind of repression. Therefore, while some did indicate being more concerned about some types of repression, there were no consistent patterns across respondents in terms of how they considered or were affected by different types of repression.

Others explicitly indicated that the form of repression made no difference, because they were either effectively deterred by all types of repression or were committed to continuing their political work regardless of the specific form of repression they might experience. When I asked Jessica, who had been arrested at a protest and who had been violently slammed to the ground and pepper sprayed by a police officer, whether she was more concerned about being arrested again or experiencing that kind of violence again, she explained that both were situations she was equally interested in avoiding at all costs, at least until her kids were grown and no one was dependent on her: "I'd say I'm equally scared. And I feel like it's safest for my family if I don't really associate with a bunch of people who are maybe doing things that attract interest to them, because I don't want to attract that kind of attention, now that I know how easy it is to get caught on a list and be surveilled and oppressed. . . . I just try to keep more my radical side hidden, in general. I really just want to fit in, you know, get through my family years.... I just have no margin of f-ck-up in my life. I work and I feed babies."

For others, these risks were too connected in their mind for it to even make sense to think about what kinds of repression they were more concerned about. Brad explained,

> I see the state and police and the feds as just waiting for any chance they can get to just f-ck us, to tear apart communities, to rip our projects to shreds, to halt our campaigns, to ultimately pacify us or send us away so that we won't ever come back together. And so, I see surveillance as a way to legitimize them being able to come in and use that violence against us whether it's raiding... our house, or arresting us, or pepper spraying us, or shooting us.... I see surveillance as absolutely a part of the threat of violence. It's the lead into that, the catalyst. So they're all very, very much connected.

Multiple people also talked about arrest as an inherently violent act. Kyle told me, "An arrest in my mind, if it's a false arrest, is a violent thing. I mean, you're being put in a cage for no reason by like scary dudes." Sani, in reference to being arrested when he and others occupied a university lab, told me, "I mean, once you're in that system, the whole process is violent." Starr et al. (2008) have made claims that echo these sentiments and urge researchers to recognize the interconnections between different forms of violence. As they put it, "overt, bodily violence against protesters is part of a dense continuum of state activity.... The density is important because bodily violence is neither clearly the worst thing that can happen to an activist nor is it entirely separable from other types of repression, over which it looms as an explicit or implicit threat.... By referencing one another, both bodily violence and other types of repression have a cumulative force and impact" (Starr et al. 2008, 2–3). Because different forms of repression were so interconnected in activists' actual experiences, and also in their minds, isolating the relative effect of different types of repression, or their relative weight in activists' decision making, may be more challenging for scholars than has been assumed.

Repression Severity

The above findings underscore Earl's (2005, 2011a, 2011b) warning against assuming different types of repression are commensurate and can be ranked against each other in terms of how costly or repressive they are. Given this, perhaps it is not the type of repression that activists experience that makes some more likely to be deterred than others, but rather the severity of these experiences. Repression severity might be a better measure of the costliness of

Table 3.3
Severity of Repressive Experiences, by Persistence/Disengagement

	Obs.	Mean	Std. Error	Std. Deviation	95% Confidence Interval	
Persisted	32	1.30303	0.2363102	1.357499	0.8216822	1.784378
Disengaged	13	1.58333	0.2599048	0.9003366	1.011287	2.15538

repression than repression type, and, if rational choice scholars are right that it is the costliness of repression that gives it a deterrent quality, this might best explain who persisted and who disengaged. Perhaps it is those who shouldered the most significant burdens of repression or had the most traumatic experiences with the state who were deterred, while those who had relatively minor experiences were not. But, as I will demonstrate using both basic methods of difference and qualitative examples, severity also fails to explain the different reactions to repressive experience among those that I studied. Together with the findings about repression type, this suggests that people have very different responses to objectively similar experiences of repression.

All respondents were assigned a severity score, measuring the number of severe repression experiences they had undergone. The score ranged from 0 to 4 and, on average, respondents had experienced about 1.4 severe types of repression.[6] Table 3.3 displays the average severity scores of respondents who persisted and those who disengaged.

Those who disengaged had an average severity score of about 1.58, and those who persisted had a severity score of about 1.3, at first glance suggesting that severity of experience might help explain the disparate effects. However, a two-sample *t*-test revealed that there was no statistically significant difference between the mean severity scores of the individuals who disengaged compared those who persisted ($t = 0.6618, p = 0.5116$).

This can be seen qualitatively as well, as many of those with the most severe stories of repression persisted, while others with less severe experiences disengaged. When Kyle was first grabbed from the crowd at a large protest on the East Coast and told he was under arrest, he wasn't too concerned. He'd been arrested a handful of times at protests back in Arizona, where he went to college. He knew that it was not uncommon for police to make mass arrests, or randomly snatch individuals from the crowd, only for the courts to drop the charges later for lack of evidence. Several hundred people had been arrested in this way in the few days prior to his arrest, so he was hardly surprised when it happened to him. He felt strongly about voicing his opposition to the war in Iraq and knew he had every right to do so. He assumed that the experience of being arrested would be more inconvenient than anything else. But as he was being processed, he started to notice that he was being treated differently than the others, and he started to worry. To deal with the high number of arrests, the city had set up a large warehouse to hold the arrested protesters. Kyle explained, "Inside of [the warehouse], they had these huge chain link cages that they put like a hundred to two hundred people in. . . . Well, they put me in one by myself and all the other ones were like packed full of people. So I knew something weird was happening, you know? That's when I really knew that something strange was going on."

Eventually, he was told he was being charged with seven felonies for allegedly setting a fire during the march, a fire that had supposedly burned a police officer. They claimed he had planned the whole thing—that others at the march were in on it too, but that he was the mastermind. He had no idea what they were talking about. He was bonded out after a week in jail but spent the next ten months traveling back and forth from Arizona fighting the charges. Insisting on his innocence, he refused to take a plea bargain. He had to drop out of college and couldn't work because of the frequent travel for court dates and the great deal of time he was spending to help build the case for his innocence. With the help of friends, he pored over hundreds of hours of footage from the protest, looking for proof that he was nowhere near where the fire was set.

For the last two months of the legal ordeal, he moved to the city where he was being tried so he could devote himself fully to the case. His friends threw him a going away party when he left. Their support was invaluable to him, but the party was bittersweet. He would be back in only a few months if he won in trial. But if he lost, he might be spending the next seven years in prison. This possibility had been hanging over him for several months, and at times was hard to bear. He told me, "I don't think, unless you've been there, you can know what it feels like. Every night, lying in bed, going to sleep thinking, 'I'm going to prison for nothing, for something I didn't do, something that was fabricated.' It was really, really hard . . . and every morning, waking up and being like, 'I'm still in this.'"

Even when, just a week before the trial, a photographer came forward with footage that proved conclusively that he was nowhere near the fire when it started, he was still worried. The way he saw it, the police had worked together to fabricate this whole story, so what's to say they wouldn't somehow find a way to, as he put it, "perpetuate this lie"? Even now, with proof of his innocence, he was worried that the truth didn't matter. But, fortunately for him, in this case it did. The new footage was damning for the state's case and all charges were dropped. He sued over the wrongful arrest, and years later eventually won a sizable settlement. But the nearly year-long nightmare left him traumatized and, like many others who are arrested at protests (Earl 2005), he learned that sometimes "the process is the punishment" (Feeley 1992).

After such an experience, many would probably steer clear of protests altogether. And at first Kyle did, only because his lawyer told him not to attend any protests while the charges were still pending. But not long after the charges were dropped, he decided to attend a protest again. He told me, "I didn't want to feel like it knocked me off my horse," so he went despite his fear. At the protest, he had a panic attack. He thought he heard two police officers talking about him, and was sure "they were, any second, about to come and get me." He had similar episodes of intense anxiety at several subsequent protests, but he kept going to them anyway and, over time, the anxiety lessened. Even today, over a decade later, he says he still feels anxious when he sees a police officer. But he doesn't let fear drive his decisions or stop him from standing up for causes he cares about. He explained, "When I attend protests now, I don't generally screen them based on like: 'This is too risky for me to go or not.' I just go to the ones I feel interested in, and have time for, and feel like it's a good cause." Despite having one of the most severe and distressing experiences with repression of those I studied, he continued to show up for social issues he cared about. This was also true of many of the other activists I spoke with who paid the highest costs for their activism.

Meanwhile, others with less severe experiences, like Jessica or Emma already discussed, were effectively deterred by these incidents. Rudiger, who has been arrested at a protest but has never faced any serious consequences, legal or otherwise, for his activism, has completely disengaged. While he has never been able to confirm that he has been under surveillance or been in a group that was infiltrated, the possibility of this happening has had a strong chilling effect on him. Like many of those I talked to, he was more concerned about informants, people who are offered a lighter sentence in exchange for providing information on others, than about undercover officers. He avoided friends who were involved in drugs for exactly this reason, as did several of the other people I studied. He was not only worried about people who might have gotten in trouble and "turned," but also those who could in the future, if they were to get caught for drugs or anything else they might be involved in. This made him incredibly paranoid around anyone he thought had, or could possibly have in the future, any criminal charges. This fear, along with other factors, led him to disengage from activism, even though his personal experiences of repression were relatively mild compared to others I spoke with, like Kyle. He explained his disengagement, telling me, "It's a combination of financial issues and avoiding some of the people. Especially the people that I suspect as past or future informants, but also other people that have become involved in things that have been destructive."

Of course, there were also those who had severe experiences and were effectively deterred, like Gerald, who, as already described, avoided involvement in anything political after he spent two years in prison on terrorism charges. And there were several who persisted in activism and had only ever experienced planned arrests that did not carry the possibility of doing real time. Still, the bottom line is that, as with repression type, repression severity does little to explain why some activists disengage following these experiences while others deepen their commitment.

Conclusion

While there was variation in both what activists experienced and how they responded to experiences of repression, their reactions did not seem to depend on what type(s) of repression they had experienced, nor its severity. One exception is that individuals who had experienced arrest were more likely to persist than those who were never arrested, but this could be a function of the almost complete saturation of the sample in terms of arrests and so should not be overinterpreted. Individuals also did not generally indicate being more willing to risk some types of repression over others when asked hypothetical questions about how they would respond in various situations. Instead, individuals were generally deterred by repression across the board or radicalized across the board. Because individuals seem to respond so differently to objectively similar costs and risks of repression, this suggests that attention should be turned to the factors that shape the subjective perception and experience of repression. To this end, the following chapters will explore the social factors that alter this calculus and make some individual activists more resilient in the face of repression than others.

4

Shaping Experiences of Repression through Prevention, Preparation, and Support

The fact that differences of repression type and severity are not enough to explain disparate effects on subsequent participation suggests that individual activists respond differently to apparently similar experiences of repression. To understand why this is the case requires examining the subjective experience of repression. At the very least, it requires examining how and why the costs of repression, even of the same type and severity, are higher for some than for others. In this chapter, I will demonstrate how groups work to lower the costs and risks of repression for individuals, and the consequences when they fail to do so. This is the first of three main ways that I argue social movement organizations and communities shape how individuals experience and respond to repression. In the following chapters, I will go further and demonstrate how being socialized into protest groups shapes how activists think about themselves and about the goals of protest—and how both, in turn, have consequences for persistence in the face of repression. Together, I argue, these constitute three major ways that groups influence individual rationality in collective action.

In this chapter, I focus on how activist organizations and networks often engage in practices aimed at reducing the risks and costs of participation for members. Some of this is in line with RAT and reminds us of the utility that this perspective provides. Recall that my core theoretical argument is that the field will be best positioned to understand repression effects (and collective action more generally) if RAT and more culturally focused theories are synthesized into a holistic approach. To this end, I start with demonstrating how RAT's focus on costs and benefits sensitizes us to an important way that groups impact the effect of repression on individuals—by mitigating the risks and costs of repression—and provides a useful starting point for examining the collective construction of individual rationality in relation to repression and to collective action more generally.

Reducing the costs of repression includes working to prevent repression where possible, preparing individuals for the possibility of repression, and providing supports that can help mitigate the costs of repression for those who bear the brunt of it. Through cultures that emphasize security, activists work to protect each other from infiltration and surveillance. Through cultures that often treat repression as an eventuality rather than a possibility (and provide members with training to prepare for this eventuality), activists work to reduce the shock and deterrent power of repression. And finally, through networks that provide material and emotional support, movements work to redistribute the costs and burdens of repression and lessen the blow for those who are targeted by or happen to incur the wrath of the state (e.g., those who are arrested at protests or who experience police violence, surveillance, or other forms of state repression). Through these practices, groups reduce the risks and costs that repression poses for individuals, and therefore, actually shape their experience of repression. In doing so, groups have the power to influence whether or not individuals are deterred by these experiences. In fact, I find that individuals who have a repressive experience in which they fail to get adequate group support or preparation are far more likely to disengage than those who felt supported through and prepared for these kinds of situations.

The Costs of Repression

As rational choice scholars and others argue, repression can be very costly for the activists who experience it. This was clear throughout interviewees' discussion of their experiences. Repression can carry both material and emotional costs and, given the high price that many pay, it is no wonder that some are deterred. After providing evidence of the costs, both material and nonmaterial, that activists described as resulting from state repression, I will then spend most of the chapter detailing the ways that groups work to mitigate these costs for individuals, and the consequences this has for persistence.

Direct Financial Costs

Repression, especially getting arrested, can be expensive. Sometimes it is very expensive. Emma, as mentioned in the previous chapter, locked herself to construction equipment to stop a controversial construction project in her community. She was charged, along with the others she was arrested with, a combined fine of $60,000 for the action. The city argued that several firefighters and police officers had to work overtime to cut them out and arrest them, and that the company was unable to proceed with construction for that day, estimating these costs and damages to total $60,000.

In the end, only Emma and one other activist were fined, even though several others also participated in the action. The two had an injunction against them, after another act of civil disobedience against the same development project, that forbade them from setting foot on the site. For violating the injunction, and inconveniencing the city and company, Emma and one other activist were saddled with the fine. Their fine was eventually reduced to $4,000, but even paying this smaller debt was a significant burden for them. Emma told me it was hard having this debt still hanging over her head more than two years later, in part because she hates the idea of being made to pay for something she doesn't support.

Kyle, the college student whose lengthy legal battle was discussed in the previous chapter, said his family, especially his mom, spent tens of thousands of dollars on his legal defense. Over a decade later, after winning a lawsuit over the case, he was finally able to repay her. When I asked him how it felt to win the suit, he said, "It mostly just feels like breaking even."

While direct financial costs, such as fines or legal fees, were clearly a concern for some, this was actually less common than many of the other costs that will be discussed. In fact, only five interviewees discussed incurring or being concerned about direct financial costs of repression. This may be because, as will be discussed, these costs are easier than others to be shared within a group, making it less likely that individuals will have to bear them alone (although this does still happen).

Career and Educational Costs

A more common concern, and one that is less easily mitigated by the group, is that related to the career and educational consequences that can come with being arrested. One man, a teacher, told me that he worries about his job prospects in the future because of his arrest for alleged property damage at a protest. He explained that, even though he was cleared of all charges, his arrest was high profile enough that it still comes up in a cursory internet search on his name. "That's like the number one thing that pops up, you know . . . anyone could search my name any time and see that," he worried.

Others also argued that, even in the absence of a conviction, their arrests had consequences for their careers. This is, in part, because some background checks show arrests, not just convictions. Bryan, now a nurse, told me, "It still affects me, which it shouldn't because I was found innocent. I was acquitted, but when you run a criminal background, it does come up." Actually, he explained, several different charges come up from the same arrest, because the state kept dropping charges and filing new ones in an effort to get something to "stick." As a result, it looks like many separate offenses on a background check. He explained, "It looks like two pages of this charge, that charge, and it's all either dropped or acquitted, but I have had employers discriminate on that." And if that wasn't bad enough, when he finished nursing school and was waiting on his nursing license to start a new job, someone from the sheriff's department called the Board of Nursing to call their attention to his arrest (despite that fact that he was not convicted), resulting in his licensing being delayed significantly and causing him to lose the first job he was set to start.

Dana was a graduate student when she was charged with vandalism of a police station, and it affected her life and education tremendously. She still doesn't know exactly why she was accused of the crime. What she does know is that, about a month before, she had attended a community meeting about a new police anti-gang initiative in her neighborhood. She had made a public statement during the time allotted for this purpose and had submitted her name and address in order to do so. Her statement was, to some, quite inflammatory. She not only argued that the initiative would lead to increased police harassment of neighborhood youth, but she likened the police themselves to a gang and said that, more than anything, she wanted them out of her neighborhood. About a month later, she was driving out of town with friends to go hiking, when, suddenly, as she told me, "this unmarked car, like cut us off very aggressively. I was like, 'Oh my god this is like, this is one of those like crazy drivers—road rage drivers. Is he going to assault us?'" Instead, several police cars came "out of nowhere," their sirens blaring, and surrounded them. The man in the unmarked car got out, flashed his police badge, and told her she was under arrest. When they took her to the police station, she said she had no idea what she was being charged with. But she heard a police officer say to another, "Yeah, that's her."

Sitting alone in the interrogation room for what felt to her like forever, still unsure of her charge, her mind began to go wild: "Oh my god, I'm being charged with something terrible," she said she was thinking at the time. She could tell by how she was being treated, and how everyone was looking at her, that, whatever they thought she had done, it was serious. She was terrified that she might be incarcerated and, when the detective finally came in to interrogate her, she was already coming up with a plan for finishing her graduate studies from prison. When she found out what she was being charged with, she was relieved. Not long after the community meeting where she had made the provocative public statement, chalk graffiti referencing a recent case of police brutality was left on the side of the police station. Although the security camera footage of the crime was low quality, it showed a person around Dana's height and with long hair like hers. With this vague resemblance as their only evidence to go on, she reasoned that they must have been trying to connect her to the crime because of the public statement she had made (which had given them her name and address).

She maintained that she had nothing to do with what happened at the police station and decided to go to trial to prove it. The trial lasted for three days, but the entire legal process took almost a year and a half. With the low-quality, very inconclusive video footage as their only evidence against her, she was found not guilty. Even though she wasn't convicted, she explained: "It definitely affected my life . . . my mug shot was blast all over the news. I almost lost my job." Her academic department was even worried about funding repercussions because the police were making statements about how her department, and the university, was supporting an anti-cop criminal.

Palma, now a professional community organizer, has also worried about the potential educational consequences of being arrested. She was threatened with expulsion by the college she was attending at the time when she was arrested at an immigrant rights protest. They claimed that the highly publicized arrest was giving them a bad name, but she argued that her choice to get arrested had nothing to do with her school. Eventually, they allowed her to stay. Still, she wishes now that she had brought attention to the school's threats, which she felt were particularly unfair. But, at the time, she just wanted the problem to go away and to be able to continue her studies.

It is no wonder, considering what happened to Palma and the others, that one respondent told me that the main reason people drop out of activism is that "it disrupts a comfortable life." In all, almost a quarter of interviewees brought up concerns about the career or educational consequences of having a criminal record or from the publicity of being arrested or otherwise repressed. This is a high incidence, considering that there were no questions prompting discussion of this, or even questions asking more generally about the problems or costs they faced due to their arrests or other repressive experiences. These stories and concerns came up in response to very general questions asking what happened when they were arrested or otherwise experienced repression, and about what they were feeling and thinking at the time.

A story told by Cory, the political science major arrested at an Occupy protest who was discussed in the previous chapter, suggested that police are sometimes aware that activists are concerned about these career and educational consequences and use them as a point of intimidation. He described being taunted by the police in jail: "It wasn't as much physical violence. They tended to avoid that. A lot of it was fear, which is worse in some senses . . . the kind of fear that they instill in you, of basically ruining your life. . . . I can see the psychological impact that has on somebody who is middle class." The police initially told him and the others they would be charged with a felony (they weren't) and that, as a result, they would have trouble getting jobs in the future: "They were like, 'Oh you guys are just a bunch of kids and you just ruined the rest of your life. Good luck getting into school, and good luck getting into a job.'" He felt like the message they were sending him was: "If you continue a path of resistance, you're gonna lose all of the privileges you have by being a member of this class, by being a middle-class, white American. We're going to make you like everybody that's in here [jail]. . . . It's terrifying."

Time Costs

Direct financial costs, and the potential for career and education consequences, are not the only material costs that those who experience state repression must contend with. Another significant cost is time. As already touched on in many of the stories, the legal process, especially if one decides to take the case to trial, is very lengthy and time consuming. Many echoed this in their stories. Jenna was one of several arrested in an action that stopped Operation Streamline (a controversial federal program that processes undocumented migrants en masse) for one day by locking themselves to the buses that transport the migrants. She told me that she was fully prepared to get arrested that day. She wouldn't have participated in the action if she wasn't. But she wasn't prepared for how long and difficult the legal process following the arrest would be. "Going to trial was a tiring, tiring process," she told me. Kyle, as previously discussed, had to put his whole life on hold while he worked to prove his innocence: "I had to stop everything I was doing in my life. And I had to be apart from my family and friends. . . . It showed me how powerful the state can be."

Even when charges are dropped, the process of being arrested and going through the legal system can be incredibly costly and can often deter people from protesting, even if only temporarily. Multiple people talked about not going to protests when they had charges pending, even if they went right back to it as soon as they were dropped or otherwise resolved. Many activists were aware of the fact that this, rather than securing convictions, was often the function of protest arrests, especially mass arrests. One man, who has been arrested five times at protests, said, "I have never ever had an arrest go to court. It never goes to court. So, to me, that's used as a repressive tactic. Like they're arresting people for charges they know won't stick. Otherwise, they would be prosecuting us. . . . And so it's used to like remove people from the protest." This is exactly what Earl (2005) has argued, applying Feeley's (1992) classic argument that "the process is the punishment" to the issue of protest arrests. Some activists were even aware of this argument made by socio-legal scholars. Zach, who, as discussed in the previous chapter, has had wide-ranging repressive experiences, including being indicted on federal terrorism charges, told me, "It was through all that that I became acquainted with the idea 'the process is the punishment.'" Regardless of conviction, which is fairly rare with protest-related arrests (Earl 2005), being arrested at a protest often costs individuals time and money and can sometimes even cost them educational and career opportunities in the future. The punishment—the costs that individuals incur—is often a result of the process itself, regardless of the legal outcome.

Emotional Costs

Being arrested cost Kyle a great deal, even though the charges were dropped when video evidence proved his innocence. The costs of this experience, for Kyle, were not just the material costs of the legal fees or having to move across the country to make the case for his innocence, or even the disruption to his education and employment that he experienced as a result. The experience was also incredibly traumatic and took a significant emotional toll on him. The charges hung over his head and filled him with intense anxiety for months, and even after they were resolved, he still had trouble attending protests and seeing police officers without having a panic attack. Even years later, the experience still haunts him, even though it hasn't stopped him from participating in activism. He told me:

> I know that it's not true that if you get struck by lightning it makes you more likely to get struck by lightning, but that's how it feels like to me. I feel like I'm marked and now I have to be extra careful when I go to protests. Which is probably not true, but it could be. And that's part of it. I feel like I've developed like a serious paranoia around it.... But, if it's valid, then is it paranoia? I don't know. I guess I'm preoccupied, not paranoid. I have a reason to be concerned because it's happened before.

Kyle's feeling of being "marked" sounded remarkably similar to something that Zach told me. He said, "I mean, like I'm still [pause].... A lot of the times I feel so branded. I just go outside and think I'm gonna get f-cking tackled, you know?"

The psychological difficulties that Kyle and Zack describe are not uncommon. In fact, despite the fact that I never directly asked about it, several interview respondents told me they had actually been diagnosed with post-traumatic stress disorder (PTSD) because of their repressive experience. Tyler told me he started going to therapy and was diagnosed with PTSD after being arrested at an Occupy protest and finding out he was on a watch list. He told me, "To this day, I still get nervous if a cop walks into a coffee shop. And he may just be there buying a coffee, you know, but it scares the shit out of me. I freeze, I get nauseated, sometimes I just, like, stop breathing, and sometimes I go into anaphylaxis just because a cop walked into a place that I'm in. And I've never had that feeling before, before Occupy really, even with all of the other activism that I did." Charles told me that he was diagnosed with PTSD after years of being involved with Earth First! and being targeted by the FBI. Mia said that, following multiple experiences where she witnessed police violence at protests, her knees still buckle every time she sees a police officer, and that she is pretty sure she has PTSD.

For Zach, the emotional toll from his experiences was so heavy that he attempted suicide. Telling me about the period that led him to make a "nearly successful" attempt to take his own life, he explained:

> When I was in court and looking at that time [in prison], I was looking forward to that ending and that being over. And then, that happened, and then I'm on probation and then I'm looking forward to the end of probation. And then, I kinda thought to myself, "Wow, I used to look forward to getting food with my friends. I used to look forward to, like, bands and shows and doing things that made me happy. Now I spend a really long time looking forward to things that are just slightly less worse." There was no end of it for me, is what I decided.

Social Costs

Many experienced social costs as well, and these constituted another major nonmaterial cost of repression. Angela had a "falling out" with some family members who did not support her antinuclear civil disobedience and her decision to go to prison. She is still estranged from them years later. Describing her feelings about this, she told me "I wish there was a word stronger than sad . . . heartbroken." Chris told me that the only thing that really caused him any hesitation about being part of a civil disobedience action at a political rally, for which he knew he would be arrested, was how his conservative family, back home in the Midwest, would react. Just as he feared, the protest made the national news and his family saw it, leading to difficult conversations.

Not only relationships with family, but also with friends, were sometimes strained by repression. Zach told me that while he was under federal investigation for ecoterrorism, "it got harder and harder for my friends to even be around me. . . . Like one of the things that the FBI did was go out to the outskirts of the city to a different suburb, and they went to this club that a friend of mine worked in—not even a friend! I knew this person by first name only and we've never hung out! They interrogated not only her, but her boss about her knowing me. Which meant her getting in trouble, which meant her friends being pissed off at me."

Mitigating Costs, Shaping Experiences

Activist groups work hard to reduce these material and nonmaterial costs for individuals and to protect them from the worst consequences of state repression wherever possible. In doing so, they work to shape the experience of repression for individuals. They do so in at least three ways. When possible, they work to prevent repression and protect individuals from it. Because this is not always possible (or desirable, as repression can also be strategic for a movement), groups also work to prepare individuals for repression so that it will be less of a shock, and easier to manage, when it happens. And, finally, groups work to mitigate the costs of repression by providing support to those who experience it and, by doing so, share the burden of repression collectively rather than expecting individuals to carry it on their own. As I will describe, I find that preparation for and support through repressive experiences are both critical for explaining why some disengage, while others persist, after such experiences.

Preventing the Costs of Repression

Activists I spoke with were often very aware of the history of repression in the United States, including programs like COINTELPRO, and of recent ways in which the state's capacity for both covert and overt repression has been expanded, as discussed in chapter 2. In the interviews, and in the zines and other activist publications recommended by the respondents, there is a clear effort to learn from the past and make movements less vulnerable to repression. Books like Brian Glick's *War at Home: Covert Action against U.S. Activists and What We Can Do about It* (1989) are read widely, as are zines that discuss various tactics for reducing the risk of state repression for those engaged in dissent.

Many told me that their experiences of repression changed how they organized and participated in social movements, in efforts to protect themselves and those around them, even if it didn't stop them from participating entirely. One man told me that even though he still goes to protests, "I definitely go about it differently. I don't carry signs. I don't dress the way I normally would have back in the day. I just like dress as normally as possible. . . . Like I'm there for the protest but I could easily just like walk away and look like a nonparticipant." While he found it useful to be able to distance himself from the protest if needed, others (often those who identify as anarchists) sometimes work to create anonymity with other protesters through what is called a black bloc. In a black bloc, individuals wear all black and cover their face, hair, and other identifying features to avoid identification. The goal is to provide anonymity by making individuals indistinguishable from one another. The more people who participate in this tactic, the more effective it can be and the harder it can be for authorities to single anyone out for arrest. Usually this is combined with Kyle's strategy of being able to pass as a non-protester, as those in the black bloc usually wear "civilian" clothes under their black clothing to change into if needed. As the zine *Blocs, Black or Otherwise* explains,

> The goal of the bloc as a tactic is to have everyone look as similar as possible, so that, ideally, no single individual can be identified within the anonymous mass. This helps to keep everybody safer. If only some people within a bloc take these precautions, the cops can more easily spot and target individuals and groups, which is dangerous both for those who are acting within the bloc and for those who are not. Those who make the effort to stay anonymous can draw extra police attention; those who don't can be more easily identified, which can make them easier targets. Neither of these situations is desirable. . . . Even if you do not plan on committing any crimes, even if you don't mind the secret service capturing your image for their files, you still do a great service to others by masking up and increasing the number of people who are disguised, thus making it more difficult for the police to keep up with all of you. Those others might not just be criminals, either; they might be foreigners who don't want their participation in radical activities to be used as grounds for deportation, or teachers who don't want to risk losing their jobs.

Another zine makes a similar point about the power of this tactic to protect those who might be more vulnerable than others to repression: "Cultivating anonymity can actually make actions more inclusive since the presumption that everyone is willing to be identified excludes people without status, people on probation or parole, people who for demographic or other reasons are more likely to be targeted for retribution, and people who have jobs they might lose if it came out they're radical." In this way, this tactic is advocated for as a way to more evenly share the risks of repression and keep everyone safer.

Many of those I interviewed, but certainly not all, talked about employing this tactic at some point. However, nearly everyone talked about more mundane everyday precautions that they sometimes take to protect themselves against repression—precautions that are often referred to under the concept of "security culture." A popular zine titled *What Is Security Culture?* defines security culture as "a set of customs shared by a community whose members may be targeted by the government, designed to minimize risk." It goes on to explain, "having a security culture in place saves everyone the trouble of having to work out safety measures over and over from scratch, and can help offset paranoia and panic in stressful situations. . . . The difference between protocol and culture is that culture becomes unconscious, instinctive, and thus effortless; once the safest possible behavior has become habitual for everyone in the circles in which you travel, you can spend less time and energy emphasizing the need for it, and suffering the consequences of not having it."

Security culture has been adopted, to varying degrees, in many activist circles, especially more radical ones, since the 1990s and is described by activists as a direct response to the history of state surveillance and infiltration (e.g., COINTELPRO), and to recent increases in covert surveillance. People I talked to described going to great lengths to prevent monitoring of themselves and others, and about the importance of making these practices ubiquitous. Security culture is less about providing cover for illegal activity than it is about creating a climate in which people can organize without undue interference and while minimizing the amount of information that is gathered about activists, understanding that this information could be used against them or their friends in unforeseen ways. Security culture rejects the notion that "if you aren't doing anything wrong, you have nothing to worry about," and instead advocates for the normalization of practices that increase privacy and security for everyone involved in social movements.

Security culture is especially important for planning direct action or actions that require an element of surprise, and to avoid arrest or other repressive consequences. Keeping a tight lip about some planned actions, avoiding talking about or coordinating some actions on social media, email, or on the phone, encrypting communications, not taking pictures at protests or posting them on social media, vetting and vouching for newcomers, all fall under "security culture" and were all discussed by those that I interviewed. Zines related to digital security culture talked about the importance of password protecting phones, using secure message apps that include end-to-end encryption, or even encrypting one's entire phone. Several respondents talked about not using Facebook or social media (not just for political organizing, but not using these platforms at all) because these tools would make them more vulnerable to being tracked and monitored. Others only used "burner phones." Several talked about not having cell phones near them or taking the batteries out of their phones when they talked about actions (to prevent them from being remotely turned on and used as "roving bugs," as discussed in chapter 2; Esquivel 2013).[1]

Some talked about only working with people they had known for years, or systems in which a core group of activists would each be allowed to invite only one trusted person to join a small action. As Tyler told me, "Stick around people you know and trust, never go anywhere alone, and then you don't have to worry about getting infiltrated because you've always got your friends there at your side." Some of this might seem like overkill or bordering on paranoia. But these concerns are often rooted in real cases of infiltration and monitoring and in a desire to learn from and correct for these past vulnerabilities. As one zine put it, "Security culture is about understanding and controlling the ways that information moves through our movements and scenes so that it works for us and not the state."

A few experienced activists worried that younger generations of activists are less security conscious, or that security culture has generally become more lax in recent years. Max, for example, said,

> You know, when I was younger you'd take your battery out of your cell phone before you even left to go to the meeting. That's when GPS tracking was first getting into these things, and like even if you turn it off and the battery is in, they can still like turn it on and listen. I don't know if any of that stuff is true. I didn't care if it was true, we just took the batteries out of our phone. And now I go to these organizing meetings, and people are on their phone and using it! Like we're all tracked there, they could look at GPS and locate all the activists in [the city]. Like oh, they are all in the same building tonight. Like what's going on right now?

When I asked him why he thinks it has become more relaxed, he told me that he thinks there is a certain level of protection that comes from living in a society that is now so thoroughly networked and dependent on technology: "I think that there is such a high volume of information on everyone. . . . I think we just blend into the noise way more."

Activists also try to protect themselves and each other by identifying infiltrators and expelling them from the group or otherwise minimizing the harm they can do. Sometimes undercover officers show up to public protests or planning meetings. Other times they even try to become part of the group and befriend individuals. Most respondents told me that these types of infiltrators, the undercover officers, were usually easy to spot. Oftentimes, they were identifiable because there was a clear lack of cultural fit between the undercover officers and the activist group. In this way, one of the strongest defenses that activist groups have against infiltration is having a distinctive, nuanced subculture that is not easy for an outsider to mimic or learn convincingly.

From some of the stories I heard, it seemed that undercover officers often failed to do even the most cursory research about the group they were trying to infiltrate. Ron said he and other environmental activists started to suspect two men of being undercover because they often talked about and watched football. As he told me, laughing, "Hippies don't do that." It turned out they were right. The two men were later discovered to be undercover officers. In another case, Keith told me about how everyone became suspicious of one man because he showed up to a potluck of environmental and animal rights activists with a bucket of Kentucky Fried Chicken. At a potluck where most, if not all, people were vegans or at least vegetarians, and guests were expected to bring healthy home-cooked meals, showing up with a bucket of KFC was a strong tell. Months later, this man conclusively exposed himself when he dropped his police-issue gun during a scuffle at a protest.

Other times, it was an individual's appearance that was a tip-off. As Bryce told me, "You would march in the streets and they had the worst undercover cops ever.... They looked like they got out of playing tennis. Like, you know that you're not convincing us, right?" Others talked about undercovers who went to the lengths of dressing "like an anarchist" (i.e., in all black) to pass as a protester in a crowd but gave it away by wearing $200 sneakers. Other times, regardless of what they wore, someone would be suspected because they had what activists considered to be a "cop haircut." Others talked more generally about how some people just had a "cop look" they could pick out. Gary told me, "If they're around long enough you can just look at them and tell that they are police officers." Nick described one time that he was sure there were two undercovers at a meeting he attended: "It was almost like when you see an extra on television. And they're behind the principal character who's in focus, and you can tell that, lips moving, all of that, but there's nothing being said.... It was like that.... And no one had ever seen them before."

Other times, undercover officers were obvious to those I interviewed because they tried too hard to seem like activists. Dana told me there were people who came to protests and meetings that were "clearly undercover." When asked how she knew, she explained, "Just by the way that they dressed and their attempt to be like 'in' and use language that didn't come off—just mannerisms that were bad, like they were trying to be cool." Doug told me about a time that he and others spotted someone at a protest, standing by himself on the periphery. He was wearing clean, "starched" jeans and a white bandana around his neck. In an attempt to figure out if he was undercover, Doug and his friends went up to him, said "Hi," and asked him his name. He responded, according to Doug, by saying, "I'm with, uh, I'm with Anonymous. Anonymous sent me." He said they knew right then that he was probably an officer, or some type of infiltrator, who apparently was not aware of the decentralized, informal, and (of course) anonymous nature of the Anonymous movement.

Tyler told me about someone he met who was staying around the Occupy camp and who said he was homeless. He wasn't known to any of the activists, or, even more concerning, to any of the people who were homeless at the camp. Tyler had been working and volunteering with the homeless for years, so he quickly knew that some things did not add up about this man. When he began to suspect that he probably wasn't really homeless, the only logical conclusion was that he was an undercover officer: "He had on nice shoes, his nails were not dirty, and his beard ... it looked like he usually trimmed that beard. And his clothes looked like they'd been picked up out of a leftovers pile ... so he looked like he was trying to look homeless . . . why would anyone do that unless they were a cop? Why do you pretend to be homeless?" Similarly, Gary told me that sometimes undercover officers at protests will try to look "dirty," but it doesn't look natural, as it would if someone simply bathed less frequently. Instead, he explained, it looks like an otherwise very clean person had smeared dirt on themselves.

Sometimes spotting an undercover officer is even easier. Several people told me variations on a story of an officer who was exposed by an activist who worked as a barista at a Starbucks that the officer frequented in uniform. Here, Bryan, who was at the meeting where she exposed him, tells the story:

> This cop would come in [to Starbucks] every day, order the same thing, and flirt with her. He would be hitting on her every day in uniform and she f-cking hates cops but she's like on the clock and in uniform, so she is trying to be polite. . . . And so this guy comes in [to the planning meeting for an upcoming protest] and he's got like an anarchist T-shirt and he's got a bandana around his neck and he's like, "I'm from Mexico City and I was involved with this protest and that protest and f-ck the cops, f-ck the cops, man. I wanna get involved in this. I am so excited." And she was just like, "A double shot mocha with extra whip?" He says, "Excuse me?" And she says, "A double shot mocha with extra whip. Get the f-ck out of here."

Not only did this undercover officer miss the mark with his over-the-top outfit and overly eager anti-cop talk, but he also failed to look around the room enough to realize that there was someone there who could easily identify him.

But infiltrators are not always this bad, or this easy to spot. Most people I interviewed were more concerned about informants than undercovers, both because they are more able to pull off the act, but also because it constitutes a much deeper form of betrayal. Informants are individuals who are, or were at some point, involved in activism themselves or at least socially tied to activists, who provide information on others in exchange for legal leniency (sometimes on a protest-related charge, sometimes on unrelated issues such as drug charges). In many cases, this can mean returning to activist groups or rekindling old friendships while wearing or carrying a listening device.

Activists use zines to spread tips for better security culture and as a way to engage in collective learning and correction following cases of infiltration by informants or undercover officers. Activists use known cases of infiltrators, like "Anna" and Brandon Darby, discussed in chapter 2, to build profiles of infiltrators and circulate information, through zines and other means, about how to spot an infiltrator, and what to do if you suspect someone of being an infiltrator. In addition, websites and publications are used to track known infiltrators and informants, so that this information can act as a warning to other activists who may meet these individuals in the future. Some of the main signs to look out for, that came up repeatedly in zines and in interviews with activists alike, were individuals who ask prying questions, push for illegal or violent actions, have inconsistent backstories or ideologies, always have resources and are eager to share them (despite having no clear source of income), and tend to cause or exacerbate interpersonal drama and divisions in the group. While keeping an eye out for these signs can result in guardedness and suspicion within activist groups, and this may sometimes be an impediment to mobilization (Montgomery and Bergman 2017), in most cases that interviewees discussed, their suspicions were confirmed and they feel strongly that their guardedness has successfully protected themselves and their friends. It is difficult to determine the impact of these repression prevention practices on my interviewees' persistence in activism. For one thing, engagement in these practices aims to provide protection for the group, not just for the individuals who engage in the practices. Second, it is difficult to say how much repression that might have otherwise occurred is prevented by these practices. For these reasons, it is not possible to determine the impact of these repression prevention strategies on the persistence of those I interviewed. Still, these practices are an important part of any discussion on the ways that activist groups work to reduce the costs of repression. When it comes to preparation and support, as will be discussed now, I am better able to measure and clearly demonstrate the impact these practices have on the subsequent participation of those I interviewed.

Preparing for the Costs of Repression

In one zine on security culture, the authors warn, "Do not let any of this give you a false sense of security. Be careful! Assess your relationship to risk honestly; don't do anything if you're not sure you could live with the worst possible consequences." While preventing state repression is often a goal of many activists, this is not always possible (or desirable), and no tactic of avoiding repression will be foolproof. Therefore, the risk of repression is always present, whether these kinds of precautions are taken or not (and whether laws are broken or not). Because of this, groups not only work to protect individuals from repression; they also work to prepare them for it. Physical and mental preparation for repression can make a significant difference in how individuals respond to a repressive experience. This is what Earl (2011b) found in her analysis of deterrence and radicalization among activists arrested at the 2004 Republican National Convention protests. She argued that individuals who had more realistic expectations about the risks they were taking on by protesting were more likely to be radicalized, and not deterred, by the experience of arrest. These more realistic expectations came from prior experiences with arrest, as well as through civil disobedience trainings. Similarly, Davenport

(2014) argues that "the effect of repression on SMOs is conditioned by the challengers' attempts to prepare its members for repressive behavior" (p. 10). He refers to this mental preparation as "reappraisal," a term borrowed from psychology. He explained, "SMOs train themselves to identify what is taking place around them, putting the experience in the appropriate category, which then serves as the basis for subsequent action" (p. 43).

Fitting with this, I find that, by preparing activists for repression, activist groups help to buffer individuals against the shock of repression. In fact, four-fifths of those who discussed having a repressive experience for which they felt unprepared subsequently disengaged, while only one-fifth of those who did not express having such an experience disengaged. This difference is statistically significant (Pearson $\chi^2(1) = 8.1818$. $p = 0.004$). Multiple interviewees also expressed that an unexpected arrest was far worse than an expected one, and a few talked about how police violence was much more upsetting to them when they didn't see it coming. As Ally, a college student who had recently been arrested at a protest aimed at pressuring her school to divest from fossil fuels, told me, "I'm not opposed to getting arrested again, but I feel it needs to be an intentional choice on my part, something that I've prepared for and I know I'm going to get arrested." Similarly, Nepsted (2014) argues that making a conscious decision to accept repression (particularly arrest and incarceration) was key to continued participation in the high-risk, antinuclear Plowshares movement.

When individuals go into a situation without an understanding of the risks, or are unprepared for the possibility of repression, and it does occur, the experience can be far more upsetting than it would have been otherwise. Jessica, the young mother who disengaged from activism following a violent arrest and being placed on the law enforcement watch list, was deterred after just one, albeit particularly traumatic, experience of state repression (and this was still before she had her child). Because she was not well-integrated into the community of the others involved in the protest, she was completely unprepared for the experience. She explained that there were meetings leading up the protest where others were helping each other to be prepared for the possibility of police violence and arrest, but she wasn't part of these meetings and felt more generally like many of the more seasoned activists didn't see her as one of them. Because she was unconnected and unaware of what was being planned or might be expected, she showed up to the protest completely unprepared. She was unprepared physically, wearing a tank top and skirt with no underwear (which turned out to be a very painful mistake when she was later doused in pepper spray), a tangible reflection of her lack of awareness of and preparation for the situation. She explained, "Other people were more prepared. . . . A lot of people had hoodies, you know? Like ample clothing on. Bandanas, like those little surgical masks that cover their faces. . . . People had meetings and were talking about it. They went together.

There were all these people who were like, 'I'm ready to get arrested,' but I wasn't one of those people. I showed up alone." Ben was arrested at the same protest. Like Jessica, he was unprepared for the experience and subsequently withdrew from activism. In fact, he didn't even know there was going to be a protest until right before it started. He had slept over at his friends' house after a party. In the morning, others at the house said they were going to the protest and he decided, spur of the moment, to tag along. It was his first protest and turned out to also be his last. At the protest, he was pepper sprayed, arrested, and charged with assaulting an officer. As a result of this incident, he was also placed on a law enforcement watch list. All of these consequences were completely unexpected for him, and he was mentally unprepared for these possibilities.

Others, who are more socialized into activist culture, are less likely to be caught off guard by repression the way that Jessica and Ben were. In activist meetings and trainings, there is often discussion of how to respond when police use force against you or arrest you, or how to talk to police, or rather how NOT talk to them, to avoid incriminating yourself or others. Sometimes this involved role-playing to mentally prepare oneself to deal with these situations. Emma talked about doing a "role-play" with others before the action where they locked themselves to construction equipment—for example, how to react if the police used pain compliance techniques to get them to unlock, including pepper spraying them at close range, using Q-tips to apply pepper spray to their eyes, and using pressure points and choke holds. She said it was helpful, not just for the practical knowledge about how to counter specific pain compliance techniques the police might use, but also just to prepare herself for the possibility that the experience might be very uncomfortable. Others had similar stories about researching and role-playing police pain compliance tactics before a lockdown civil disobedience action. These types of actions, in particular, require a great deal of preparation to fortify individuals for the repression and discomfort that might result. Not only do police sometimes use pain compliance techniques to try to get activists to unlock, just the experience of being locked in an uncomfortable position, sometimes for many hours, can be incredibly difficult. Locked-down protesters are unable to get away and are often unable to use their arms. Many activists talked about how incredibly vulnerable they felt in this position. Preparation, both physical and mental, is critical. As one activist who participated in the lockdown action against Operation Streamline told me, sometimes this meant going as far as wearing adult diapers in anticipation of being stuck there for many hours.

This kind of preparation in advance of civil disobedience demonstrations, whether lockdowns, sit-ins, or other types of actions where success often depends on the activists' ability to endure and withstand discomfort and violence, is not new. During the civil rights movement, activists also engaged in role-play exercises. For example, before the lunch counter sit-ins, demonstrators sometimes practiced not reacting while other activists taunted them, spit on them, and poured drinks on them, to prepare the demonstrators for the hostility they would have to withstand from white counterprotesters (Cosgrove 2013). In a similar spirit, Jared and his friends went as far as spraying each other in the face with pepper spray so they'd already know how it feels, and how best to respond and not panic, if, or as they saw it, when, the police used it on them. He explained, "In our circle of friends—people who had been around for a while—I think they are pretty prepared. I don't think there's a lot that can be thrown at them that they haven't practiced." Another activist told me that although he hasn't gone to this length to prepare for protests, he knows others do, and that it makes sense: "You never know how your body is gonna react. . . . You, know, inoculate yourself." But he added, "I think it takes a certain amount of courage to get there, because then you're admitting to yourself that the cops really are that bad. And I know in my head there's like a deeper level, like my taxes are paying for these people, and I have to do a role-play to like prepare myself for their inevitably kicking my ass? Like there's some internal disconnect that has to happen to do that."

These preparations, even though some may seem extreme, are an important way that groups reduce the costs of repression, by helping individuals to mentally and physically ready themselves, and by making repression taken for granted as a risk of participating in protest. When activists take on the mindset that repression is highly probable, or even inevitable, and take steps to prepare themselves to absorb it, this can reduce repression's potential for deterrence. This is shown by the fact that those who discussed having a repressive experience that they felt unprepared for were much more likely to disengage following the experience than were individuals who expressed having adequate preparation for the consequences they experienced. Again, this difference was dramatic: an 80 percent disengagement rate for those who had felt unprepared compared with a 20 percent disengagement rate for those who felt adequately prepared (Pearson $\chi^2(1) = 8.1818$. $p = 0.004$).

Support and the Sharing of Repression's Cost

The final way that groups can reduce the costs of repression for individuals is through providing support to those who experience it. This is especially important when costs and risks are unpredictable and unevenly distributed (and therefore fall on some individuals more than others), as is often the case with repression. By creating systems in which those who are less directly impacted chip in to relieve some of the burden of those who are more directly impacted, costs are redistributed and shared among the group. When these support networks are strong and functional, this not only has benefits for those receiving the support and makes it less likely that they will disengage following repression, but this support also builds a sense of solidarity and comradery among activists and helps to build stronger movements that are more attractive to newcomers.

I found that individuals who described not receiving support they needed during an experience of repression were far more likely to disengage than those who did not express ever having such an experience. While nearly 70 percent of those who had an experience in which they lacked support disengaged, less than 10 percent of those who expressed always having the necessary support from others did so. This difference is highly statistically significant (Pearson $\chi^2(1) = 16.9365, p = 0.000$). It is important to note that to say someone had a repressive experience where they felt unsupported does not mean that they didn't also have support in other ways or in other repressive experiences. In fact, every respondent talked about receiving some support from others at some point. The real distinction is whether or not they also discussed, in addition to the support they did receive, a situation in which they did not have the support that they needed or wished they could have had. After describing the types of support, both material and nonmaterial, that activist groups develop to reduce the costs of repression, I will discuss, using the words of my respondents, why this kind of support is so critical to both individuals and the groups they are a part of, and why, when this is lacking, individuals are so much more likely to disengage.

Activists often develop their own legal, financial, and medical support systems for the purpose of sharing the costs of repression (Starr and Fernandez 2009; Starr, Fernandez, and Scholl 2011; Zwerman and Steinhoff 2012; Nepsted 2014). In addition to these more tangible forms of support, activist networks often provide emotional support that can help take the sting out of experiencing repression and make it a collective rather than an individual experience. When people know others "have their back," they are more willing to take on possible risks of repression. And when risks and costs are shared, this can strengthen solidarity, collective identity, and the affective ties between activists. While an experience of repression can sometimes strain relationships with unsupportive family members and others, it often simultaneously strengthens ties to those in the activist community who provide the understanding and moral support that outsiders cannot. This is done not only through informal friendships or conversations among activists, but also through institutionalized forms of emotional support such as organized debriefing sessions after repressive incidents and attending fellow activists' court dates. Some organized forms of support, such as having a group meet someone as they are released from jail and take them home, are as much a form of emotional support as they are a form of material or logistical support.

Legal Support. When they needed it, most respondents found that their friends and others in the activist community stepped up to make sure they got the legal defense they needed, and the funds needed to cover it. Just as was the case in previous protest cycles (Zwerman and Steinhoff 2012), lawyers often offered to represent them pro bono because they wanted to support their First Amendment right to protest or the political causes they were fighting for. Everyone who was arrested described receiving a pro bono lawyer, fundraisers to pay legal fees, or some other kind of legal support. Not a single person said they were completely responsible for their own legal representation. In fact, Zach told me about a demonstration that he organized, where seventeen people got arrested and "like forty lawyers in town" signed up to defend them, pro bono.

Cory talked about how much it meant to him to have lawyers from the ACLU step up to defend him and others arrested at an Occupy protest: "Everything was pro bono for us—we didn't have to pay a cent." He said he actually felt a little guilty about having access to this privilege while others do not: "If it wasn't for the ACLU, we all would have been f-cked. The only reason we were able to get out of the situation like that was because we had ACLU support and . . . your general prisoner doesn't have that . . . it's kind of like a 'get out of jail free' card—it literally is a 'get out of jail free' card."

In many cases, a legal team is assembled and money is collected before an action, even before they know if anyone will be arrested. This not only helps to make sure the support will actually be ready to mobilize when needed, it also helps activists to know, going into the action, that this support is there for them. Some talked about designating a dedicated "legal lead," an activist who would not get arrested and would work to coordinate the release and defense of those who were, before an action. Chris talked about how, knowing that a bail fund had been created ahead of time, and that pro bono lawyers had already volunteered to defend them, made the choice to participate in a civil disobedience lockdown at a political rally much easier. Proactively setting up collective funds to pay off any fines that individuals might get as a result of an action is a way to, as Ally put it, make "getting arrested accessible financially."

In addition to pro bono lawyers, groups like the National Lawyers Guild provide legal observers at many protests. Legal observers are trained to collect information that can later be used in court to defend arrested protesters against criminal charges or to make a case that the civil rights of demonstrators were violated. In addition, the National Lawyers Guild also provides "Know Your Rights" trainings to activists so that activists and others will be more likely to exercise their rights in interactions with law enforcement, such as their right to remain silent, to not consent to a search, and to ask for a lawyer. Finally, for large protests, legal hotlines are often set up for activists to call if they are arrested, or for dealing with other legal issues. The legal hotline number is circulated ahead of time and activists often write it on their arm or other part of their body with permanent marker, so that they will still have the number if they are arrested and all their possessions are taken from them. Lawyers willing to provide pro bono representation are critical, but they are only one part of a much larger legal support system that exists to help protesters.

Following an arrest, it is also common for friends and fellow activists to put on events, such as concerts or parties, to raise funds for legal costs and collect bail money to get fellow activists out of jail as soon as possible. Dana talked about how, when she was arrested, her bail was almost $1,000 and her friends pooled their money and paid it right away. One woman told me that people put together a website to support her and others arrested at an immigrant rights protest, to publicize what happened, and to gather donations to fund the legal defense of those who had the most serious charges. Emma talked about a similar website and crowd-funding effort established to raise bail money for her and others. A local band even went on tour and raised a few thousand dollars for the group of arrestees.

Medical Support. Activists also work to provide medical support to each other in the event that they are hurt by police at a protest. Street medic teams are often organized to provide medical aid to protesters who are pepper sprayed, tear gassed, struck by police, or are otherwise injured or in need of medical help during a protest. Multiple respondents spoke of the importance of having this support in moments of pain and panic when they were injured by police. Others spoke of how the mere presence of these medics made them feel safer, knowing that others were there looking out for their well-being and armed with basic medical supplies and knowledge of how to counteract chemical weapons and other tactics used by the police.

Bryan, a nurse, has been very involved in organizing street medic teams in his town and described the evolution of this support network over time. He described one protest where the police responded with much greater violence than expected. They only had six medics there, but as he told me, "I swear to god, a hundred people got pepper sprayed in that crowd and just the number of victims was stunning and we were utterly unprepared . . . and this was not young, healthy black bloc-ers. It was old people in wheelchairs and babies in strollers. This was like really expected to be like a green zone [low-risk] march and it was really not good. . . . It was a bit of a disaster and so, since then we try to never let there be a protest without our presence." He explained that, since then, they don't make assumptions about whether a protest is likely to result in police violence or not. He explained, "We try to be ready for anything . . . we do that for two reasons. The first is that we were so confident that time that nothing was going to happen and it went the other way," but also because the presence of medics has been used in court as proof that protesters planned to break the law and might also be used by police as an indicator that some protesters at an event are planning to be more confrontational or disruptive. "And so instead," Bryan explained, "we always just show up ready for anything, even if, you know, it's a candlelight vigil, so it doesn't provide any extra information or clues."

Although Bryan's group tries to attend all the protests they can and organized street medic teams are much more common now than ten years ago, even now medics are not at every protest. But when they are not, many people told me that they could count on someone to have Maalox to treat pepper spray, as well as other basic medical supplies. Activists also often take it upon themselves to have these items on hand to share with others who may need them. In my observation at protests, any time someone needed something—whether it be Maalox to treat pepper spray, or simple things like water to avoid dehydration or a snack if their blood sugar was low during a long march—there was almost always someone within shouting distance who had a stock of these supplies on hand. Sometimes this is formally planned by organizers ahead of time, but a good deal of this kind of support to treat or prevent medical issues at protests happens organically, and being prepared to help others is often taken for granted as part of activist culture.

Other times, activists who know each other well form groups to look out for each other and provide basic medical help to each other if needed. The second time Brad was pepper sprayed at a protest, he told me he was prepared. He went to the protest having made the decision that he would stand his ground despite whatever violence he encountered, unlike the first time when he didn't yet know what to expect. But it wasn't just his previous experience with pepper spray that emboldened him; it was the social support he felt going into the protest: "There was very much a system. Nobody was left unattended. Everyone was taken care of. Everyone was taking care of each other. Everyone was helping out."

Jenna said having street medics there when she participated in a lockdown "really helped to make me feel a lot less physically at risk," not just in relation to dramatic risks like police violence, but also more mundane (but still potentially serious) risks like dehydration and sunburn. These lockdown actions make support by others, who are not locked down, imperative. As Max explained about the same protest, the medics made sure he and the others who were locked down stayed hydrated on that hot Arizona day. This meant the medics had to physically pour water into their mouths, as they were unable to use their hands. This reliance of protesters on each other is made especially clear in the case of a lockdown protest like this where those locked down might not be able to take care of these basic needs without assistance, but a similar system of support operates in a more subtle way at marches and other demonstrations as well, as everyone works to make sure that the basic needs of all are met.

Activists' networks also sometimes institutionalize ways to support individuals' general well-being and health as well, not just treating immediate injuries or physical discomfort at protests but addressing longer-term issues of trauma and burnout that can result from repression, and from activism in general. Events providing free therapeutic services to activists are becoming increasingly common, as activist culture increasingly stresses not only self-care, but also "collective care," as some respondents referred to it. Multiple people I interviewed said that they offered free or discounted massage and other types of physical therapy to fellow activists dealing with trauma or injury following protests. As one interviewee, a massage therapist who often provides her services to fellow activists, said, "Being an activist can be traumatic." Repression and other costs of being an activist can lead to trauma and exhaustion, and these kinds of services provide important physical as well as emotional support. There are also sometimes trauma or healing centers set up at large protests where people can get these healing services, talk to a therapist, or talk with other activists who have had similar experiences (Starr, Fernandez, and Scholl 2011). This is one of the many ways that activist communities sometimes work to create support systems that support not only the legal defense and immediate physical health of protesters, but also their mental health and well-being.

Other Material Support. There are other kinds of material support, besides legal and medical support, provided to activists as well. For example, Johnny set up a childcare network to make it easier for parents to attend protests and not worry about their children getting hurt by police. Sometimes this meant having somewhere parents could take their kids before the protest and pick them up after. Other times, it meant creating what he referred to a "child bloc." The child bloc is a special area of the protest where children and their parents can march separately from the rest of the march. "That way," Johnny explained, "if the police did act against more radical parts of the march, the children were safe." From people who organize free childcare or child blocs, to the street medics, legal observers, people staffing the legal hotline, pro bono lawyers, and many others, there are many people who help to make protesting a little less risky for others and who work to provide the material support that gives people the courage to attend protests, challenge authority, and get arrested, all while knowing there are whole teams of people, some they don't even know, who will have their backs. Sean, who has been arrested several times and experienced police violence at protests on more than one occasion, told me, looking back on all the people that made it possible for him to take the risks that he has, "I mean, I see this whole network of people around me . . . they are all important roles. There were lawyers that got, they got me out of jail. . . . There were others doing other things and were helping out in ways that were completely necessary. There are all these roles, all these levels of people" who make it possible for the few who most visibly put their lives and bodies "on the line" to do so, he explained.

Over the course of their lives and careers as activists, people sometimes shift from the front lines to the supportive roles, or vice versa. For example, Gary, an activist lawyer, told me that, after the second time he was arrested while in law school, a mentor told him he needed to decide whether he wanted to be the person who got arrested or the person who defended the person who got arrested. He chose the latter and since has devoted a significant amount of his legal practice to defending protesters.

Emotional Support and Solidarity

Activist cultures also work to provide emotional support to individuals who have experienced repression, both through institutionalized events and through more informal means. Just as with the forms of material support already discussed, these forms of support are critical to activist persistence in the face of repression. As will become clear later, when this emotional support breaks down, this can be just as consequential as a lack of legal, medical, or other material support.

Institutionalized Emotional Support. When Jessica and I arrived at the spontaneous protest discussed in chapter 3, Jenna was one of those under the Border Patrol vehicle, literally putting her body on the line to prevent the young father from being deported. She told me later that she felt very supported by the fact that when she started texting and calling people from underneath the vehicle, they responded immediately, and in no time there was a supportive crowd of more than a hundred people surrounding the vehicle. She was able to mobilize a large network of people in a relatively short amount of time, and their presence made her feel much safer. The position she was in was an incredibly vulnerable and risky one. She didn't anticipate how tight it would be under the car, or that the underside of the running vehicle would be so burning hot as it idled, only inches from her skin, for hours. She was worried about being burned by the underside of the car, but she at least felt that she had some level of protection from being run over or brutalized by the police or Border Patrol. She explained that as soon as people started arriving, "I wasn't super afraid of getting the shit beaten out of me because there was going to be a bunch of people there." When she was taken into Border Patrol custody, a campaign quickly formed to call and demand her release, along with the two others who were detained. From the irritated tone of the person who answered the phone when I called to participate in the call-in hours later, it was obvious that many, many people were calling. When she was released, Jenna said, "People were lovely. They took us from house to house, because my car was at one house and my cell phone was at another house [because different people had taken her keys, cell phone, etc. while she was under the vehicle] and just like fed us and it was so nice."

As they did for Jenna, activist groups often coordinate to meet people when they are released from jail after being arrested at a protest, to make sure they have a way home, food, and a sympathetic ear. Patty told me that when she was released after being arrested at an Occupy protest, she wasn't sure what she was going to do. She thought she was going to have to walk home but wasn't even sure exactly where she was. Instead, there was someone from Occupy waiting for her. It wasn't even someone she knew, but they knew she was going to be released and made sure she wouldn't be alone when she was. She explained, "As soon as I walked out, my name was called . . . there was someone from Occupy there to pick me up and take me home, and he had some food for me." Many others talked about people waiting for them when they were released from jail, with clothes, food, cigarettes, or other things to ease the hardship of the confinement experience and welcome them back as a hero.

Another woman described being very sad and scared when she was finally released from jail, in the middle of the night downtown. She was worried that she would be all alone with no way to get home, but to her surprise, there were people waiting for her with pizza and blankets. Another talked about his surprise when he was finally released from jail and found almost 200 people, at two in the morning, waiting to greet him, cheer him on, console him, and show their solidarity with him: "I had no idea. I could not have imagined. And to walk out the door and be like, 'What the f-ck?' That was something really special." Since then, he explained, this has become institutionalized in his town. "Now that people get arrested all the time, there's a f-cking protocol. Like everyone is going to come down, they're gonna do a concert outside of the jail, we're gonna bring bongo drums, we're gonna order pizza . . . we all know how it's done." Jared told me that knowing ahead of time that there would be dedicated jail support and people waiting when he and others got out of jail was really reassuring.

Groups also organize court solidarity events, so that the courtroom is filled with friendly faces when activists go to trial. When Max and others went to trial on "littering" charges for leaving water for migrants crossing through the desert, so many people came out to support them that some people were unable to fit in the courtroom and had to line up outside. At the time, he was a youth adviser at his church, and some of the high schoolers he worked with even left school to be at his court appearance, which he found particularly touching. Likewise, Suzanne told me, "I can tell you that when I went to court and my friends would be there in the benches to witness, I felt supported." Through the lengthy legal process, she explained, "I felt very well loved."

And for those who went through long-term incarceration, support was especially important for staving off the isolation of prison. Gerald, who spent two years in prison, said that the letters of support he received while incarcerated, not only from people he knew but also from complete strangers, were a huge help through the days of loneliness, depression, and separation from his wife and children. But the letters began to dry up toward the end of his sentence, making the remaining time much more difficult. Angela, the nun who went to prison for antinuclear activism, also talked about how much it meant to her to get letters of support in prison. A group called the Anarchist Black Cross organizes letter-writing parties and sends letters and literature to political and politicized prisoners around the United States (Hackett 2015). Online and through networks of activists, names and addresses of long-term political prisoners (also sometimes referred to as prisoners of war) are circulated so that anyone can write them. As one such listing explains, "Writing a letter to a political prisoner or prisoner of war is a concrete way to support those imprisoned for their political struggles. A letter is a simple way to brighten someone's day in prison by creating human interaction and communication—something prisons attempt to destroy. Beyond that, writing keeps prisoners connected to the communities and movements of which they are a part, allowing them to provide insights and stay up to date."

Informal Emotional Support. Emotional support to those experiencing state repression also comes in more informal ways, from friends and fellow activists. Max told me he didn't really need much organized support when he was arrested for "littering" because, as he explained, "I mean, I lived in a house full of activists. I think there's a default support there." And Dana also talked about an instance in which some of her activist roommates were arrested alongside her, and that built-in support in her home made a huge difference. Multiple respondents talked about people throwing parties for them after their charges were dropped, or they got off parole, or before they went to court to face the possibility of doing significant time in prison. One talked about a party he threw for a friend before he went to jail, complete with a band, a banner saying that he was a "badass," and a pig piñata painted like a police officer and filled with marijuana and candy. Even very seasoned older male activists who prided themselves on their toughness and decried what they saw as the weakness and navel-gazing of young activists who emphasize "self-care," like Charles, saw the value of this kind of support. He told me: "We provided each other emotional support in our own rough way, not in a touchy-feely way."

Sometimes, the best support comes from others with whom one is arrested. Suzanne told me that, when she was arrested dozens of times over the course of Occupy, she was worried because she wasn't sure what the legal consequences would be, but knowing others were with her made a huge difference: "It was scary. It was scary because we didn't know the outcome. We didn't know if there would be financial penalties or jail time or what the outcome would be. It was frightening, but then again, I wasn't alone. I wasn't the only one. There were others in the same boat." Jenna told me about how the first time she was arrested at a protest against land mines, she was arrested alongside many veteran activists. On the bus to the jail, she sat next to a man who was in his sixties and had been arrested many times before. "He was really supportive," she told me. "It felt like he was a mentor for arrest." One woman talked about how seeing a familiar face in jail, someone she knew from the community who was arrested at the same protest, made a world of difference. "We didn't talk much, 'cause we were super f-cking bummed to be in jail. But just that 'Hey? Are you okay?' meant a lot." In a context in which she was scared and the guards "seemed like beasts just barking at you," "it's a lot to be seen and respected and cared for as a human with so little words."

This kind of support is important because, as Bryan explained, even though activists often try to have a tough public face, many also need a space where they can be vulnerable. He explained, "You can get out [of jail] and say, 'I'm not scared of anything. F-ck you—I'm not scared at all,' and then you go in a quiet place, in privacy and f-cking cry and cry and we'll have a massage therapist come and then we are going to bake you your comfort food. When you get out, we are going to find out what your comfort food is and just like nobody is going to know because you know that we will protect your privacy and you can just process through that shit and then go home."

Similarly, Tyler told me that what he thinks other activists often need most, and what he tries to provide, is someone who believes them: "I see it happen with activists being called crazy, being put down, being shushed if they mention that police have harassed them. So I think that just making it clear that these things actually happen, and being there for people, and I think just saying, if someone says something like that, I pull them aside later and say, 'I totally believe you, man, I hear what you're saying.' 'I hear what you're saying' is a huge thing, I think.... I don't even tell them that I've been harassed by cops. I just tell them, 'I hear you. I feel you.'"

The Importance of Support for Individuals

This kind of emotional support and solidarity among activists facing repression can help to take the sting—and the stigma—out of spending time in jail or prison, experiencing police violence, or otherwise being repressed by the state for political activity. This kind of support is critical to increasing the odds of persistence, as opposed to deterrence, for individuals in these situations. In fact, as already mentioned, nearly seven in ten individuals who had an experience in which they felt unsupported subsequently disengaged, while only 10 percent of those who never expressed feeling unsupported did so (Pearson $\chi^2(1) = 16.9365, p = 0.000$).

Like preparation, support is not always provided equally to all repression targets, but instead is often more accessible to those who are more experienced and well integrated into activist groups. When people do not get the support they need, for whatever reason, this—more than the repression itself—can cause them to question their participation. Sani said that, even though it didn't lead him to disengage, the most disempowering action he has ever been involved in was one where "there was no clear legal support or even real jail support that was organized, so all the people that were arrested were left fending for themselves." He continued, "[T]he lesson that I learned from that was just to never be a part of an action . . . unless you are deeply committed to follow through with it and make sure that you have some sort of support prior, not as an afterthought." Max had a similar experience with an action he was involved in. He explained, "That one was an interesting case of what we understood everything to be versus how it played out. . . . We were kinda left on our own. And we weren't a tight group. I mean, we all kinda came together with different people dreaming to do this action, so . . . it was people I didn't even know. There was no affinity with that group."

For several others, feeling unsupported was a major factor precipitating their disengagement. The $4,000 fine Emma had received from the construction project action was still unpaid at the time of my interview with her, and she was worried about her wages being garnished. She explained that there were benefits to raise money for those arrested with her, but that the money went to a few charismatic people and overhead costs for the organization involved in the action, so none of it helped her. It was not necessarily the cost of the fines themselves that caused her to reconsider her involvement following this episode, she explained, but the fact that those she expected to have her back didn't. In addition to not receiving this material support she thought she could count on, in the aftermath of the action some in the activist community were critical of her and others' choices related to this action. This lack of moral support played a major role in her subsequent disengagement from activism. She conceded that their criticism may have had validity to it, but it wasn't given in a constructive way and it left her feeling "embarrassed and disappointed." She explained, after that, "I was really quick to disown other people too, because we were being disowned."

These kinds of experiences, where the target of repression is blamed or criticized by others, seemed to be particularly hard on those I talked to and was a common thread among many who have since disengaged. In fact, one-third of those who disengaged had a story of feeling criticized after an experience of repression, whereas only one activist who has persisted had such a story. This difference is statistically significant (Pearson $\chi^2(1) = 8.1818$, $p = 0.004$). Bryce stopped going to protests in part because of an experience with police violence where he felt some leaders did not support him and others, but instead "threw them under the bus," as he put it. After this experience, he explained, "It kind of got to the point where I got to wondering, 'What's the point of a march?' I think, over time, we always had that kind of thought in the back of our heads anyways." Another man, who has also disengaged, discussed this same protest and the way he also felt that some of the organizers, and "their whole narrative of what happened," blamed him and other activists rather than supporting those who had borne the brunt of the crackdown by police at the march.

Debra was the one person who described having an experience where she felt criticized by other activists in the wake of being repressed, and yet has persisted. After her arrest at a political rally protest, she felt traumatized and drained and even considered taking a break from organizing and participating in protests. What upset her more than how the police treated her in this experience was that she felt criticized rather than supported by others in the organization she was protesting with. She told me she planned to talk with others in the group soon (the arrest had just happened days before), adding, "I don't know, maybe it's just different emotional styles." Whatever the reason, the disconnect she felt from the group in the aftermath of the arrest was as hard for her as the arrest itself. Although she did end up persisting in activism and is still very active today, this experience gave her serious pause.

Overall, these stories were rare in comparison to the stories of overwhelming support. The overall image that emerged from the interviews, observations, and content analysis is of a culture in which much effort goes into making sure that the burden of repression is lightened for those who experience it. This is done through the creation of strong systems of formal support, and a strong culture of informal support. But as these stories remind us, this support system, at times, breaks down. And when it does, it has serious consequences for the likelihood of continued participation for those who feel unsupported.

The Importance of Support for the Group

In addition to benefiting those who bear the brunt of repression's costs, these support networks can benefit the larger group and the movement that they are a part of in important ways; they also increase solidarity and comradery among activists and help to build a more attractive movement with more opportunities for people to participate in diverse ways. While it is difficult to measure the effects of these benefits for the individuals I interviewed, many argued that systems of support have further-reaching benefits than simply for the individuals who are targeted for repression.

Strengthening Ties of Solidarity

Support helps to prevent deterrence, not simply by reducing the costs of repression, but arguably by also strengthening the ties between activists (Nepsted 2014). When costs are shared and targets of repression receive support from the broader community and from others going through the same experience, strong bonds can develop that may not have developed in the absence of repression and the supportive response of others. Many people talked about the experience of going through repression with others as a bonding experience. One man was still a teenager when he was first arrested at a protest. He was arrested with more experienced activists and, being the youngest, everyone looked out for him and helped him through the experience. "I felt like I . . . built a family bond with people that I had just met, or people that I had hung out with but didn't really feel like a serious connection to. . . . I felt like these were important people now." Carl explained, after being arrested at a civil disobedience action, "Besides the person that introduced me to the action itself, I didn't know any of these people beforehand," but, "there's a certain kind of bond that forms with these people when you do these sorts of things. And I can unequivocally say that I hold these people in the highest regard."

Shane even argued that the power of arrest to connect and bond people with each other could be used as a benefit to movements. He told me, laughing, "It's a great organizing tactic. . . . It's like how they send people to prison over stupid little crimes and then they like learn how to commit better crimes. I'm like, 'Oh, you're giving me a whole bunch of comrades. Thanks!'" And Bryce argued that this comradery that develops from experiencing repression together also makes groups less vulnerable to repression in the future. He described the culture of Earth First!, a culture forged through particularly intense repression, this way: "It went beyond just like feeling comradery or whatever . . . it felt like your friends, almost like besties . . . it felt like a really tight kinship almost, like you couldn't really break it apart. I think they might try, like feds or cops might try and get undercover agents involved and stuff, but . . . it's even harder with a group like this, Earth First!, because they're so tight."

Movement Building

Kyle worried about the fact that people were spending so much time helping his legal case and raising money for his legal defense. He explained, "All that just to get my ass out of trouble. That energy and time and money should go into the activist cause . . . instead of just like helping somebody that's getting screwed." But others argued that building this kind of support is all part of movement building more generally. Ron said of fundraisers he organized to provide legal support: "We sold T-shirts and bumper stickers and we had little rock concerts. And, uh, that's part of the campaign as far as I'm concerned. Fundraising is also about educating and connecting people."

These kinds of support networks also create opportunities for more people to be involved in a movement and fill different roles. Jenna told me that she takes comfort in the fact that she doesn't always have to be the one willing to get arrested but can still make valuable contributions. Sometimes she can be the one to plan the party for the person who is being released; she explained, "And like when I am the one who gets arrested, those people are going to have my back." In this way, there is often an assumption of generalized exchange by which activists sometimes play support roles and trust that others will play such roles for them when needed. And when changing life circumstances make it hard for individuals to continue in the kind of roles they had occupied, they can shift into other, more supportive roles rather than disengaging altogether. This is how Johnny started organizing childcare and child blocs at protests. When he became a parent himself, it became more difficult for him to attend protests, and especially to be arrested. Rather than disengage, he took on a safer, support role—one that also helped to make participation easier and less risky for other parents like him.

Creating an environment where support can be assumed might help to retain existing members, as well as attract new ones. As one zine explained,

> Part of the state's goal in repression is to send a message to future dissidents to deter them from engaging in resistance efforts by demonstrating the intensity of punishment people can expect if they engage in such efforts. Our support for those faced with state repression can send the message that our movements take care of our own, and that we have each other's backs—no matter what the state dishes out. . . . In demonstrating our capacity to support our friends through state repression, we can make it less intimidating for people to consider engaging in activities that entail considerable risk.

Providing support also makes it less likely that agents provocateurs will be able to entrap impressionable or less socialized activists, or that activists, if arrested, will "flip" and become informants out of fear. If the support—material and otherwise—is there, there is less of a reason to cooperate with law enforcement. Suzanne told me she worries most about the people who are involved but not well integrated into the group: "Especially if there are vulnerable individuals who aren't well connected who don't have a social network. . . . That's where our security is. If you've got a lot of connections, a lot of ties, if something happens to disrupt the web, it pulls those strings, and other people are involved in monitoring. But if you're isolated and alone, you don't have that same social security." A man who has worked to support imprisoned peace activists for decades told me, after discussing recent cases in which agents provocateurs were able to entrap activists because they lacked sufficient support and integration into the activist community, that he believes movements have a responsibility to those who join them. He explained, "We have a responsibility as a movement. We've created this scene in radical and progressive movements in conflict with the state. It attracts people who are marginalized, passionate, vulnerable. The movement accepts them, but then cops pluck them out. We now have a responsibility to support them. We have responsibility to train and prepare people, have frank discussion about worst possible consequences."

Finally, building and maintaining systems of material and emotional support to sustain each other through repression and other challenges can also be a way for activists to model the kind of world they are working to create. It can be a way, in the here and now, for radical activists to embody the ideals of mutual aid and cooperation that, for many, are central to the more just, post-capitalist future they are fighting for. In this way, these support networks can be understood as one manifestation of prefigurative politics, a key feature in today's antiauthoritarian movements (Dixon 2014). At its core, the idea of prefigurative politics is that the means of fighting for change must necessarily reflect the ends being sought. As Dixon (2014) explains, many radical activists believe that how they "get there" will fundamentally shape what "there" looks like. In other words, "the means prefigure the ends" (Dixon 2014, 85). Prefigurative political practices, such as the systems of mutual aid discussed here, or participatory democracy practices discussed elsewhere (e.g., Polletta 2004), create a way for activists to get a glimpse of and feel the promise of even their loftiest of ideals without having to wait for a "new world" (Dixon 2014).

Conclusion

As rational choice scholars would expect, repression is costly, but organizations and groups also do a great deal to lower these costs for individuals. They do this by working to buffer and protect each other from repression, through practices that increase anonymity, privacy, and security. They also work to prepare and fortify individuals against the possibility of repression through trainings, role-plays, and a culture that focuses on acknowledging and accepting the risks of repression. Finally, activist communities build formal and informal systems of support that are activated in instances of state repression. These support systems work to meet both the material and emotional needs of individuals who experience repression. Because the costs and risks associated with repression are often more unpredictable and unevenly distributed than other costs of participation that rational choice scholars think about (e.g., time), mechanisms for reducing these costs often take the form of collective chipping in to reduce the costs for the relatively small number of people who experience the highest costs. Because people can generally take for granted that this support will be there if they need it, this fortifies them to take on risks and be bolder in their actions than they might be willing to do on their own.

I found that adequate preparation and support were both associated with dramatically lower rates of disengagement. Those who had experiences in which they felt unsupported in or unprepared for repression were far more likely to disengage than those who did not report such experiences. Examining the ways that groups reduce the costs of repression provides new ways to think about why repression sometimes deters and other times backfires. While scholars have generally assumed these outcomes are mostly a function of the features of the repression (e.g., its form, timing, consistency), there is also variation in the extent to which these cost-reducing practices are in place or work to benefit all those who need them, and this may be just as consequential as the actions of the state. The ways of mitigating costs of repression discussed in this chapter are not always evenly distributed within movements. Resources and information flow through activist networks, meaning that those who are better connected are also better protected, prepared, and supported. Poor planning, conflicting interests, and hierarchies and schisms within communities or movements can lead to some individuals feeling "disowned" or "left to fend for themselves," with serious consequences for their continued participation.

Therefore, the extent to which groups and movements develop effective and inclusive ways of preventing and preparing for repression, and supporting those who experience it, is an important factor shaping how repression is likely to impact their mobilization. While this may seem like an obvious point, previous research has done little to examine the role that movements themselves play in determining repression's effects on them (Zwerman and Steinhoff 2005). This chapter has taken a step toward rectifying that, by examining the ways that individuals' experiences of repression are fundamentally changed by the prevention, preparation, and support provided by the groups of which they are a part. The way that groups work together to reduce costs of participation (including repression) for individuals is a key part of the story, but, as the following chapters will demonstrate, to stop here would be to miss some of the most powerful ways that group culture can shape individual rationality.

5

"The Attempt Is Meaningful"

Redefining Protest's Ends

As the last chapter made clear, support and preparation provided by activist groups can make the experience of repression easier on individuals by lowering the costs, both material and nonmaterial, that they must bear. In doing so, they alter individuals' experiences of repression, in keeping with expectations of rational actor theories of collective action. I will now argue that groups also influence individuals' response to repression by providing a new lens through which to understand the risks and rewards of participation in collective action. Participation in protest cultures influences the ends that individuals strive for, but, just as importantly, they influence how they evaluate whether they have achieved these ends and whether the costs they have incurred in doing so are worth it. As Becker (1953) demonstrates, socialization in a counterculture (whether that of marijuana users in the 1950s in his study or that of leftist activists today in mine) can powerfully shape how individuals interpret new experiences. In this chapter, I will demonstrate that how activists learn to give meaning to their efforts and sacrifices has consequences for sustaining participation through experiences of state repression.

To be clear, my argument is not that groups simply help individuals to feel more efficacious or provide constant reinforcement that collective efforts are successfully creating change, making the sacrifices repression entails more palatable in a cost-benefit trade-off. While that would be consistent with previous research on perceived efficacy and protest participation, I instead document pervasive pessimism shared by my respondents, but also the ways that groups help activists to render their participation, and their sacrifices, meaningful despite what is often a lack of tangible success. I demonstrate how activists collectively expand what it means to be effective—making it less tied to tangible social or political change—and come to see the means of resistance as ends in and of themselves. Furthermore, I show how repression, rather than being perceived as a blow to themselves or their movement, is often taken by activists as further proof of the power of their collective action. Being "reoriented" in these ways, or in other words changing how they think about the purpose and meaning of protest and repression, is especially important for activists who have experienced repression. My argument in this chapter is not that protest groups buoy participants by showcasing their successes, but rather by helping them to repackage their goals to be more process-oriented and by helping them to see repression not as a cost that must be balanced but as independent evidence of the importance of their cause, actions, and sacrifices. Furthermore, I demonstrate that viewing participation and repression through this lens is associated with persistence.

"Ultimately, We're All Losing": The Pessimism of Protest

Keith was driving alone in a remote area when the police pulled him over. He quickly realized it was more than a routine traffic stop. The officer asked him increasingly specific questions about his past—who he knew and where he'd lived. He could hear a voice coming through the police radio, feeding the officer questions. He thought he heard the voice say that his name was on some kind of "list." The officer asked him about specific individuals by name, radical environmentalists who were wanted for engaging in forms of direct action that would soon become legally redefined and prosecuted as "domestic terrorism." He told them nothing. Eventually, they let him leave, but as he drove away, he couldn't shake the eerie feeling that he was being watched.

Over the years, Keith has also been arrested for civil disobedience more times than he can remember—"dozens at least"—and saw a good friend go to prison for years on the word of someone she thought was a fellow activist—and lover—who turned out to be on the payroll of the FBI. Through all of this, he has remained strong in his convictions and in his resolve to risk everything to defend wild spaces and a planet in peril. When I asked whether it gave him pause when someone he knew was revealed to be an undercover officer sent to get information on him and his friends, he laughed. "No, I drank the Kool-Aid years before . . . I was all in."

Much of the previous research on perceived efficacy and protest participation would assume that Keith must be willing to risk all this—his liberty, his livelihood, maybe even his life—in part because he believes his actions will make a difference. But, approaching his fiftieth birthday and thinking back on over twenty years of activism, he told me, "Ultimately, we're all losing. Everything. In my opinion, the earth is sunk." I asked why he still engages in protest and political organizing despite this grim outlook. After a long pause he replied, "Huh . . . I don't know. I guess I don't know what else there is to do."

To my surprise, when I asked activists about times they felt like political campaigns or actions they were involved in achieved something, and about times they felt defeated or ineffectual, respondent after respondent found it difficult to point to any "successes" but had ample stories of "failure" and moments of defeat and disillusionment to share. Their answers reflected despair much more often than hope. Like Keith, many believed that they were losing, or had already lost. They spoke of fighting to stop seemingly unpopular anti-immigrant legislation that was ultimately signed into law. They recounted organizing, protesting, and canvassing to protect Mexican American studies programs in public schools, only to see those programs dismantled and their books banned. They described multiyear struggles and trips to Washington, D.C., to protect sacred indigenous lands and critical animal habitats that were eventually destroyed. Many simply replied "over and over," "too many to count," or "there are a lot more of those" when I asked about efforts that they considered to be failures.

Jenna told me, reflecting back on all the campaigns and causes she has worked on over the years, "I mean, take the campaign that I first started working on: land mines have still not been banned. And I would say that the vast majority of political campaigns that I have worked on have not had the tangible result that we were looking for." Similarly, Jessica summed up her involvement in the immigrant rights movement by saying, "It seems like the bad guys always win and the shitty laws always get passed. You know, I don't know that any protest I've ever participated in has produced a tangible sociopolitical result." And Victor, a forty-year-old activist who has worked on a variety of causes for years, but especially for indigenous rights, said he was unfazed when a campaign he worked on failed, because "I'm not an optimistic person. Everything else, we always lost. So, it's no big deal to lose again. . . . I don't think we can beat them. Like that's the basic rule."

For Victor and many others, failure had become the default expectation. One environmental activist told me, explaining the surprise he felt when he and others successfully saved a grove of redwood trees from being logged, "We weren't used to winning much." Gary, an activist and lawyer who has spent much of his career representing protesters arrested or hurt by police, explained, "We're used to being small, used to failing. . . . We don't expect to win." Many respondents spoke of having little hope that the issues they cared about and worked to change would ever get better. One woman told me, with tears welling up in her eyes, "I'm jaded. I have no hope. . . . My heart has been broken for years."

As a society, we often celebrate those movements, like the civil rights movement, that were unequivocally successful at producing social and political progress. As social movement scholars, we also tend to focus on those movements, groups, and protest events that achieve some measure of "success." But as my respondents' stories make clear, often the aims of specific campaigns or movements are not realized. Despite the concerted efforts of groups of activists, ancient trees are cut down, regressive laws are passed, and wars rage on. In the face of what often feels like a long string of failures, punctuated by the occasional success, persisting in activism can feel like walking a thin line between hope and despair (Montgomery and Bergman 2017). To engage in collective action is not only to put forth effort with no guarantee that it will pay off; it is to invest oneself in an enterprise in which victory is always possible, but rarely probable. As I will argue, accepting—and even expecting—failure, as most of my respondents do, may (almost counterintuitively) help protect activists from disillusionment and disappointment and encourage commitment in the face of repression.

Efficacy and Protest Participation

That activists would expend great effort, and risk serious consequences, despite pessimism about the impact of their actions or the chances for social change, is puzzling considering that much of social movement research assumes that people participate in protest, in part, because they believe they can have an impact. Perhaps most famously, McAdam argues that, to mobilize, people must not simply believe that something is unjust; they must also believe that it can be changed (1999). Putting it in the terms of rational actor theory, Ennis and Schreuer (1987) argue that efficacy or "participants' sense of being able to make a difference" is "a social psychological 'reward' which may affect decisions to support, oppose, or ignore a campaign" (p. 395). Opp (1989) argues that perceived efficacy, even more than selective incentives, is the primary driver of participation in collective action. He further argues that when people are integrated into a group or community working for change, they no longer think in terms of their own efficacy, but rather in terms of their collective efficacy, giving them a greater sense of power than they would have on their own (see also Klandermans 1984; Macy 1991; Marwell and Oliver 1993). As will be clear, I go further and argue that not only does being a part of a group alter one's sense of efficacy in achieving a given goal; it may also provide alternative definitions of what it means to be effective.

Studies on a variety of different types of protest actions across diverse movements, from the labor movement to the environmental movement, have shown that perceived efficacy is a key factor explaining participation (for a review, see Einwohner 2002). However, just as is the case with research on social movement participation more generally, the majority of this research on the role of efficacy in micro-mobilization centers on the initial decision to join a movement, not on longer-term persistence. Sustaining a sense of efficacy arguably becomes more difficult the longer one is involved, as the optimism and enthusiasm of the new recruit gives way to the disappointment, failure, and uncertainty that often characterize activist work (Einwohner 2002).

The few studies that have focused on perceived efficacy and longer-term persistence (Voss 1998; Einwohner 2002) have demonstrated that a sense of efficacy is a collective achievement that requires work to be maintained rather than a preexisting attitude. For example, Voss (1998) demonstrates how groups must engage in intense reframing following a major loss. She documents how labor unions frame defeats or setbacks in ways that encourage continued commitment. To sustain losses and not collapse, she argues, movements needed to develop what she terms a fortifying myth: "an explanation of defeat that linked current failure to future triumphs, keeping hope alive so that activists could mobilize support when new political opportunities arose" (p. 139). Through studying the discourse of British "new unions," Voss identifies specific fortifying myths—stories that the unionists told themselves to justify persistence in the face of failure. For example, they told themselves that the defeat was still a "moral victory," it was actually a partial success, it was merely a temporary setback, or that it moved them one step closer to inevitable victory. These stories "put a positive slant on defeat [and] gave workers reasons to believe that their sacrifices had not been in vain" (p. 145). Meanwhile, in the United States, the Knights of Labor were silent following their strike defeats, and Voss partially credits their demise to the fact that they did not work to construct such "fortifying myths."

Drawing on Voss's work, Einwohner (2002) examines how animal rights activists think about the efficacy of their efforts. The activists she studied worked to keep morale high and put a positive spin on their efforts through "fortifying strategies." They found evidence of progress in even the clearest of defeats, framed their efforts as small steps toward a far-off goal, celebrated victories when they could, and claimed credit for progress that may or may not have been a result of their efforts. She refers to these strategies as forms of "efficacy work," just as previous studies have documented how protest groups engage in emotion work, identity work, and framing work. The animal rights activists' efficacy work helped them to hold onto just enough hope to continue. In documenting this, Einwohner demonstrates that a sense of efficacy matters for continued participation, not just initial recruitment. Just as importantly, she also highlights how individuals' sense of efficacy is highly malleable and collectively constructed. Just as Festinare, Reiken, and Schachter (1956) show in their study of failed prophecy in an end-of-days cult, collective experience and interpretation of "failures" is often key to individuals' persistence through moments that might otherwise lead to doubt.

Beyond Efficacy

While Voss and Einwohner both document the ways that activists work together to hold onto hope in order to motivate themselves to fight another day, I argue that groups sometimes redefine "success" and "failure" in even more fundamental ways and, furthermore, that their ability to do so may be an important boon for weathering state repression. Voss and Einwohner demonstrate how activists convince themselves that, despite apparent failures, they are still making progress. However, I find that sometimes activists may actually move away from thinking about their participation in terms of efficacy entirely and instead give meaning to their participation, and their sacrifices, independently of the achievement (present or future) of tangible political change. I identify four ways that activists I interviewed exhibit this kind of reorientation in thinking about the ends of protest: (1) redefining success to include nebulous, process-oriented goals; (2) redefining success to include resistance itself; (3) redefining success to include repression; and (4) explicitly resisting the language of efficacy.

Those who exhibited one or more of these discursive signs of reorientation were more likely to persist in activism despite their experiences of state repression. I find that while this factor was not significantly associated with persistence for the entire sample, it was significant for all those who described having the support and preparation for repressive experiences that they needed ($n = 31$). This is because lack of support or preparation is so strongly associated with disengagement, as discussed in the previous chapter, that redefining success makes little difference to those who have felt unsupported and unprepared. These individuals are highly likely to disengage, whether reoriented or not. However, reorientation does explain why some, despite having received adequate support and preparation, disengage while others persist.

More specifically, I find that while all of those who were supported, prepared, and reoriented persisted, only three-quarters of those who were supported, prepared, but not reoriented persisted (Pearson $\chi^2(1) = 6.1466$, $p = 0.013$). Both rates of persistence are high simply because persistence among those who always felt prepared and supported was very high, about 90 percent. Still, among those who felt supported and prepared, the adoption of alternative ways of thinking about efficacy and the purpose of protest helped explain why some persisted in the face of repression while others did not.

To be clear, my argument is not that this reorientation toward different ends of protest simply leads to persistence (or that the lack of it leads to disengagement), but rather that the two are associated with each other. This may be, in part, because this perspective can help sustain individuals through disappointment and sacrifice. In addition, individuals who persist despite repressive experiences may rely on this discourse to rationalize their continued participation and to give meaning to what appears, from an outside perspective, to be a high-risk, low-reward activity. Below I document each of the four ways that activists I interviewed talked about success and failure in ways that made their participation meaningful to them, regardless of the chances for tangible social change. Through this discourse, they construct a narrative in which their efforts are not in vain, despite their pessimism about the possibility for change and despite the high costs they have already paid.

Expanding the Definition of Success

When asked about times they felt they achieved something through their political efforts, some activists simply shrugged. Others laughed. Not only were pessimism, stories of failure, and assessments of general ineffectiveness incredibly common, but even when people did talk about past efforts that they considered to be "successes," these were often not successes in the way social movement scholars would usually conceive of or measure it. By including outcomes such as gaining attention, raising awareness, and building movement capacity as "successes," even when the goals of the campaign or action were not achieved, activists expand what it means to be effective.

Palma told me that when the DREAM Act did not pass, after months of putting much effort and time into a campaign to support it, she took the loss hard. It was the first time she was heavily involved in a political campaign and she had high hopes for its success. She explained her thought process at the time: "We did everything . . . how could this have happened? You know I was in my house, in my room crying for like a whole day and my family was coming in and hugging me. I just couldn't—it didn't make sense. We had done actions. We had done petitions. And we had done calls. We had done so many things. I thought that, like, there was no way it wouldn't pass."

Consistent with the findings of previous research on the importance of perceived efficacy for initial recruitment, Palma came to activism with a sense of optimism and, apparent in her description, a belief that if she and others tried hard enough, change was not only possible, it was probable. Now, after this and other failed campaigns, she feels this perspective was naïve. She realized that there are many factors other than her effort that determine whether a campaign is successful. Her main takeaway from the experience, once she got over the initial shock of the defeat, was "that the people in power are not the people that should be in power." As a result of this realization, she shifted her focus to getting out the vote in the Latinx community, in an effort to elect candidates that better reflected her community. She also developed a more expansive sense of what it means to succeed. As will become clear later, to her, standing up for herself and for her beliefs became a victory in and of itself. Her story suggests that even if perceived efficacy is what draws people to movements, perhaps it is a relaxing of what counts as "efficacy" that helps them to stay and, more specifically, to stay despite the risks and costs of state repression.

Gaining Attention, Raising Awareness

When they could think of a "success" at all, about one in five respondents saw a time they raised awareness or gained attention as their greatest example of a "success," even though they may not have achieved their stated goals. For example, Emma talked about the ultimately unsuccessful campaign against a resort in her community, a campaign for which she was arrested twice, incurred significant fines, and literally put her body on the line by locking herself, by her neck, to construction equipment. The resort went ahead as planned, but her actions and those of other activists brought significant attention to long-standing local issues surrounding Native land rights, water consumption, and environmental protection. Because of the action of a small group of activists, she argues that the resort became something that almost everyone in her small town now has an opinion about. To her, that is a victory, even if it isn't the one she was originally seeking. Brad, who was part of this same action with Emma, explained, "We shut down construction, I think for like two or three hours and then all got arrested, but . . . the goal we had . . . was just to bring the issue into the media spotlight, which was a wild success."

Similarly, Kyle told me about a protest he attended where activists came from all over the state to disrupt a neo-Nazi rally in Phoenix. He considered their counterprotest to be a success, not only because it got media attention, but, more specifically, because it produced a spectacle in which the police and the neo-Nazis appeared to be on one side, marching together, while the police pepper sprayed and dispersed the anti-racist counterprotesters. They made the police look bad, and even as if they were in collusion with the neo-Nazis. For him, that made the protest a success.

Operation Streamline continues to prosecute and sentence seventy migrants every weekday in Tucson. Still, the activists who locked themselves to each other and to a bus transporting the migrants to court, as part of a campaign to end Operation Streamline, told me that they considered this action to be a success. Aaron explained that the action not only interrupted "business as usual" for Operation Streamline for that one day; it also brought media attention, including major outlets, such as the *New York Times*, the *Washington Post*, and the *Wall Street Journal*, to a legal process that had previously been, as he put it, an "open secret." And the consequences for the seventy migrants on the bus were very real: they were deported immediately but did not receive a criminal record and did not have to spend months in immigration detention. Beth, who also participated in the action with Aaron, explained, "It's a little victory. Is the war won? No. And I don't know how to win the war, I just know the things that are immediately in front of me."

Jessica explained that the only positive impact she believes she has made is that she has hopefully exposed others to new information or perspectives. Pressed for specifics, she recounted a time when she and a few other activists went to a busy shopping mall during the holiday rush. They stood amid the crowd of frenzied shoppers, singing carols to the tune of popular Christmas songs but rewritten to promote an anti-consumerism message. Seeing shoppers stop in their tracks or look on in dismay validated her efforts, as she figured that her actions, if nothing else, might have led even just one person to think twice about their choices. By focusing on bringing attention and awareness to issues they care about, Jessica and the others construct a definition of success that is less dependent on whether or not the action, campaign, or movement achieves its stated goals. In doing so, they protect themselves from disappointment and make the costs they have already paid (and, in many cases, continue to put themselves at risk of) feel worthwhile.

Building Movement, Building Community

While some expanded the definition of success to include getting attention or raising awareness, others (about one in ten respondents) argued that otherwise "failed" campaigns were successful because they helped to make new connections or otherwise build community and movement capacity that could later be mobilized for other campaigns.

Ron and others worked tirelessly to save an old growth forest when he lived in the Northwest, only to see the trees cut down. Still, he considered it to be one of his more effective campaigns because it planted seeds for later success. He explained that at first it seemed like an utter failure:

> We ran the campaign for two or three years without much success and I really thought . . . we had come to the end of the line. . . . We lost the trees, and we also had a SLAPP suit filed against us, and they even read us the Riot Act—I mean, I didn't even know that was a real thing, but that one demonstration, we were charged with rioting. We faced a lot of felony charges, and long jail sentences. There were hunger strikes, and all kinds of support, jail support demos. . . . And it seemed like they had worn us out after three years, and we didn't have much to show for it.

But, in fact, they had succeeded in building a movement. He went on,

> The actions that we did, the campaigns that we did there, you know, they paid off a lot down the road. . . . We had trained quite a few activists. We had built a network of a number of organizations. We had fine-tuned our tactics and our messaging. . . . The movement got kick-started again, and when it did, it wasn't just us at the helm. You know, it was a lot of other people too. . . . It took us a couple of years to realize what we had actually gotten done. . . . People were pretty depressed when the grove was cut. . . . That was the object of the whole campaign. But really, that was the last one that got away. And no others would go down without a fight. . . . So looking back at it, I think those actions were some of the most effective ones that we had done.

For Ron, this experience was a reminder that the immediate goal is not all that matters. The social and organizational by-products of the process of working toward that goal are sometimes just as important. Furthermore, for him this experience demonstrated the fact that any given campaign, even one that lasts for years, is part of an even longer struggle. Taking a wider view and "playing the long game" helps Ron and other activists to maintain a sense of efficacy through defeats. It also helps them to better weather and persist through repression, as his discussion of the civil and criminal legal consequences they had to contend with made clear.

When I asked Victor about the greatest success he had experienced, he began his story with a disclaimer. "It's gonna sound ironic, because it was, in fact, not a victory . . . ," he began. He described a protest he attended against House Bill 2281, which was eventually signed into law. HB 2281 would prohibit Arizona schools from teaching classes catering to students of particular ethnic groups or that "promoted the overthrow of the U.S. government," among other stipulations (Santa Cruz 2010). Victor and others worried that the law, if passed, would be the end of the Mexican American studies program that had been in place for years in Tucson public schools, a program that many argued had been very successful at improving educational outcomes among Mexican American students through teaching culturally relevant curriculum. The protest drew activists from all over the state, including Victor, to the state capital:

> It was 100,000 people. It had to be. Like, it was a sea of people. And the reality is we were losing. We were losing in the courts. We were losing all over. Like according to the national media, we didn't win it. . . . But there was so much energy in the movement. There was so much fire in people. . . . You started seeing leaders emerge. You started seeing things aligning, like who should be speaking, who should be in the back, who's better at managing, who's better at

> making posters, who's better at making phone calls. . . . All that was happening naturally. And there were strong kids coming out of the high schools, and even the middle schools. They're, to this day, still involved, you know. . . . We succeeded in organizing our community.

To him, even though the bill was signed into law, the movement against it was successful because of the way that it brought people together, brought young people into activism, and helped solidify roles that would make future campaigns easier to get off the ground. Sani made a similar argument when describing a campaign in which local indigenous high school students got involved. Seeing them mobilize and become politicized was particularly fulfilling because, as he explained, "You know the times that I feel like, even if we don't win a campaign, the times that I feel like are the most rewarding for me personally is when people are just empowered and they recognize that they don't need some specialists, activist nonprofit group to mediate their desires for justice."

Kyle told me that one of his "biggest successes" as an activist was forming a collective with others and running an infoshop (a community center that provides political books and zines and a space for meetings and other events) for several years. He explained, "Something that came out of that period of protest was creating a countercultural subculture in Tucson that was very strong and vibrant for many years. . . . I definitely remember feeling really proud of what we had created: this alternative space for people to be able to discuss things and plan and organize. . . . I was creating a space that didn't exist before and I felt really proud of that."

Cory argued that the greatest success that came from the Occupy movement in his town was the connections that it fostered, networks that he argues still remain and are ready, if needed, to be mobilized again. He explained,

> The ties are still there. Even though Occupy no longer remains and people call it a failure. I don't think it was a failure at all . . . it was able to lay the ground structure for what could be at future movements, and the people that I met there are still just as, just as active, they're still as interested in the cause. And the people who were really there, the people who were there from day to day . . . are still there, but they're under the radar now. So it's a situation of like, they could be—they could become active at any time. We are kind of just waiting for this moment that's right, I guess. It's kind of just this endless discussion about when to hit the "go" button, when to actually start something . . . you kind of have to wait until there's a good moment.

By focusing on the creation of new networks, social spaces, and organizational infrastructure as successes in and of themselves, Cory and the others are able to reframe what might otherwise be considered defeats as ground gained toward future victories. While this discursive strategy, and to a lesser extent defining awareness raising as a success, can still be seen as potentially tied to a hope for future political change (as Voss 1998 and Einwohner 2002 also document), it also expands, and makes looser, what counts as effective. As I will describe, the next three strategies expand the idea of success even more fundamentally, making it coterminous with resistance and repression and explicitly resisting the notion of thinking about their efforts in terms of "success" and "failure" altogether.

When Means Become Ends: Resistance as a Victory

Not only do groups redefine "success" for their members to include things like movement building and awareness raising, but over time, as people participate in social movements and become socially, emotionally, and ideologically invested in them, the means of protest increasingly become indistinguishable from the ends. When this occurs, participation in movements becomes less instrumental and more expressive. What I mean by this is that the purpose of protest becomes less about seeking a tangible goal, like a political change, than about expressing one's opinion or indignation about an issue. Resistance itself becomes the end. When talking about experiences that they considered to be "successes," it became clear that many saw the act of protest, in and of itself, to be a success regardless of what came of it. Over a third of respondents engaged in this type of rationalization of their efforts.

For example, when I asked him to tell me about a time he felt he was successful, Nick told me about a protest he attended at which there was open confrontation in the streets between anti-racist activists, neo-Nazis, and police (the same protest discussed by Kyle earlier in this chapter). When pressed about why this protest was a success, Nick explained, "I think because people just weren't even afraid. It was the summer SB 1070 [a controversial anti-immigrant law in Arizona] passed and I think people, at that point, were just like, 'This is where we're drawing the line.' I think there were moments of like—I don't even want to say 'heroism'—but moments in which people stepped outside of what I think they thought they could or would do." He went on to explain that all he and others really did was hold a line against the police. He was proud that they held their ground for as long as they did and that when the police did advance, it was only a couple of feet at a time. But he added, "That was like a moment which, in terms of what was accomplished, you know, it's tough to say. Because sometimes what you want to accomplish is that people have a realization that they are the ones making the decisions about what they do."

The day that Lonnie Schwartz, the Border Patrol agent who shot Mexican teenager José Antonio through the fence along the U.S.-Mexico border, was found not guilty of second-degree murder, protesters blocked an interstate exit ramp for hours. Late into the night, the activists blocked traffic, chanted, and played music. They made it clear that they weren't going anywhere anytime soon. There was even talk of staying all night, so they could also get more coverage on the early morning news. At one point, an unnamed masked protester leaned over to me and said, "Wow, we actually did something this time." Even with only his eyes visible, I could tell that he was smiling. The "something" they had done was disrupt traffic, get media attention, and make it known that they disagreed with the verdict. Their victory was in the fact that they didn't let the acquittal go without notice, and that they hopefully sent a clear message that they would continue to put pressure on the state to hold the officer accountable and get justice for José Antonio and his family. The prosecutors announced days later that they would pursue lesser charges of manslaughter against Schwartz—that they weren't going to drop the case despite the outcome of the murder trial. Would this have happened regardless, protests or no protests? It's hard to say. But for that young man, that wasn't really the point. They had already succeeded—they had "done something."

As one respondent put it, thinking back on many protests he had been a part of, "I guess that I feel like my expectations were always somewhat low. . . . I think our definition of a win was to just to be there and just voice our opinion about how things were being done." He went on to elaborate that "it was important that we do it," despite the fact that he never felt as if the protests he organized and attended were really going to impact the big issues he cared about. An activist who has given her time, home, and resources to aiding and advocating for the rights of immigrants, especially LGBT immigrants, echoed this sentiment, saying: "So far, the success has been in continuing to struggle in a really unjust world and maintain our humanity . . . but the laws that get passed seem to be getting worse and worse, so it's hard to claim a lot of victories." Similarly, an older activist said of his past involvement in radical environmental activism: "Our victories, I think, were mostly in that we demonstrated a collective tenacity and uncompromising position that went on for years and years." Furthermore, for Zach, withstanding repression and threats of incarceration was a victory: "I mean, it takes, it takes a lot of confidence to look at things that have a great deal more power than you, and decide that you're going to . . . do this anyway. And the fact that, like, I accomplished that and have gotten through, like, really difficult times . . . that's the victory for me."

Sean told me about a campaign he was a part of in which he and others spent years engaged in legal battles and civil disobedience to try to stop a power plant from being built. Ultimately, the power plant was built anyway. But he was happy that they were able to bring attention to important issues; for example, they used the trial of arrested protesters as a stage for scientists to testify about climate change and the environmental impact that the power plant would have. Even more than that, he said it was satisfying just to give the company so much grief for so long. The company was clearly inconvenienced by the constant pressure put on them by the civil disobedience demonstrations, and they spent large amounts of money countering movement messages in the media and battling movement lawyers in court. Just being a thorn in their side for years and working together with everyday people against a modern-day Goliath "felt good"—regardless of the outcome. Similarly, when I asked Frank what kept him fighting for peace and immigrant rights, he answered, "I mean, what else would I do at this point? . . . I mean, we might ultimately lose, but I want to make the bad guys suffer if we do." Jared explained that, when he attended a large protest at a political convention, their goal was to shut down the meetings. They didn't succeed in doing this, but for him it was still not a loss because, as he put it, "At least they knew that everyone around them was angry with them. . . . That felt good."

Dana told me, of her past efforts, "The attempt, I guess, is meaningful, even if it doesn't turn out." By making resistance meaningful in and of itself, divorcing efficacy from tangible achievements and attaching it to such outcomes as expressing anger or giving opponents a hard time, activists make the means of protest coterminous with the ends. This is what Hirschman refers to as "striving" and what he argues gives our lives meaning (1986). As Ferree (1992) explains, "In such behavior, effort expended is not a cost but rewarding in itself; striving to affirm a value is done 'for its own sake'" (p. 33). I would argue that coming to see the attempt itself as meaningful and letting this, rather than a desire to achieve "success" for one's cause, become a motivation to act is key to facilitating and sustaining collective action. As one woman put it:

> I mean, there are definitely moments of despair, like deep despair, where you feel like it's all just like a waste of time. But I think some of it is just knowing that I'm not sitting on my hands, even if sometimes it doesn't feel very tactical. Knowing that I'm trying is really important. . . . Just knowing that there are lot of other people too in the world that care . . . I think really seals it. Even though it seems irrational sometimes. It's going to have to be irrational in order for it to really happen. If everyone were truly reasonable and people thought about what they're up against, I think people would just sit at home.

What her sentiments reveal is a sense of needing to "do something," to not sit idly by, regardless of whether or not this action "feels very tactical." Many others shared her belief in the importance of just "knowing that I'm trying." As she explains, this might not be rational in a narrow sense, but it may also be necessary for collective action to occur and to be sustained. This perspective of giving meaning to the attempt, I argue, may be at least as effective at facilitating and sustaining collective action as would convincing themselves that they are effective.

Some talked about how what made resistance meaningful to them, regardless of the outcome, was the way that it brought to the surface social conflict and suffering that they felt was always there, just below the awareness of most people. Not only does resistance make this conflict visible to others, but it can also be satisfying to activists whose worldview make them aware, sometimes painfully so, of injustice. Russo (2018) similarly shows how "solidarity witness" activists derive meaning from acts of ritual protest that bring to light the suffering of victims of the United States security state.

This dynamic may be all the more pronounced when that resistance is met with state repression. Emma described how, at the height of her involvement in activism, her ideological commitments were like a lens she couldn't remove. She saw politics in everything. She described not being able to turn on the lights, or the faucet, without thinking about where those resources were coming from and about the desecration of animal habitats and of indigenous lands and cultures, or just the way that "everything is rooted in imperialism." At times, this hyperawareness felt paralyzing. Now, no longer intensely involved in activism, she still believes that "nothing is apolitical," but she tries not to let these concerns eat at her the way they used to. But she described feeling, at that time, a need to express and make explicit the conflict that she felt with the world around her. Similarly, Brad told me, after talking about a situation in which the police violently dispersed a protest he was at, "I mean, it felt good to have the conflict within yourself towards these ideologies like white supremacy, anti-immigrant stuff, like this intense animosity toward whatever, you know—call it your enemy. It felt like I started to have that internal conflict be external as well, like seeing the conflict up front."

These confrontations, even though they may be risky or result in physical or legal consequences for activists, give activists an opportunity to make explicit the sense of conflict and indignation that they feel and work to sharpen the boundary between activists and their opponents. As Eric Hoffer argues, sometimes what one is fighting against is as strong a motivation as what they are fighting for. As he put it, "Mass movements can rise and spread without a belief in a god, but never without a belief in a devil. Usually, the strength of a mass movements is proportionate to the vividness and tangibility of its devil" (1951, 91).

The importance of resistance for bringing ever-present social conflict to the surface and challenging systems of authority and domination, regardless of the outcome, was not only expressed through respondents' discourse; it was also present in the written manifestations of activist culture that my respondents recommended to me. A zine entitled *What They Mean When They Say Peace* argues that when protesters are disruptive or even destructive, as some were in the protests in Ferguson, Missouri, following the shooting of Michael Brown, they are, as the author(s) put it,

> reminding us of the conflicts that remain unresolved in our society. . . . They are not disturbing the peace; they are simply bringing to light that there never was any peace, there never was any justice in the first place. At tremendous risk to themselves, they are giving us a gift: a chance to recognize the suffering around us and to rediscover our capacity to identify and sympathize with those who experience it. For we can only experience tragedies such as the death of Michael Brown for what they are when we see other people responding to them as tragedies.

Through discourse that makes the surfacing of social conflict an end in and of itself and reframes engaging in struggle as a victory, activists fuse the means and ends of protest and make resistance less vulnerable to losses or to costs such as repression. In the process, participation becomes less instrumental and more expressive. Sometimes, this transformation can occur over the course of even a single experience of collective action. When I asked him what he was thinking and feeling at the first protest he ever attended, a protest against police brutality, Bryce admitted, "I was thinking it was, like, a big waste of time for the most part." But he continued, "But then, like marching through the streets . . . I didn't feel like it was a waste of time by the end." Being at the protest, meeting others who cared about the same issue he did, and being exposed to families who had been directly impacted by police brutality changed his perspective. By the end of the protest, he came to the same conclusion that Dana had—that the attempt itself was meaningful. This is what Ferree (1992, 35) was referring to when she argued that "getting people to act can, under some conditions, literally change what and how they see." Becker (1953) makes a similar argument in his classic work—that "motives" and "dispositions" are often emergent from (collective) experience rather than preconditions for it. As Neil Gross explains, "Means and ends are not always given prior to action, as assumed in most rational choice models, but are often emergent from action, as lines of activity are initiated that lead actors to see themselves in new ways, to value different kinds of goods, and to become attached to problem solutions they could not have imagined previously" (2009, 367).

In this same vein, Benford (1993) argues that activists develop "vocabularies of motive" to justify their participation to themselves and to others over time. In this way, "benefits are interactionally defined and redefined in the course of participation" (p. 208). Contrary to most work on micro-mobilization, he does not treat attitudes—like a sense of efficacy or a moral obligation to participate—as attitudes that precede action. Rather, participating in collective action contributes to the development of these ways of thinking about and motivating their behavior. I argue that this continual redefinition of "benefits" is especially important when costs are high and success is uncertain.

Furthermore, resistance may especially feel like a victory for those with the most to lose. Palma described what she was feeling when she came face to face with police at an immigrant rights protest: "We were sitting down, and you could see police officers in full gear—riot gear—walking towards us and it was just great to face them." She was still undocumented at the time, so the stakes were high. She knew going into the protest that it put her at risk not only of arrest, but of deportation. She knew that she could potentially be separated from her family and sent back to a country she had only lived in as an infant.

Her mom had begged her not to go to the protest. But for Palma, resistance was worth the risks. She explained that she had grown up in fear of the police, and when she was younger, she tried to avoid doing anything that might draw attention to herself or her family. She explained, "My mom always told me, you know, 'Just do good in school, just stay quiet, don't cause attention, and it'll be okay.'" But when SB 1070 passed, she explained, "I realized that wasn't the case. That it didn't matter how quiet I was, that it didn't matter how good of a student I was, that it didn't matter that I was in college, like none of that mattered. A group of people did not want us here and they did not want me here."

When SB 1070 became law, for her the risks of sitting idly by were suddenly raised. The law allowed for the prosecution of legal residents for "human smuggling" if they housed an undocumented person, even if they were related to them. Giving a ride to an undocumented family member could theoretically even result in charges of "transporting an illegal immigrant." In the wake of its passage, Palma's mixed-status family had to change how they functioned on a daily basis. They stopped visiting their grandparents, who were residents. She could no longer get rides with her brother, who was a citizen. She decided it was time that she learned to drive. In fact, one of the very first times she drove on her own, it was to attend a protest, against her mother's wishes. She had never even been downtown before, let alone to the capitol building where the protest was being held. Having lived in fear and rarely venturing out of her immediate neighborhood, all of it was new to her.

She knew that protesting was risky, but at least these risks were chosen. Plus, if she were arrested at a protest, there would be a whole community of people rallying around her. She explained that undocumented immigrants who are picked up and are not politically involved often don't have this built-in support. They can be arrested and deported, and no one even knows, she told me. She went on to explain, "I run the risk every day. I can go to school and be arrested and deported. I can go to a friend's house and be arrested and be deported. And so, with this, at least I'm making a statement and letting them know . . . I'm gonna face it." Adam, a white American citizen who has been involved in the immigrant rights movement for years, made a similar argument. He said that, in his observations, people who were politically active were less likely to be deported. "Being politically active provides a certain protection," he explained, because people will mobilize on their behalf. He explained, "Not all the time, but lots of times, there have been people who are politically active who . . . it felt like it stopped them from getting deported . . . not the fact that they're political, but the fact that people mobilize around them."

At that first protest, Palma met other people, especially other young people, who were also undocumented like she was. They were proudly proclaiming that they were not afraid, and she was inspired by them. She explained that meeting them "became a reason to continue fighting, 'cause prior to that I felt really alone and so I was in and out of depression like, 'What am I gonna do with my life?' . . . I was sad, I was depressed, I thought that I didn't have any power or agency over what was happening. Seeing other people like put their lives on the line . . . it's been inspiring." She explained that, through coming together with others, acting together, taking risks together, she found courage that she had lacked on her own. Now a professional community organizer, it is her mission to help others find this courage as well. She explained, "We need to connect more with people and have more human interaction, have more of an awareness with each other, and how like we're affected by all these systems that are in place . . . it takes putting ourselves into spaces where you have a whole room of other people fighting right alongside of you."

That experience where she said it "felt great" to face the riot police—a tangible representation of a justice system that she felt persecuted by—ended in her arrest, along with several others. As she had hoped, she received an outpouring of support from the community. People called the jail and Immigration and Customs Enforcement (ICE) and advocated for her release. To her surprise and the relief of her family, she was not deported. In fact, with time, she was able to gain legal residency. Eventually, her mom, who had been so scared of her daughter becoming politically involved, started attending protests with her. Palma told me, "It's been amazing to see my mom break the fear . . . to see her now, out there, and being like, 'I'm afraid but I'm not gonna let it paralyze me.' . . . So now . . . my dad's involved, my little sister, my brother, they're all involved. . . . So for me that's been the most powerful thing, like having my family not live with that fear is the best feeling."

But when her mom went so far as to volunteer to be arrested at a protest, Palma was worried. She joked that the tables had been turned; now she was the one worrying about her mom. She didn't want her mom to be in jail alone (she was the only woman who had volunteered to be arrested at the action), so Palma decided, at the last minute, she would get arrested with her. That worried her too, because she knew if she was "on the inside" she couldn't coordinate support for her mom the way she could if she were not arrested. But she decided to get arrested with her mom and trust that others would support them "from the outside," which they did.

At a protest on the fifth anniversary of the passage of SB 1070, the crowd recited chants like "undocumented, unafraid" and "*sin papeles, sin miedo*" (without papers, without fear). These chants are a reminder of the fact there is a double fear that needs to be overcome for undocumented protesters—the fear of arrest that others must also face, plus the fear of deportation or other consequences related to their immigration status. For those who are undocumented, the costs of protest and of repression are simply much higher. But, as Palma's story makes clear, there may also be a greater satisfaction in overcoming this fear. When the fifth anniversary protest ended in front of Sheriff Arpaio's jail (this was before Joe Arpaio was voted out of office), someone on a megaphone shouted defiantly in the direction of the building, "Arpaio, you've been looking for us. We're all here. Come and take us."

This idea that asserting one's agency through acts of dissent, even when defeat is certain or nearly certain, can be an end in and of itself is not new in research on social movements. Rachel Einwohner's (2003) work on the Warsaw Ghetto Uprising argued exactly this and, in many ways, turned political opportunity theory on its head. Here was a case of people joining in collective action, literally at the expense of their lives, not because they believed they could win but precisely because they knew they could not. Directly contrary to the dominant paradigm, she argues that it was precisely the sense of utter hopelessness that motivated the Jews in the Warsaw Ghetto to rise up. They had nothing left to lose and, by resisting, they could at least gain a death with dignity and honor.

Wood (2001) also argues that we should not underestimate the "pleasure of agency" (p. 272) and of defiance in the face of otherwise paralyzing fear (p. 279) as a motivating force for collective action. Like Einwohner's study of the Warsaw Ghetto Uprising, the case through which Wood demonstrates this—peasant resistance in El Salvador in the 1970s—is one of extreme oppression, violence, and risk. But, in the contemporary United States, even for undocumented protesters like Palma (and certainly for those who enjoy the privilege of citizenship, as most of my respondents do), the threats are far less severe and defeat far less certain than was the case for Jews in the Warsaw Ghetto or peasants in 1970s El Salvador. Considering this, the fact that so many respondents also saw struggle and confrontation as victories in and of themselves and described what could be considered the "pleasure of agency" (Wood 2001) and the dignity of resistance (Einwohner 2003) suggests that these previous findings, and the challenge they posed to extant understandings of what drives mobilization, may be far more general. As Einwohner and Maher (2011) remind us, threat is subjective. A situation must be assessed and framed as threatening if it is to raise the costs of inaction and move people to act collectively. I would argue that even in situations that are objectively less extreme than the Warsaw Ghetto, what matters is whether people collectively define, or redefine, a situation as less tolerable than the consequences that might come from resisting it.

When Costs Become Rewarding: Repression as a Sign of Success

Not only can resistance be reframed as a success—so can repression. When repression is framed as indicative of the importance or strength of the movement, it is no longer simply a cost, it is also a sign of "success." This is why, as one activist involved in support of political prisoners told me, you sometimes see "resistance courting repression." In fact, a full two-thirds of respondents described repression as proof of their efficacy, or that of their movement.

Brad told me that he's noticed a trend lately where the police will come to protests but, as he put it, "just leave us alone." I asked him what he thought of that, and he responded, "It definitely feels like, 'Why aren't the cops paying attention?' . . . It's hard to not take personally in the way of our effectiveness, but it does feel like maybe we're more trivial than is actually worth spending time on policing, you know?" Victor also explained the rise and fall of repression over the time he has been involved in activism in terms of the strength of resistance. He explained that repression was less intense lately (this was in 2016, before the presidential election), but "maybe they don't think—maybe they think we are marginalized again? I'm not sure, but to a certain extent, it kinda dropped off. Like it flared up for a while and now it's back to a little less. But at the same time, we're also a little less." Another woman simply asserted, "If you're effective, they squash it."

Several people involved in Occupy talked about the police response to that movement being a result of the fact that the movement was threatening powerful economic interests and bringing attention to inequality, which, as one woman put it, "terrifies the power structure." Keith told me that he feels like groups like Earth First! were targeted for repression because the environmental movement was, at that time, growing both bolder and more popular: "In the late eighties there was a real environmental movement that was getting more radical, and the American people were largely supportive of it. Not like today. It was an ideological war, but it was definitely also a very practical one. Because America, without the repression of that movement, could have looked a lot different. People were clearly wanting to have real, more conservation-minded laws, more serious efforts for clean air and clean water and to save our forests, and all that stuff was real. And now we've suffered a tremendous loss and backsliding since then." Carl told me that, when he received a Facebook friend request from someone he didn't know and later figured out was law enforcement, his response was: "It caused me to go all in . . .'cause when they pay attention that means that you are doing something right." Similarly, those who knew they were on a law enforcement watch list or had been in some way associated with the label of terrorism by law enforcement described their feelings about this, using words like "exciting" or by saying "I was kind of proud of it" (even if they also admitted it was scary and unjustified). Frank told me that when he read a police report about a protest he organized, in which the police disparaged him, he considered it "a mark of pride" that they would talk about him in that way. Bryan added, after admitting it made him feel good to know he was on a list, "I know it's kinda juvenile. . . . But I think any activist that pretends like that [pride] is not there is lying to you." Giving credence to this, Charles told me laughing, "I've thought about doing a FOIA on myself, but it would be embarrassing if there was nothing there."

This way of thinking about the meaning of repression was not only apparent in interviewees' discourse, but at public protests as well. At a small rally in front of McDonald's after a march to raise the minimum wage to fifteen dollars, fast-food workers and their supporters sang along as a local folk singer played the old union standard "Which Side Are You On?" At one point, between songs, he asked the crowd if anyone in the audience was "an agent," presumably meaning an FBI agent or other law enforcement officer. After no one responded, he added, "Well, I hope there are a few here. Because when the agents come, you know you're on the right track." In zines and other activist written materials, there are indications that this kind of thinking is common, and even sometimes problematic for movements. In the popular zine *What Is Security Culture?* the author(s) explain, "Always be prepared for the possibility that you are under observation, but don't mistake attracting surveillance for being effective . . . don't get caught up in the excitement of being under surveillance and begin to assume that the more the authorities pay attention to you, the more dangerous to them you must be—they're not that smart."

Resisting the Language of Efficacy

Not only did many activists rely on these discursive strategies to construe their actions as meaningful or effective, despite their general pessimism; some even rejected the language of "success" and "failure" entirely. When I asked him to recall a story of success, Zach said: "I don't prefer to speak in terms of success." When I asked Adam to tell me about a time he felt he had failed to achieve something he was seeking, he replied, "Well, failure is not the right word." To the same question, Dana responded, "I guess nothing really ever felt like a defeat . . . in terms of success or failure . . . a lot of times we didn't reach the goal that we hoped for, but I think it was always still very possible." To her, the fact that most battles are lost is not really the point. It is enough that a few are won, or even that, in theory, they could be. Not interpreting past actions as failures helps activists to feel that sacrifices made and costs paid were worth it. Debra explained, "I can't think of anything that I'm sorry for in my activism. . . . I mean some won't work out the way we want them to, but I never feel like they are a failure."

Not measuring the meaning of his participation in terms of the achievement of tangible political goals helps Kyle to feel better about all that he has invested, and all that he has lost. He described his involvement in activism as "banging your head against the wall for your entire twenties trying to make social change just to see shit get worse." But this doesn't necessarily mean it was for nothing. He explained, "It's still important. And I don't regret the time and energy I put in to like fighting over the years. . . . I never expected it to necessarily get better." Karen argued that there is no such thing as a pure win, or a pure loss, when the issues you are fighting are systemic: "It's just a larger fight. . . . And larger fights are ongoing. So, even when it's a win, you don't really win. And you lose, but it isn't over. You haven't actually lost." Victor even argued that when people are too motivated by tangible success, they will eventually burn out because there are not enough successes to keep them going. He said of some people who join but quickly lose steam and drop out: "They're not seeing a lot of successes. A lot of people like successes on paper. . . . They get tired, they decide 'well, I'll just stay home from this one today.'"

Conclusion

Through making the definition of success flexible enough to include outcomes such as gaining attention or building a movement, through framing resistance as inherently meaningful and as a victory in itself, and through interpreting repression to be a sign of an individual's or a movement's effectiveness (and resisting even thinking of their efforts in terms of efficacy), activists work to motivate continued participation and make themselves less easily deterred by defeats or by costs such as those associated with state repression. In all, roughly three-quarters of interview respondents relied on one of these discursive strategies to give meaning to their actions and find ways to feel that their efforts are worthwhile, despite overwhelming pessimism. Groups and individuals who have paid higher prices for their activism, because they have been suppressed by the state, arguably have a greater interest in engaging in discourse that rationalizes these sacrifices.

These discursive strategies were also significantly associated with persistence among those who have felt supported in and prepared for their experiences of repression. When activists are reoriented in how they think about the ends of protest, participation becomes less instrumental and more expressive. In the process, participation also becomes less vulnerable to increasing costs, like those from repression, and less dependent on achieving stated aims. This finding contributes to our understanding of how groups work to keep individuals involved in the face of repression. It also presents a challenge to rational choice theory, as the "free-rider problem" becomes less relevant when the public good that collective action ostensibly seeks is no longer the main "point" of protest for those who engage in it. Through redefining the ends of protest, protest groups not only make individuals more resilient in the face of repression; they also fundamentally shape individuals' rationality as it relates to their participation in collective action.

6

Activist Identity Salience and Repression Resilience

Chapter 4 showed that by providing support and preparation, protest groups work to lower the costs of repression for individuals. Chapter 5 showed that by redefining the ends of protest and making the meaningfulness of protest less dependent on achieving tangible success, protest cultures make collective action less instrumental and goal-oriented and more expressive. In this chapter, I argue that protest cultures also provide individuals with a source of identity and that, when this activist role identity is particularly salient, participation becomes foundational to one's sense of self and comes to feel like "second nature." As this happens, costs and benefits fade into the background, participation becomes less of a conscious "choice," and alternative lines of action become increasingly difficult for individuals to imagine. As a result, participation also becomes more resilient to the potential deterrent effects of repression. Therefore, movement culture works to produce commitment in the face of repression not just by shaping actors' experiences (i.e., costs and benefits) or motivations (i.e., their ends). It also shapes individuals' identities by internalizing social movement participation as a fundamental aspect of self in ways that can make participation taken for granted, even (or especially) when it becomes costly.

Research on identity as a driver of participation in social movements has often focused on the initial decision to join a movement. But to understand the potential role of identity in explaining persistence in the face of repression, we must understand the fact that, once recruited, the personal identities of some, more than others, become deeply invested in activism. I argue that the concept of identity salience (Stryker 1968), and role identity salience in particular (Callero 1985), can sensitize us to this variation among activists. I demonstrate how this variation helps explain why some persist in the face of repression while others do not. I find that those whose narratives suggest that they hold, or at some point have held, a salient activist identity are more likely to persist in activism following repressive experiences. I then explore how a salient activist identity develops, suggesting that it is often rooted in early experiences of activism, deepened through experiences of repression that "test" this commitment, and sometimes challenged by the introduction of a new salient role identity (namely, that of "parent").

Ultimately, I argue that examining the role of identity in sustaining participation in social movements presents a challenge to rational choice theories. To reduce identity to a selective incentive, as some have done (Friedman and McAdam 1992), misses the more fundamental power identity can have in guiding action. Identities have the power to shape behavior across situations, independent of the costs and benefits inherent in these situations, and shape how individuals understand their situations and choices. As a result, identities, especially those rooted in ideological and moral commitments, can provide a foundation for action that is independent of the costs and benefits inherent in any given choice. As Grecas (2000) argues, "To the extent that ideology becomes the grounding of identity, a person's being becomes contingent on the maintenance of that ideology and thus sets limits on the capacity to change oneself or the ideology. Self-identity is gained through ideologies, but sometimes at the expense of a capacity for choice" (p. 99).

Identity and Social Movement Participation

Classic theories on identity and participation focused on the preexisting identities or dispositions that make some individuals more likely to join movements, and this thinking has carried over into some contemporary studies as well. These theories argue that people come to join movements because they lack a sense of identity and purpose in their lives and look to movements to fill this void (Kornhauser 1959; Klapp 1969), or because they have a spoiled or stigmatized identity that they hope to replace or salvage (Kaplan and Liu 2000). Others argue that people are attracted to social movements out of a desire to validate an existing identity (Pinel and Swann 2000).

While these theories and empirical works view identity (or lack thereof) as an explanation for initial participation, more recent studies in the constructionist and interactionist traditions have brought our attention to the fact that identity can also be a product or achievement of participation (Snow and

Machalek 1984; Snow and Anderson 1987; McAdam 1988; Hunt and Benford 1994). However, we still know less about how identities, once forged or deepened through social movement participation, may act back upon participation, fueling and sustaining it over time (Hunt and Benford 1994; Perez 2018).

It is also important to note that while many past studies on identity and social movement participation have examined how personal identities become aligned with the collective identity of a specific organization or movement, or why individuals become committed to one social movement organization rather than another (e.g., Hunt and Benford 1994), I am interested in how an activist role identity develops through participation and, in turn, helps to sustain participation over time, as individuals move through a variety of movements and organizations. While ties to specific organizations or individual activists are often important for recruitment into activism (Snow, Zurcher, and Ekland-Olson 1980; McAdam 1986; McAdam and Paulsen 1993), I agree with Stryker (2000), that, once this connection has been made, participation can work to cultivate an activist identity with a force of its own, independent of the specific relationships and context in which it was forged. In fact, Diani (2004) has argued that the importance of network ties for social movement participation may be primarily owed to the power of these ties to reinforce identity, which in turn drives participation. Nearly all of those I interviewed have worked on multiple causes and with various organizations over their careers as activists. As others have found (Driscoll 2018), what is consistent, despite moving from organization to organization or even movement to movement, is that they are (or were) an "activist."

Activist Identity Salience

Identities are "internalized . . . categories that carry prescriptions for acting, thinking, and feeling" (Kiecolt 2000, 111). Identities are often trans-situational, meaning that "persons 'carry' these categories across situations, predisposing them to perceive and act in situations in line with extant identities" (Stryker 2000:28). Stryker (2000) argues that because identities are not only trans-situational, but are also motivational, "moving people to actions expressing their meaning behaviorally" (p. 28), and are reinforced through being expressed through action, over time, "identities can become functionally autonomous of the circumstances that gave rise to them" (p. 36).

Role identities are those that carry prescriptions based on collectively constructed understandings of what it means to play a particular role within a group, institution, or interaction (for example, "activist," "father," or "teacher"). These understandings form an identity standard that individuals occupying the role generally aspire to meet. Therefore, the desire to confirm one's role identity through enactment of this standard, particularly in interaction with others, can powerfully guide behavior (Burke 1991). By providing a foundation for consistency of action, I argue that role identities problematize what Swidler refers to as the "unit act fallacy" of the rational choice perspective, "the notion that people choose their actions one at a time according to their interests or values" (1986, 276). Identities, as schema through which individuals interpret experiences and motivate action across different situations, dispose individuals to certain lines of action.

A central insight of identity theory is that people have multiple identities, some of which are more salient than others (Stryker 1968). Stryker defines identity salience as "readiness to act out an identity as a consequence of its properties as a cognitive schema" (Stryker 2000, 34). To measure the salience of activist identity, I examine how respondents talk about themselves and their participation. These "narratives of the self" are a form of identity work (Kiecolt 2000, 121) and therefore, regardless of factual accuracy, are illuminating in that they provide a window into how individuals think of themselves, past and present, and who they aspire to be.

I consider discourse in which individuals describe their activism as inseparable from their sense of self, as something they feel "compelled" or morally obligated to do, or as something they cannot (or could not) imagine not doing, as evidence of a trans-situational, salient activist identity. This discourse was generally produced in response to questions about whether, or how, specific experiences of repression caused them to reconsider or think differently about their participation in activism or the risks they were willing to take, but sometimes came up at other points in the interview as well. Therefore, individuals are coded as having a trans-situational, salient activist role identity if they relied on one of these three kinds of discourse (activism as inseparable from their identity, activism as a compulsion or moral obligation, or activism as something they can't or could not imagine stopping), even if they have since disengaged in response to their experience(s) of repression. For example, when Dana's close friend, another activist, was under surveillance, she said that this didn't cause her to reconsider her involvement. She attempted to explain why: "You know, I don't know why. I guess that it should have. But maybe . . . my brain was protecting me. Because I think that at the time, that . . . was my life. . . . Getting out? I just couldn't even think of it . . . that would be terrifying to lose my, what I considered my identity and life at that time. . . . If I stepped out I would lose my life pretty much—like where I lived, my friends, just kind of . . . everything. So, yeah, I never considered that."

Dana's reflection, when asked about her choices in the context of an interview, that "I guess maybe it should have [caused reconsideration]" suggests that her behavior at the time was not subject to the kind of calculated decision making that rational choice theories assume or that my question forced her to think in terms of. Still, over time, in the face of mounting consequences from multiple experiences with repression, Dana eventually grew weary and did eventually disengage from activism. Therefore, having a salient activist identity is no guarantee that one will not be deterred by repression, but, as I will demonstrate, it does make deterrence less likely.

Below, I will describe in detail these three types of discursive evidence of a salient activist role identity. After coding activist discourse for these indicators of salience, I find that of those whose "narratives of self" indicated a salient activist role identity (53 percent of the sample), nearly 90 percent have persisted. Of those who do not talk about their past or present selves in this way (47 percent of the sample), only about half have persisted after experiencing state repression. This difference is statistically significant (Pearson $\chi^2(1) = 5.2780, p = 0.022$).

"An Activist Even When I'm Not": Activism as Inseparable from Self

Like Dana, a few explicitly stated that they saw their personal identity as inseparable from their political efforts. For example, Brad said of his efforts in starting and running an infoshop, a community center that provides political literature and other resources to a community, and a space for activist meetings and events: "It was my entire identity, like, that's who I was while I was doing that . . . it was so a part of my identity that when the infoshop failed, I failed, you know. . . . In reality, I should have separated my personal successes and failures from the project or organization I was a part of, but that's how deeply like engrossed I was in what was going on." Victor, a Latino and Native man in his forties who has been active in movements ever since attending protests with his family as a child, described how being an activist permeates his entire life and is integral to who he is. He told me, "[Being an activist] means that I am working to make the world a better place—but like actively working to make the world a better place. Like, I'm an activist even when I'm not an activist. Like, I'm an activist at a job site where some guy says something sexist and I'm like, 'Hey, that's pretty f-cked up, homie.'" But for most, the salience of their activist identity was not so explicitly expressed, but was, as I will now discuss, nonetheless apparent in how they described their participation as a compulsion, or as something they could never imagine not doing.

"My Rent on This Earth": Compulsion, Guilt, and Obligation

In justifying why they continued to put time and energy into their political work, often at great risk to themselves, and often with little hope of achieving the changes they sought, many respondents said things like Suzanne did: "It's like I don't have a choice. I feel a calling, like this is my life's work. This is what I should be doing. This is what I'm equipped for, and it's very fulfilling. It's like . . . compulsion." Activism does not feel like a choice but rather a "compulsion" to Suzanne, in part because she feels well "equipped" for it. When one's personal identity is attached to and adapted to a certain social context or activity, participation feels seamless. Rather than a conscious choice, it feels like a "natural" expression of one's internal self. Development of a salient activist role identity, like Suzanne's, is both the result of committed participation over time and can help to maintain that participation, including when it might otherwise be called into question by the incurring of costs like those associated with state repression.

Fully one-third of respondents described participation in social movements as something that they felt compelled to do, that they "had to" do, or as something they could not simply choose to stop or "turn off." They explained that, as long as they are aware of an injustice, they "have to" do something about it. Exemplifying this, John explained that for him, the "choice" to be involved in movements for social justice was not only independent of any potential outcome but was something he didn't really think of as a choice at all. He told me that, to him, it was no more a choice than what he would do if he saw a dog dying on the side of the road. He couldn't live with the decision of leaving it there to die alone. Even if there was no hope that the dog could be saved and there was nothing he could do, he still would not leave. He would see no other option than to stay by its side until it died. To him, this is what it means to be an activist: to bear witness, to be in solidarity with those most affected by injustice, to show up and to fight, regardless of whether you can win.

Another activist told me that his "conscience" keeps him involved because "the injustice hasn't stopped. It hasn't gone away. Unfortunately, it's never going to go away. . . . If something f-cked up is happening, I feel compelled to say, 'No, you can't do that.'" And another told me, "If there's a social ill, I feel compelled to do something about it." This language of compulsion was common and points to something that rational choice assumptions about behavior and how repression should impact participation do not account for. When being active in social movements feels like a compulsion, and one is surrounded by a milieu that requires participation and sacrifice to maintain an activist identity, repression is rarely enough to cause a change of course, or even a serious reevaluation of that course. For example, Beth told me that repression wasn't a major consideration for her once she has decided to be involved in a cause, because "I think that the things that I get involved with are always things that I feel like are part of my being or my identity or like things that I just can't live with."

Similarly, Gary, the activist lawyer, described his political convictions as something he can't "turn off." He explained that, as for people he has seen come and go over the years, what they seem to lack is not passion, but this sense of compulsion or obligation. He explained, "They come in all hot and excited and then they realize, 'Wait a minute, this is really hard. This takes a lot of effort.' And it's easy to just turn it off. I can't. But other people, I guess, can." When I asked him why he felt as if he can't turn this off in himself as others seem to be able to, he elaborated, "I mean, it's not possible. I know what needs to be done. I've seen the truth, and I couldn't just one day be like, 'I guess I'll go work at like a regular [law] firm and like just get a BMW, and just pretend like things are good.' It's just not possible for me. It would have to be the end of my life for me to stop doing it."

Charles, despite being arrested multiple times, sustaining permanent damage to his back after being pushed into a ditch by police when he and others attempted to block logging trucks, and suspecting that he was under surveillance for years, told me that discontinuing his political organizing "was not an option because of what I knew and believed. I couldn't turn back or walk away." Similarly, Aaron described shifting his political priorities and tactics over time, but never considering disengaging altogether, despite having been arrested multiple times. He told me, "I feel like I could never—it's part of who I am. I would never stop completely. So I don't think that's possible. I'd be so depressed."

Many not only spoke of their participation in activism as more of a "compulsion" than a choice, but also as a moral imperative and as something they would feel guilt or depression over not doing. Mia said of her involvement in the environmental and women's movements: "It's my rent on this earth." She also said she knows "tons" of people who have dropped out of activism because of experiences with state repression: "It's working. As I often say, they've won." But she added, "Repression is intense, but when I disengage, I feel worse. I get depressed." Debra, who has worked on peace, Palestine solidarity, feminist, and anti-racist organizing for many years and continues to devote large amounts of her time and energy to this work despite health problems, told me that, for her, staying involved was critical for her mental health. She worries that if she were to hear about injustice and do nothing about it, she would "internalize the anger and the sadness." As she put it, "I just feel that for my own health—mental and physical and spiritual even . . . I have to be involved."

For her and others I spoke with, a sense of compulsion and a desire to avoid anticipated depression and guilt if she were to disengage seemed to drive her to continue despite her doubts about the efficacy of her participation and despite the costs she has paid. Angela, the eighty-five-year-old nun who spent several months in prison for participation in an antinuclear protest, said, for example, "I don't think that I could sleep at night if I didn't. Like . . . that responsibility is . . . foundational for me or something." And Ally, a twenty-one-year-old college student who had been arrested only days earlier at a protest against fossil fuels, told me, "I don't feel like my life is worth living unless I am actually doing something to bring attention. . . . It makes me feel like I'm doing something meaningful with my life . . . to continue to live this way."

This sense of compulsion, to do something in response to injustice and the belief that, if they did not, they would be resigned to depression and guilt was common among those I interviewed and provides insight into why many persist in activism despite what are often high costs and uncertain rewards. When activism becomes more of a compulsion and less of a choice, the costs of repression become less and less consequential for individual behavior. This "compulsion" is an expression of a deeply held activist identity. Over time, if protest norms are internalized and participation becomes routine, the concepts of "choice," "costs," and "benefits" become increasingly less germane to explaining continued participation.

"I Don't Know What Else to Do": Taking Activism for Granted

The final, and closely related, piece of evidence of a highly salient activist identity is when individuals take participation in activism for granted, to the point where they can no longer imagine other lines of action, as their activist identity becomes more internalized and less conscious and calculating. Keith exemplified this with his response to my question about why he still engages in protest and political organizing despite believing that, as he put it, "the earth is sunk." After a long pause he replied, "Huh . . . I don't know. I guess I don't know what else there is to do." Similarly, Debra said, "I don't think I could live with myself if I don't. I mean what would I do? Watch TV all day? Or just give up? I'm not that kind of person that could live with denial." Frank simply asked, "What else would I do at this point?" Of course, we all know that there are, in fact, many more things they could do with their time and energy than organize and participate in protest. But this is how some respondents described it: activism was not only something that they felt they couldn't stop, but they were at a loss as to other possible courses of action. At this level of habituation and taken-for-granted-ness, we may even say that these activists have developed not simply an activist identity, but an activist habitus (Crossley 2003).

Just as asking them about their "successes" and "failures" in activism revealed that these were often not the terms in which they thought about the meaning of their participation (as discussed in chapter 5), being questioned about how their experiences of repression factored into their subsequent decisions about participation seemed to catch many off guard, suggesting that they were not used to considering their participation in such calculating terms. In all, a fifth of respondents expressed not being able to imagine other courses of action other than continuing to participate in social movements. As previously noted, this, along with the other kinds of discourse indicative of salient activist role identity, was strongly associated with persistence following repression. When one's life and sense of self are built around being an activist, the option of changing course is not even on the table for many. For Zach, even facing prison time didn't cause him to seriously reconsider his political involvement because, as he explained, "I didn't know anything else at the time. That's what I was doing, where my heart was. And literally my entire lifestyle was based around that."

This level of attachment to an activist identity demonstrates the power of subcultures to orient actors and shape their behavior. However, maintaining such an identity requires significant social reinforcement. Even a momentary lack of the social reinforcement that helps individuals to maintain this activist identity has the potential to create space for doubt to creep in. For example, when asked if concerns about repression ever made him reconsider what he was doing, Charles first said "No," but then he qualified his response: "It was okay when I was at the Earth First! office with others. But when I was on the road alone, it was hard. . . . I remember being in a spring snowstorm in a decrepit motel somewhere on tour with Earth First! and thinking, 'What the hell am I doing?'" He went on to explain that an activist friend of his had just been sent to prison, and another to the hospital. But it was only when sitting alone in that motel that any of this really led him to wonder if he was in over his head. This, and the way that others describe how investment in an activist identity prevented and protected them from reevaluating their behavior in the wake of paying the high costs of repression, and even given the pessimism about social and political change that many expressed, lends credence to the power of activist culture to shape individual rationality in ways that make it less vulnerable to fluctuations in costs and benefits. Of course, as Charles's story suggests, this socialization is still often partial and must be maintained. When it is not, even if just temporarily, the weight of the risks can begin to feel heavier and participation less taken for granted.

Activist Role Identity Development

Given these findings suggesting the power of a salient activist role identity in making individuals more likely to persist in the face of repression, I explored evidence from my respondents' narratives of how such an identity develops. Their stories suggest that a salient activist role identity develops over time, often rooted in early transformative experiences and tested through repressive experiences.

Activist Origin Stories

For many, their first memorable experiences of activism came when they were quite young. Multiple respondents were even second- or third-generation activists. In all, about a quarter of respondents described having their first protest experience as a child, before the age of fourteen. About half were between the ages fifteen and twenty. The remaining quarter were young adults when they first became involved, ranging in age from twenty-one to twenty-eight. Experiences at younger ages seemed to have more power in forming one's sense of self and in creating inertia that continued to propel participation many years later. In fact, I found that 80 percent of those who went to their first protest before age twenty-one persisted, compared with slightly less than half of those who came to activism after age twenty-one (Pearson $\chi^2(1) = 4.8011$, $p = 0.028$). My argument is less that youth participation directly leads to adult participation, although this has been argued elsewhere (Flanagan and Levine 2010), but rather that such early experiences and "origin stories" anchor narratives and give the activist identity greater weight for individuals. Early experiences carry more significance because we understand new experiences, in part, through the lens of our pasts (Bourdieu and Wacquant 1992, 60).

Angela, now in her eighties, told me that she first attended a protest when she was only ten years old, with her grandmother. She was now proud to say that she had passed down this tradition to her own granddaughter: "My granddaughter is in college and she's already been arrested twice. And I'm so proud of her. You can imagine." She added, with pride, that her son has also been arrested at protests a few times. Many described being as young as three or five years old when they were first introduced to activism. Sani grew up going to indigenous rights protests with his family. He barely remembers the first protest he went to, because he was only three years old, but he has seen the pictures of himself in a family photo album. He explained, "It probably wasn't even the first protest, but I was three years old and my family was protesting forced relocation of our relatives. . . . I was three years old and I was holding up a sign that says, 'BIA [Bureau of Indian Affairs]: Don't kill me. I'm only three.'"

Ally even participated in acts of protest on her own before she found others to join with. When she was seven, she refused to sing the national anthem in class. When she was eight, she started a petition against her city council's plan to ban outdoor cats to protect wild bird life. She even set up a booth downtown to collect signatures. She explained, "I took that very personally because I loved my cat, and my cat loved the outdoors." She explained that although this isn't a cause she would get fired up about today, she took this early experience, and the empowerment she felt from it, as a sign that activism was integral to who she was.

Tyler's introduction to activism was also self-initiated and came young, when he was six years old and camping with his family in the redwoods of California. He and his family camped in the same area every summer, and the trees—those "ancient beings" as he called them—held a special significance for him. When his family and other campers heard of plans by the park service to cut down some of the trees to build a lake in order to attract more tourists, they were upset. Tyler and some of the other kids from a "hippie" family that lived in a school bus got the idea to chain themselves to the trees in attempts to save them. Tyler "thought that sounded like a great idea," but when he told his mom, she thought it was too dangerous. She spoke with some of the other adult campers and a small group of them organized to chain themselves to the trees instead. Tyler's mom also took the kids around to nearby campgrounds collecting signatures for a petition to save the trees, a protest activity she considered more appropriate for young children. Tyler explained that he and the other children even wrote and performed a song about saving the trees, "and we would go around, getting people to sign the petition by singing." When park officials came out to deal with the adults who had chained themselves to the trees, the children presented their petition. He explained, "We got it submitted to the right people to change those plans and those trees are still there today."

This experience was incredibly transformative for Tyler. As he put it, "It kept me going back to activism in one form or another, because it proved that it could work." This memory buoyed him through years of setbacks, repression, and trauma. As Collins (2004) describes, intense moments of collective effervescence and empowerment like these "are high points not only for groups but also for individual lives. These are the events that we remember, that give meaning to our personal biographies, and sometimes to obsessive attempts to repeat them" (p. 43). Tyler went on, "I think it's always going to be a part of who I am. My mom has said that I have always been her little hippie flower child . . . because I would sing and dance to school, and, um, she says that there's never been a time where something unjust happened around me where . . . I was able to just sit there and take it. . . . I had to speak up. I got bullied a lot in school, so I didn't like seeing it happen to other people, so I felt like I had to stick up for them." By placing emphasis on this early experience, and on other signs of his early inclination toward social justice, Tyler constructs a narrative of himself and his identity as inextricably linked to activism.

For Beth, the identity she found in activism as an adolescent was a saving grace. When she was twelve, she was in and out of foster care and didn't feel that she belonged anywhere. It was at that age she became a vegetarian and started smoking cigarettes. She jokes that those might seem like contradictory choices, but, at the time, she was desperately trying to find "my people" and figure out who she wanted to be in the world. Around that same time, she was given a pamphlet by pro-life activists that included a quote along the lines of: "I always thought that somebody should do something. Then I realized I was somebody." That spoke to her and she became heavily involved in the pro-life movement throughout her teen years. The pro-life movement was her introduction to activism, but today she does not identify as pro-life and has primarily been involved in struggles for immigrant rights and transgender rights. But regardless of the specific cause, she explained how much it meant to her to feel like she could have some impact on the world, considering that her own immediate environment had always felt out of her control: "I think activism to me is an extension of trying to have, like, a sense of control over my environment. And being like, 'No, there are things that can be done, you don't just have to live with it.' I don't just have to put up with it. And I think that also meant not putting up with, you know, bad situations that I was having at that time with my family."

Even those who came to activism later in their youth often talked about their first introduction to it as transformative. Zach was nineteen years old and working at a 7-Eleven convenience store when George W. Bush declared war in Iraq. His friend came into the store while he was working and told him he was going to leave and travel throughout the West Coast to attend protests against the war and asked Zach to join him. At first Zach declined, saying he had to work. His friend responded, "Quit your f-cking job, man! There's a war on!" Zach was apparently persuaded by this argument, quitting his job and joining his friend. On this trip, he attended his first protests and met many activists organizing against the war and for other causes. Over fifteen years later, he has never looked back.

Activist War Stories

This activist identity, rooted in early experiences of activism, often deepens over time, as individuals participate in protest and take on risks until both the participation and the risks become taken for granted. This is not a precondition for collective action as much as an achievement of committed collective action that helps to sustain it. Several respondents told stories in which they had their activist identity "tested" through an experience of repression and came out with a deeper attachment to that identity because of it. In fact, all of those who told such stories also exhibited signs of a salient activist role identity, as defined previously, while those who did not tell such stories only possessed a salient activist role identity about half the time (Pearson $\chi^2(1) = 4.2033, p = 0.040$).

For example, Suzanne told me that when she and others were occupying a public park during the Occupy movement, the police came by each night and ticketed those who were in the park after dark. Each time, this offered her a choice to leave and avoid another ticket, and the legal and financial consequences that came along with it, or to stay. She told me about her thought process the first time: "It felt like an automatic and necessary choice.... I wondered about sidestepping it, but I knew that I'd be ashamed of myself. I knew that it would not feel good to do that." After that first time, it got easier and even more automatic. Eventually, she accumulated more than forty of these tickets, each of which carried a fine and potential jail time.

Like Suzanne, others talked about key experiences of repression as opportunities to affirm their commitments. Once these commitments were affirmed through this experience, subsequent risks became easier, and less conscious. Patty has been arrested over thirty times, but the first was the most memorable. The police had announced that anyone who reentered the park where the protest was being held could be arrested. There were several police officers standing in the middle of the park, but she nonetheless decided to go back in. She walked into the park, stood on a large rock, and held her hand up in a "peace" sign. She recounted, "[The police] were about six feet away from me, and I just stood there with my hand in the air for maybe three minutes, maybe five minutes, it's hard to know at a scene like that. My heart was pounding... But I wasn't scared in the moment. I was in line with my values and I don't think I had ever tested those values. And it felt really... primal. It was like: 'This is my true self.'"

After this first arrest, she not only continued to put herself at risk of arrest, and was arrested many times after, she actually got a tattoo as a reminder to herself of that event, and of her "commitment to peace." This commitment, represented by a permanent mark on her body, was forged through being tested in a moment of risk. By taking this risk, she felt able to express her "true self" and live in line with her values in a way she hadn't before. The experience was powerful for her and set her on a path of more highly committed and riskier activism.

When Cory was arrested along with around fifty other people after refusing to leave a park during the early days of the Occupy movement in his city, he was expecting it. "Probably going to get arrested in the park tonight. See you all when I get out," he posted on Twitter shortly before. He gave his cell phone and wallet to his friend, keeping only his ID so he could show it to the cops when he was arrested. By midnight, his friend and everyone else who didn't want to get arrested—families with kids, people with criminal records, others with too much to lose—had left. The fifty or so people who remained were from all walks of life, but they had one thing in common: they were willing to get arrested. They represented a range of ideologies across the political left but had enough shared values to spark fruitful political discussions. For Cory, that was the best part of the whole experience, and it was unlike anything he'd ever been a part of. A college student and a political science major, to him this was true democracy in action. For about an hour and a half, while the police assembled and made plans to arrest the group, the protesters sat and talked politics. To him, that was what the Occupy movement was all about—not just physically taking over public space but claiming it as space for public discourse and for community, not just for commerce.

When the police announced that they would arrest anyone who remained, he knew he would stay. He felt compelled in that moment to take a stand for his political beliefs. Plus, there were other people doing it with him. He argued that it wasn't something that required much courage, not like if he did it on his own: "I needed other people around me to do it—for me to stand up myself." It wasn't a choice he took lightly. He had to work the next day and thought there was a good chance he would be fired if he had to "call in" from jail. And he really needed the job. He told me, "Looking back on it, it actually seems like a really, really bad decision. But at the time, my emotion and rage had been building for months and months on end, and it was just a position where I felt like I needed to stand up and say something." About 300 riot cops were deployed to arrest the crowd of about fifty protesters. The cops marched slowly and methodically from one end of the park to where the protesters sat in a circle on the ground—so slowly that it took them thirty minutes to reach them. The protesters just kept debating politics. Helicopters circled overhead shining lights on the crowd. By the time the line of cops reached the circle of protesters, Cory was terrified, but also a little excited. They arrested the protesters one by one. Two cops would run out from a break in the line of riot police, grab one protester, and pull them through the riot police line and out of sight of the rest of the protesters. A minute later, they would come for the next one.

As mentioned in chapter 3, this experience and his subsequent time in jail only strengthened Cory's resolve to be involved in the movement, as it did for many of those he was arrested alongside. But he also saw a drop in the number of protesters in the park after that day, the largest and most dramatic arrest that happened at that particular Occupy site. Many of the more "mainstream" people, as Cory put it, were scared off by the mass arrest and stopped coming to the park. That was disappointing to Cory, but he was happy that most of those he was arrested with, and had formed a bond with through the experience, persisted. When he got out of jail the next day and returned to the park, he saw that others who had been arrested were already there, occupying the space. It was in this moment that he knew he had made the right decision.

For Cory, this experience was a moment of truth—was he willing to take a risk for something he cared deeply about? We can say he was radicalized by his experience of repression, but this story suggests it is not that simple. In many ways, his choice to be arrested reflected the fact that he was ready to allow the experience to radicalize him. It was an opportunity to test, express, and make real an identity he already felt. By putting himself through this experience, and by interpreting his interaction with the police and the efficacy of the protest through the lens of these commitments, he fostered an activist role identity that has propelled him to be involved in other causes since.

When Max was arrested for "premeditated littering" for putting water jugs in the desert for migrants, he and the others with whom he was arrested opted for a jury trial (which they were eligible for because the charges carried a maximum prison sentence of one year). They wanted to create a "spectacle" and make the court and prosecutor "work harder." The trial lasted for days, and they used it as an opportunity to bring attention to migrant deaths in the desert. As he explained, "We used it and grew from it." The arrest served not only as an opportunity to bring attention to their cause, but also as "a good learning moment for us to really reflect on how committed we were," because, he admitted, they were more intimidated by the charges than they thought they would be. They had long discussions about whether or not to continue putting water out in the desert. To him, it was important to continue even if it meant more littering tickets. Being tested in this way only deepened his commitment. Similarly, Gary told me that, for him, getting arrested "was important to my development as an activist, as a leftist. . . . To say there's something you're committed enough to that you're willing to get arrested."

For those who are prepared for it and feel supported in it, repression is not just a cost, or even just a sign of success (as discussed in the previous chapter); it is a test. These kinds of narratives of being tested by a difficult situation and deepening one's commitment as a result, are what Hunt and Benford (1994) refer to as "war stories." Extending this idea, I would further suggest that repression not only produces "war stories" that strengthen the activity role identity but can—especially when it is chosen or planned—also constitute a ritual. And as Kiecolt (2000) argues, rituals are an important way that activists reaffirm common values and align personal and collective identities.

Parenting as a Challenge to Activist Identity Salience

When someone takes on a new role identity, this can cause inter-role conflict and a reshuffling of their identity salience hierarchy (Stryker 2000). For example, as already discussed, Jessica's "temporary break" from activism following a traumatic arrest at a protest became permanent when she became a parent. Studies explaining the relationship between parenthood and protest participation usually rely on the concept of biographical availability, arguing that basic facts about one's life, such as parental or employment status, make some more or less available to participate than others. But inter-role conflict provides an alternative explanation for why parents tend to participate in protest at lower rates. Parenting and protest do not simply compete for one's time;

they also, potentially, compete for one's identity. After becoming a parent, Jessica reprioritized her identities not by completely letting go of her activist identity but by folding it into, and subordinating it to, her new role identity as a parent. When I asked Jessica if she was still involved in any kind of movement activities, her response not only revealed how repression combined with becoming a parent to lead to her disengagement, but also how she has retained a sense of herself as "radical" through how she enacts her new role as a parent. She replied, "No. I think my activism has moved more towards things that are less conducive to police repression 'cause I have a record and I have a family to take care of now. So now I'm more into radical mothering, radical breastfeeding, radical natural health. . . . I think that raising liberated children, which I do every day, most of the day, is like pretty much the most radical thing that I can do."

While her story suggests that, for some, becoming a parent may reduce the salience of one's activist identity (even if it is not disregarded altogether), this was not the case for others. Among my interviewees, six individuals were parents of young children (and had become parents since becoming involved in activism) and brought this up, unprompted, in discussing how they thought about their activism and repression. While, of course, such small numbers should be interpreted with caution, three of these individuals have disengaged, and credited repression combined with becoming a parent for this change, while the other three have persisted. This was not statistically significantly different than the rate of persistence among those who did not have young children (Pearson $\chi^2(1) = 1.9274, p = 0.165$). This suggests that while becoming a parent may present a challenge to the salience of an activist identity, individuals may respond to this challenge, and reshuffle their identity salience hierarchy, in a variety of ways. For example, when Johnny became a parent, it caused him to think more seriously before taking on risks and to shift the focus of his activist efforts (toward supporting other parent-activists through organizing childcare at protests and meetings and "child blocs" at protests), but he did not disengage. Actually, in some ways, his new identity provided a new reserve of motivation to fight for the causes he cared about, even if it also made him less willing to take some risks while doing so. He explained, "I've got a daughter now. . . . I want to do something to make things better for her, but I'm also less willing to put my body on the line for that." Therefore, Johnny incorporated his identity as a parent into his approach to, and justification for, his activism.

Jenna similarly integrated her identity as activist and parent in a way that reduced the challenge that parenting posed to her activism. In fact, her decision to take on parenting was inextricably tied up with her activist work. Of those who became parents, she was the only one who did so through nonbiological means. As mentioned, Jenna has been active in migrant rights and refugee resettlement for years. Through this community, she became close friends with a pregnant woman seeking asylum in the United States, and the two now live together and are co-parenting the child. They are not romantically involved and never have been, but they have made a commitment to parent together and form an unconventional family.

For the biological mother, this arrangement provides critical support, both material and emotional, that she would have otherwise lacked as a single mother in a new country. For Jenna, it provided a way for her to cultivate a sense of family in her life in a way that is an outgrowth of, rather than in competition with, her political ideals and efforts. She told me that, when she was younger, she had decided explicitly not to have kids because she valued the way that being childless allowed her to devote more of her life to, and take greater risks for, her political convictions. At the time, she was heavily involved in a peace and social justice–oriented religious community and was around people who had taken vows of poverty, gone to prison to protest nuclear weapons, and often forsaken having a family or home of their own to follow a path they saw as politically and religiously righteous. She explained, "At that time in my life, I was thinking about things like family, and not having a family, and the ways that people could take risks when they didn't have family. These people were going to jail for years, people were putting their bodies in situations with a high chance of getting harmed. I have so much respect for that. That is how I wanted to live my life." Years later, she explained, she made a decision to start a family, albeit an unconventional one, as an extension of, rather than a detraction from, her pursuit of social justice and humanitarian service.

Conclusion

As we can see from the way activists describe themselves and their participation, being involved in social movements can provide an important source of identity. In some cases, especially when this participation starts earlier is life, and is deepened through intentional choices to "test" these commitments, a highly salient activist role identity develops, marked by discourse of a compulsion to participate in movements and an inability to imagine their lives, or themselves, without it.

Philip Blumstein refers to the process of building and maintaining a sense of self through repeated fulfillment of a role in interaction with others over time as "the ossification of self" (2001). This is precisely what I find with many who persisted in activism despite experiences of repression. They have so thoroughly internalized the activist role identity through repeated enactments for years that it is now ossified, integral, and inseparable from who they are.

Such a salient activist role identity makes participation come to feel more like "second nature" and less like a conscious or discrete "choice." As a result, continued participation becomes less of a function of costs and benefits, and, in turn, less vulnerable to reconsideration in the face of costs like repression. Gross (2009) argues that culture, when it is most deeply internalized, shapes the actions that individuals even consider as possible and make them more competent at and comfortable with solving problems and responding to recurring situations in some ways rather than others. As a result, behavior becomes more a matter of habit than choice (Gross 2009). Repression is arguably best understood as a recurring—and often particularly intense—problem situation that activist individuals and groups must periodically face. When the possibility of repression is built into what it means to be an activist, and when being an activist becomes integral to how individuals see themselves and organize their lives, repression is less likely to shape individuals' behavior the way that rational choice scholars assume. The development of such an identity through participation in activist culture encourages commitment in the face of repression because actors are less conscious of each individual choice to participate in an event or take a particular risk as these choices become taken for granted as an expression of one's "true" self.

7
Conclusion

While previous research has focused on how different features of state repression help explain its divergent effects, I instead bring into focus the role that activists themselves play in mediating repression's effects. I have demonstrated how activists work together to buffer themselves against repression by shaping their experiences, motivations, and identities and, as a result, fundamentally shape the rationality of participation in collective action. In doing so, I demonstrate the value of an approach that integrates insights from rational choice and cultural theories of collective action, not only for examining repression's effects, but also for understanding protest participation more generally. After summarizing these contributions, I discuss areas for future research suggested by this study, including the need for a shift from focusing on differential recruitment and participation to what might be termed "differential persistence."

Shaping Experiences, Motivations, and Identities

In chapter 3, I demonstrated that neither the severity nor the type of repression can adequately explain persistence or deterrence following experiences of state repression. In the subsequent chapters, I identified three factors that provide new traction in understanding variation in repression's effects by attending to how individuals' experiences, motivations, and identities are shaped by the protest cultures of which they are a part. In chapter 4, I demonstrated that repression can come with a variety of costs for individuals, and I documented the lengths that activist groups often go to reduce these risks and costs. Through cultures that emphasize security, activists work to protect each other from infiltration and surveillance. Through cultures that work to train and otherwise prepare individuals for the possibility of repression, activists work to reduce the shock and deterrent power that repression can have. Finally, through networks that provide legal, financial, medical, emotional, and other forms of support, movements work to share the costs and burdens of repression and lessen the blow for those most affected. Through these practices, groups reduce the risks and costs that repression can pose for individuals, and therefore shape the very experience of repression that individuals endure. I show that having experiences of repression in which preparation or support from others is lacking is strongly associated with deterrence following repression. Not only does adequate preparation and support make experiences of repression less costly for individuals in very direct ways; when people have a sense, more generally, that others "have their back," their willingness to take risks increases. And when risks and costs are shared, this can strengthen solidarity and ties between activists and fortify the movement as a whole.

In chapter 5, I showed how groups shape not only individuals' experiences but also their motivations by influencing how activists evaluate the impact and worth of their efforts. More specifically, I argue that redefining and expanding "success" by making it less tied to measurable, tangible political change can protect individuals from the discouragement or disillusionment that might otherwise result from inevitable setbacks. Furthermore, over time, as people participate in social movements and become socially, emotionally, and ideologically invested in them, the means of protest increasingly become indistinguishable from the ends and resistance becomes defined as a victory in and of itself, regardless of what results from it. Furthermore, even repression can, counterintuitively, become interpreted as a sign of "success." Importantly, I demonstrate that activists who have been reoriented to think about success in these more flexible ways and who find meaning in their efforts regardless of tangible impact on social and political issues are more likely to continue their participation in the wake of experiences of repression.

Finally, I demonstrate that protest groups can shape individuals' response to repression through cultivating in them a salient activist role identity, as discussed in chapter 6. The development of such an identity encourages commitment in the face of repression because actors are less conscious of each individual choice to participate in an event or take a particular risk, as these choices become part of a larger strategy of action and expression of one's fundamental sense of themselves. I demonstrate that those whose discourse indicates that they possess, or have at some point possessed, a strong identification with activism are more likely to persist in activism following experiences of repression. I further explore how such an identity develops, suggesting that it is often anchored in early transformative experiences of collective action and strengthened through repressive experiences that are viewed by activists as "tests" of their commitment.

These findings demonstrate the importance of these three factors—preparation and support, alternative conceptions of the ends of collective action, and a salient activist role identity—for explaining who persists and who disengages following experiences of repression. Combined with the findings discussed in chapter 3 showing that repression type and severity do little to explain variation in responses to repression, this points to the importance of the subjective experience of repression and, furthermore, the power of group culture in shaping this. Both insights have been largely neglected in previous research on the effects of state repression, which has tended to look to features of the repression itself to explain its heterogeneous effects and which has underestimated the degree to which individual rationality is malleable and collectively constructed.

My findings also demonstrate that these collective practices and meanings through which groups can buffer individuals from the deterrence effects of repression sometimes fail. When individuals are not well integrated into communities of activists, they sometimes lack adequate preparation, both physical and mental, for these experiences and are more likely to subsequently disengage from activism as a result. Perhaps even more consequentially, when individuals lack the support they need, and especially when they feel criticized rather than supported by other activists following a repressive incident, they are much more likely to distance themselves from further involvement. Furthermore, when individuals are not socialized into thinking about the meaningfulness of their efforts in more expansive and expressive terms and instead measure their efforts in terms of more narrow concepts of efficacy, they may more quickly burn out when immediate success proves lacking, especially when this absence of reward is coupled with the high costs that can come with state repression. Finally, when individuals lack a salient activist role identity, they are less likely to persist following repression, in part because they may be more vulnerable to reconsidering their behavior when faced with the increased costs posed by repression. And for some, a less salient activist identity can result from the taking on of another important identity, like that of parent. These failures to prevent deterrence following repression provide important lessons to activist organizations and communities, and, for social movement scholars, provide new ways of thinking about the contingent effects of repression.

By demonstrating how individuals' experience of and decision making about repression are influenced by the activist cultures in which they participate, I provide a new angle for making sense of the mixed findings on repression's effects that have been identified in previous studies. While, as previous research suggests, features of the repression itself may help explain why repression sometimes deters and at other times fails to deter (or even radicalizes) activists and fuels mobilization, my findings suggest that this variation is also sometimes produced by the fact that individuals have uneven access to support and preparation that can be critical to weathering experiences of repression, are not equally socialized into thinking about efficacy in more expansive and expressive ways, and are differentially attached to an activist identity. These factors, I demonstrate, can shape how individuals experience repression and, in turn, how their subsequent participation is affected by these experiences. Future research should explore other ways in which features of activists, and activist groups, influence the impact repression tends to have on them.

From Recruitment to Persistence

Shifting the focus away from the initial decision to join a movement (as has been the traditional focus of micro-mobilization research) toward explaining persistence in activism, as I have done here, raises important questions about our extant understandings of social movement participation. For example, the findings presented in chapter 5 suggest that while a sense of efficacy might drive recruitment into activism and explain different levels of participation once recruited, as found in previous studies (Barkan, Cohn, and Whitaker 1993, 1995), detaching from a focus on efficacy, expanding what counts as success, and divorcing the meaningfulness of protest from its tangible achievement of social and political change may actually better sustain long-term participation. Furthermore, while network ties have been shown to be a highly robust predictor of movement recruitment and levels of subsequent participation (Barkan, Cohn, and Whitaker 1993, 1995), the findings discussed in chapter 6 suggest that once this connection is made, if individuals come to see activism as a fundamental part of their identity, this identity may eclipse the ties that gave rise to it, in terms of its power to generate commitment and persistence over time.

More generally, the emphasis in modern social movement theory on resources, organizations, and microstructural factors (and the rational choice assumptions underlying this emphasis) may in part be a consequence of our focus on the initial decision to join a movement, as these factors are critical for creating opportunities for individuals to become involved initially. But, as the stories of many activists in this study made clear, once someone joins a movement, this participation can change how they think about themselves and their actions. As a result, the dynamics of sustained participation may not resemble those of initial recruitment to the extent that many of our theories and research on collective action implicitly assume (and even explicitly argue, e.g., Corrigall-Brown 2011). Future research should critically examine how theories of social movement participation hold up when we shift our focus from recruitment, which has received the bulk of attention and upon which our theories have been built, or even levels of involvement once recruited (Barkan, Cohn, and Whitaker 1993, 1995), to long-term persistence, about which we know far less. While I have focused on a specific question related to persistence—persistence in the face of repression—in doing so, I have surfaced important questions about the dynamics of persistence more generally and have added to the small body of work examining differential participation (Barkan, Cohn, and Whitaker 1993, 1995) and persistence (Aho 1994; Downton and Wehr 1997; Corrigall-Brown 2011; Nepsted 2014) beyond initial recruitment.

A Synthesized Approach to Collective Action

As the previous discussion suggests, cultural factors such as ideology, identity, and emotions may come more to the fore when we seek to explain persistence rather than recruitment. Factors associated with rational choice theories of participation may be most relevant for initial recruitment but fade in importance as individuals invest themselves in movements for change. Indeed, the "collective action problem," which initially triggered so much work in the rational choice tradition, is primarily concerned with why people join with others in collective action instead of sitting by and hoping others will do so for them.

By demonstrating that even repression, which has been identified by social movement scholars as a key source of risk and cost in collective action, cannot be explained in rational choice terms alone, I make a strong case for the need to attend to how protest cultures fundamentally shape rationality in collective action. By attending to the malleability of the costs and benefits of collective action and the importance of the subjective experience of movement participation, I have modeled a more synthesized approach to explaining collective action. In doing so, I help to bridge the divide between more structural, rational actor–based theories of collective action (which have dominated the field since the 1970s) and more recent cultural approaches, which have largely developed alongside or been subjugated to, rather than brought into an equal dialogue with, this dominant paradigm. Through applying this integrated approach, I not only provide new traction on the long-standing puzzle over the consequences of repression for social movements. Doing so also brings to the fore the agency that movements have in shaping these consequences and, more generally, illuminates the means through which movements build cultures of resistance and resilience.

Appendix

To understand how activists perceive the risks of social movement participation, how their personal experiences of the costs of state repression weigh into these considerations, and how these experiences and perceptions are shaped by the groups of which they are a part, it is imperative to go to the source—activists themselves. More specifically, it requires studying activists who have been targeted for or in some way have experienced state repression, including both overt forms like police violence and arrest and covert forms like surveillance and infiltration.

This is no easy task, given the guardedness that can sometimes (with good reason) characterize activists in general, and those who have experienced repression in particular. This is probably part of why, as Zwerman and Steinhoff (2005) have pointed out, "we know much about what the state has done to social movements" but "understand little about the ways in which activists provoked, absorbed, and resisted repression" (p. 87). In the large body of research on social movement repression, there is a noticeable lack of research on how activists think about and strategize around repression (for exceptions, see Goodwin and Pfaff 2001; Zwerman and Steinhoff 2005; Hess and Martin 2006; Starr et al. 2008). For example, while many researchers have attempted to develop rankings and indices of different forms of repression, based on assumptions about what types are more or less "repressive," they have never asked activists themselves how they evaluate and weigh these different forms against one another (Earl 2011a).

Despite the at times guarded nature of this population, I gained access to interview forty-five activists or former activists in Arizona who have experienced state repression, asking them about these experiences, their history of and current involvement in activism, and how the costs they have incurred and the risks they continue to take on (for those who are still involved) shape how they think about themselves, their participation, and the movements and groups they are a part of. I also conducted content analysis of activist writings (most of which were suggested by my interview respondents, providing a window into some of the cultural resources they drew on). I also attended protests and other activist events across the state, allowing me to observe systems of support and strategies of repression resistance in action, keep in touch with past interviewees, and recruit new interviewees. After describing the setting of my study, I discuss the collection and analysis of the primary data—the in-depth interviews with activists and former activists—in greater depth.

Study Setting

Arizona is home to one of the nation's first fusion centers. The Arizona Fusion Center, also called the Arizona Counter Terrorism Information Center (ACTIC), employs more than 800 terrorism liaison officers who work across the state to monitor potential domestic terrorism threats. According to records released through a Freedom of Information Act (FOIA) request, millions of dollars were spent in Arizona to monitor the activities of Occupy Phoenix, Occupy Tucson, immigrant rights advocacy groups, and others, through electronic surveillance as well as through the use of undercover officers embedded in activist groups (Hodai 2013). The release of these documents in 2013 raised concerns among many Arizona activists, confirming suspicions about surveillance and infiltration and prompting activists to organize meetings and events focused on mobilizing within this increasingly repressive context. In addition to this covert surveillance, there have been several protests throughout the state in recent years that have ended in the arrest of, and police violence against, demonstrators. The repressive tactics of Arizona law enforcement agencies and ACTIC are not unique to Arizona, however, but rather are reflective of nationwide trends of rising surveillance, more aggressive protest policing, and—more generally—the criminalization of dissent (as discussed in chapter 2).

Arizona is not only representative of these broader trends of increasing repression; the state has also been a site of sustained and active mobilization over the same time period, in part owing to high levels of activism on regionally pressing issues related to the U.S.-Mexican border, immigration, and native rights, in addition to movements that have been equally active in other parts of the country, such as the Occupy movement. In the recent past, Arizona (and Tucson in particular) was also a major hub of the radical environmental movement, including serving as headquarters for the group Earth First! (EF!). As previously discussed, this movement has experienced some of the most intense repression in recent U.S. history because of its association with tactics that law enforcement labels as "ecoterrorism." Many of these radical environmentalists remain in the area and have continued to fight for environmental causes, as well as other social issues. Activists in Arizona, therefore, provide a prime opportunity to examine how movements work to sustain participation in the face of rising repression, both covert and overt.

By focusing on activists in a single state, I developed a deeper understanding of the specifics of the mobilization context of my subjects than would have been possible if studying activists nationwide. Arizona is home to a diverse social movement sector that includes three main interrelated hubs of movement activity—Phoenix, Tucson, and Flagstaff—between which activists regularly relocate, travel for protests and meetings, and collaborate and share information and resources. Therefore, studying activists who are mobilizing in these slightly different political climates (and in cities of varying sizes) within the same state allowed for greater variation in context, and arguably greater generalizability, than would have been afforded by focusing on a single city, or on a state with a single major hub of movement activity.

Also, because subjects all live(d) in the same state, the interviews produced multiple, sometimes several, accounts of the same instances of repression in recent years (for example, a mass arrest at a particular protest, or a specific case of infiltration). These different accounts of the same event or sequences of events, from slightly different angles, came together to create a fuller, and arguably more accurate, depiction of these events than a single account would have allowed. To further triangulate these accounts, I also read news articles related to the events that surfaced in the interviews wherever possible.

Finally, while the efforts of ACTIC have been, to some degree, focused on either suspected or self-described anarchist individuals and groups, causing some activists to dub it the "Anarchist Task Force" (although, to my knowledge, this was not a name used by law enforcement itself), in fact individuals advocating for various causes and from various activist groups have been targeted for or have experienced state repression in Arizona in recent years. Defining my sampling frame geographically, rather than focusing on a single movement, allows for greater generalizability as well as for comparison of how activists from groups with varying goals and ideologies respond to repression differently.

Interviews

The primary data used to understand activist response to repression in the state in recent years were in-depth interviews with forty-five activists and former activists in Arizona who have experienced state repression in recent years as a result of their political involvement. Because I am interested in explaining individuals' willingness to persist in activism in the face of repression, and argue that how individuals make sense of, give meaning to, and emotionally experience repression is key to understanding this, interviews with activists and former activists who have experienced repression were the most appropriate method for this inquiry. While I also collected other types of data, as mentioned previously, I relied most heavily on in-depth interviews and, furthermore, allowed these interviews to guide my collection and analysis of the supplementary archival and observational data.

Everyone I interviewed had experienced arrest, police violence, surveillance, or infiltration by an informant or law enforcement officer. Many had experience with multiple, or even all, of these forms of state repression. I started with a law enforcement watch list of "persons of interest," used by the Arizona Fusion Center and released through a FOIA request, as a seed sample. The list consisted of individuals involved in the Occupy movement, Cop Watch, and anarchist activists in both Phoenix and Tucson, among others. Of those on the list, about half were able to be reached and agreed to be interviewed, yielding eleven interviews. I then asked these respondents to identify others I should speak with who had had these kinds of experiences. I also identified additional respondents to interview through attending protests and building rapport in Arizona activist communities (as will be discussed). This resulted in interviews with a total of forty-five activists from across the state.

Those I interviewed reflected a variety of causes, organizations, as well as levels and durations of political involvement. All were leftists[1] and many, but certainly not all, were fairly radical. Their more radical politics, and sometimes more confrontational tactics, may have been part of why they were on the law enforcement list, known to others on the list, or had otherwise experienced state repression. Therefore, those I interviewed are not representative of activists more generally, but rather of activists who have been targeted for monitoring and have experienced state repression. Importantly, because I used the list of "persons of interest" (which had been circulated to law enforcement four years before I began interviewing) as a seed sample, rather than simply identifying individuals to be interviewed among those currently active in social movement organizations or attending protest events, my final sample included individuals who have persisted in activism as well as those who have disengaged over time.

As table A.1 makes clear, the sample is not representative of the state or of activists generally, as the sample is overwhelmingly white and male. Also, while interviewees ranged in age from their early twenties to late eighties, nearly half were between the age of thirty and thirty-nine.

Interviews lasted between one and six hours and were performed in subjects' homes, offices or other places of business, or in public settings of their choosing. The semi-structured interview schedule was designed to elicit

Table A.1
Interview subject demographics

	Percentage of Sample
Gender	
Male	67%
Female	33%
Race	
White	82%
Non-white	18%
Age	
20–29	20%
30–39	49%
40+	31%

respondents' thoughts and feelings about the costs and risks of participation in protest, especially state repression. They were asked about their personal experiences with state repression, the support they received in these experiences, how these experiences shaped their subsequent involvement, and how they thought about themselves, their movements, and the state (see below for interview guide). These questions were repeated for every major type of repression they had experienced (arrest, police violence, surveillance, infiltration).[2] Additionally, all interviewees were asked about how they would respond to hypothetical situations involving each of these four types of repression, regardless of whether they had experienced them. I randomized the order in which the types of repression were discussed to minimize question order effects and to allow for better comparative leverage for understanding how activists perceive and react to different types of repression differently.

Together with the content analysis of activist writings on repression (most of which were suggested by my interviewees) and the firsthand experience at public protests (including direct experience of state repression and activist support in response), these interviews provide access to the mental, cultural, and social landscapes through which my subjects navigate questions of persistence and burnout, repression and resistance, and success and failure. These data provide insight into how they think about themselves, the groups and movements they are a part of, and the government which, in mobilizing for the causes they care deeply about, they sometimes confront. By probing their decision-making processes, always with an eye to how these are constrained and enabled by the social and cultural contexts in which they are embedded, I was able to not only understand how they are impacted by repression, but more generally how their rationality is collectively constructed by the groups and milieus they are a part of.

Measuring Severity of Repressive Experiences

As discussed in chapter 3, I inductively derived a scheme for coding the severity of different experiences within each type of repression. Among those who were arrested, those who were incarcerated or who faced the possibility of long-term incarceration were coded as having a severe experience of arrest, whereas those who were arrested but released within twenty-four hours and had no chance of being sentenced to prison were coded as having a less severe experience of arrest. Those who experienced indirect violence from police at a protest, operationalized as exposure to pepper spray, tear gas, or other chemicals used for crowd control, were coded as having a less severe experience of police violence than those who were physically struck with batons, thrown to the ground, or otherwise had full contact with law enforcement officers. Again, this distinction was based on the violent experiences interviewees themselves described as more serious or concerning to them but does not suggest that the less severe experiences were not also difficult for some respondents.

A severe experience of surveillance was operationalized as those that were confirmed—where the individual knew through court proceedings, law enforcement interrogation, a Freedom of Information Act request (including that which made public the watch list used to identify interview subjects for this project), or by other means that they were in fact the target of surveillance. Less severe surveillance experiences were those in which the individual had specific reasons to suspect they were under surveillance (for example, they noticed interference on their phones when talking with other activists but not when talking with others), but never had any confirmation and could not say for certain that they had been under surveillance. While even suspected surveillance can be very worrisome for many and can affect their behavior, respondents described how having definitive confirmation that they were a "person of interest" was particularly chilling. For example, Brad told me,

> getting a police report and finding pictures of my house, the car I drove in . . . and then my known associates, like pictures of like my friends' cars parked outside my house and then parked outside their own house, like people who even weren't a part of like actions . . . and this network, like them building up a model of what my social network was. That was, you know, intimidating. And I mean, I already know that they knew all that shit about us anyways, but to see it right there—like, "Oh, that's a shitty photo of my house. Hey, that's my car."

Importantly, all those interviewed who were on the law enforcement watch list used as the seed sample for this project ($n = 11$) were aware, prior to the interview, that they were on the list. A journalist had published the list after receiving it from a FOIA request (which is also how I was able to access it), and the news of it quickly spread among the activists who were on it. Individuals on the list expressed a variety of responses to this news, ranging from pride to fear to anger, but they generally expressed that having this confirmation of their surveillance affected them more intensely than simply suspecting this might be the case (as many had before finding out about the list).

Finally, if someone confirmed or believed that someone they knew personally had been an undercover officer or informant, this was coded as a severe experience of infiltration. Those who experienced infiltration by someone they did not have personal interactions or a relationship with—for example, if they witnessed a plainclothes officer at a protest reveal their identity when they arrested someone—were coded as having a less severe experience of infiltration. Multiple people told me that the idea that someone they knew personally could betray them by giving information to law enforcement, or turning out to be a law enforcement officer themselves, was a much more disturbing possibility than the more impersonal forms of infiltration that sometimes occur in crowds or meetings. As one person said of an experience in which someone she had met and was friendly with turned out to an FBI agent trying unsuccessfully to get information from her about her partner, "It hurt on a human level." Another respondent told me, "And once, you know, that happens, you have to like rationalize every encounter you had with that person. You re-rationalize every encounter you had with that person from the minute you met them, as a relationship of opportunity."

Qualitative Interview Guide

Note: Interviews were semi-structured. The exact questions asked and the order they were asked were changed as necessary.

Okay, did you read the informed consent document thoroughly? Did you have a chance to have any questions you had answered? Do you voluntarily consent, with full knowledge, to participation in this research project?

As you noticed in the informed consent, I will never use your real name for any documents or publications that result from this project. Is there a pseudonym that you would like me to use for you?

Also, to protect your privacy and that of others, try to avoid using names or specific details such as place names that might identify someone. If you accidently use a name or specific identifying details, it is not a big deal because these will be redacted from the transcript.

To begin, I'd like to ask you some questions about how you became involved in activism and the causes you have worked on. . . .

Do you remember the first protest you ever went to?

How old were you?
How did you hear about it?
What was it like?
How did you feel being there?
Are you still involved in anything related to———?
(cause they first protested about)
If no: Why?

What other issues have you been involved with in the past?

What issues, if any, are you currently involved in activism around?

Try to think back to a time when you felt like a movement, organization, or campaign you were involved with achieved something important.

What happened?
What were you thinking and feeling at the time?

Try to think back to a time when you felt a movement, organization, or campaign you were involved with failed at creating change you were seeking.

What happened?
What were you thinking and feeling at the time?

Do you consider yourself to be an activist?

If no: Have you ever considered yourself to be an activist at any point in the past?

What does it mean to say that you or someone else is an "activist"?

Now, I'd like to ask some more specific questions about some things you may have experienced as a result of your involvement. . . .

Arrest

(1) Have you ever been arrested as a result of your involvement in activism?

If no, ask if they have ever witnessed others being arrested at a protest and still ask the following questions about their sharpest memory of this. If they say they have experienced arrest multiple times, ask them to list the incidents and then go through the following questions for each incident.

What happened?
How did you react?

If they need prodding:

Were you angry? Scared? Sad? Did you feel defeated? Empowered? Why do you think you reacted/felt this way?

If only a witness:

Did you think that you yourself might be arrested? Did you think that this might be a possibility before the protest? Were you concerned about this possibility?

If arrested themselves:

Before this incident, did you think arrest might be a possible outcome?

Were others talking about the possibility that arrests would be made at the protest? Did you talk with them about how you would handle it? Were there ever disagreements about this?

Were there other activists also arrested at the same protest? Did others seem to react to the incident similarly to you?

Did you have a chance to debrief with others who were arrested? Did you coordinate your legal strategies in any way? What was the energy like in those meetings?

Did you receive any support, financial, emotional, or otherwise, from other activists after this incident?

What eventually happened with your charges?

Did this experience cause you to reconsider your involvement in activism?

Did it change how you participated or organized?

Have you ever had any experiences with arrest unrelated to activism? Was this before or after the incident(s) you just talked about?

If before:

Did this prior experience with arrest shape how you experienced the incident(s) at the protest? In what way?

If after:

Did the experience of arrest unrelated to protest shape how you thought about the possibility or arrest at protest after?

Let's say you were planning to go to a protest and you heard police were going to be there and might make arrests. Would this make you less likely to go or more likely to go? Why?

Let's say you were at a protest and police started to make arrests. What would you do? Why?

Police Violence

(2) Have you ever experienced violence from police as result of your involvement in activism? This could include direct contact (baton, being tackled, etc.) but also pepper spray, tear gas, etc.

If no, ask if they have ever witnessed others being beaten, pepper sprayed, etc. at a protest and still ask the following questions. If they say they have experienced police violence multiple times, ask them to list the incidents and then go through the following questions for each incident.

What happened?
How did you react?
If they need prodding:
Were you angry? Scared? Sad? Did you feel defeated? Empowered?
Why do you think you reacted/felt this way?

If only a witness:
Did you think that you yourself might be hurt? Did you think that this might be a possibility before the protest? Were you concerned about this possibility?

If beaten themselves:
Before this incident, did you think this might happen? Were others talking about this possibility that police would use violence at the protest? Did you talk with them about how you would handle it? Were there ever disagreements about this?
Were there other activists who also experienced police violence at this same event? Did others seem to react to the incident similarly to you?
Did you have a chance to debrief with others who were beat? What was the energy like in those meetings?
Did you receive any support, financial, medical, emotional, or otherwise, from other activists during or after this incident?

Did this experience cause you to reconsider your involvement in activism?
Did it change how you participated or organized?
Have you ever had any experiences with police violence unrelated to activism?
Was this before or after the incident(s) you just talked about?

If before:
Did this prior experience with police violence shape how you experienced the incident(s) at the protest? In what way?

If after:

Did the experience with police violence unrelated to protest shape how you thought about the possibility of arrest at protests after?

Let's say you were planning to go to a protest and you heard police were going to be there and might use force to disperse the crowd. Would this make you less likely to go or more likely to go? Why?

Let's say you were at a protest and police started to use batons, pepper spray, or other forceful methods to disperse the crowd. What would you do? Why?

Comparing your experiences and observations with arrest with those of police violence, which are you more concerned about happening to you? How do you weigh these different risks? Which affected you more at the time? What about later on?

Surveillance

(3) Have you ever experienced surveillance, or suspected you were under surveillance, as result of your involvement in activism?

If no, ask if they know people who have been under surveillance and ask only the following questions that are still relevant. If they say they have experienced surveillance multiple times, ask them to list the incidents and then go through the following questions for each incident.

What happened?/What made you think you might be under surveillance?
How did you react?
If they need prodding:

Were you angry? Scared? Sad? Did you feel defeated? Empowered?
Why do you think you reacted/felt this way?

Were there other activists also targeted by this surveillance? Did others seem to react to the incident similarly to you? Did you talk with them about how to handle it? Were there ever disagreements about this? What was the energy like in these meetings?
Did you receive any support, financial, emotional, or otherwise, from other activists as a result?
Why do you think that you or the movement you were involved in were targeted in this way?
Did this experience cause you to reconsider your involvement in activism?
Did it change how you participated or organized? Did you begin taking any new precautions?

Let's say you were planning to go to a meeting or protest and had reason to believe your activities were being monitored. Would this make you less likely to go or more likely to go? Why?

Comparing your experiences and observations with surveillance with those of police violence and arrest discussed earlier, which are you more concerned about happening to you? How do you weigh these different risks? Which affected you more at the time? What about later on?

Infiltration

(4) Has a group you were involved with ever been infiltrated by an undercover officer or an informant, or have you or other suspected that this was happening?

If no, ask if they know people who have been infiltrated and ask only the following questions that are still relevant. If they say they have experienced infiltration multiple times, ask them to list the incidents and then go through the following questions for each incident.

What happened?/What made you think you might be infiltrated or being informed on?
How did you react?
If they need prodding:

Were you angry? Scared? Sad? Did you feel defeated? Empowered?
Why do you think you reacted/felt this way?

Were there other activists also targeted by this infiltration? Did others seem to react to the incident similarly to you? Did you talk with them about how to handle it? Were there ever disagreements about this? What was the energy like in these meetings?
Did you receive any support, financial, emotional, or otherwise, from other activists as a result?
Why do you think that you or the movement you were involved in were targeted in this way?
Did this experience cause you to reconsider your involvement in activism?
Did it change how you participated or organized? Did you begin taking any new precautions?

Let's say you were planning to go to a meeting or protest and you heard there may be an undercover cop there. Would this make you less likely to go or more likely to go? Why?

Let's say you were at a meeting or protest and you and others suspected that someone there was an undercover cop. What would you do? Why?

Comparing your experiences and observations with infiltration with those of police surveillance, violence, and arrest discussed earlier, which are you more concerned about happening to you? How do you weigh these different risks? Which affected you more at the time? What about later on?

Harassment

Have you ever felt that you were harassed or hassled by police, outside of a protest context, because of your political activity?

> What happened?
> How did you react? Why do you think you reacted/felt this way?
> Why do you think that you or the movement you were involved in were targeted in this way?
> Did this experience cause you to reconsider your involvement in activism?
> Did it change how you participated or organized? Did you begin taking any new precautions?

And . . .

In what other ways, besides those we have discussed, has the state challenged you and sought to undermine your work? What about other entities besides the police or the state?

Who are the primary players working to suppress movement activity in your community? What sorts of tactics do they use?

Over the period of time you have been involved in activism, have you noticed shifts in how the state has worked to suppress activism? How do you think this has shaped how people organize?

Now I'd like to ask you some final questions about how your involvement in activism has changed over time. . . .

When you first became involved in activism, how big of a part of your life was it? How big a part of your identity was it? How much time do you spend in a typical week on these kinds of activities? What kinds of roles and tasks did you take on?

Thinking about your involvement in activism today, how big of a part of your life would you say it is? How big a part of your identity is it? How much time do you spend in a typical week on these kinds of activities? What kinds of roles and tasks do you take on?

If they indicate some change (whether increase or decrease):

What happened?
Why do you think you became more involved/less involved?
How do you feel about this change?

For those still involved in activism to some extent:

What keeps you going? Have you ever considered stopping?

For those no longer involved at all:

Why did you stop protesting and/or organizing? Do you ever think about wanting to get involved again?

Why do you think others drop out of activism? What do you think would be the best way to prevent this?

Do you know anyone personally who has stopped or changed their participation in activism because of concerns about repression? What happened? What do you think would be the best way to prevent this?

Thinking again about the period of time when you first became involved in activism compared to today, would you say your political beliefs and passions have: Stayed the same? Become more radical? Become more moderate? Changed completely?

Why do you think your beliefs changed?
How do you feel about this change?

And a quick last couple of things. . . .

Do you know about any resources, such as zines, writings, talks, groups, or specific individuals, that are available to help activists deal with repression, or more generally with emotional burnout or trauma, whatever the cause, or to help promote activist self-care?

Is there anything else you want to add, tell me about, or ask me about the project?

Thank you so much for your time.

End Recording

One last thing: Do you have any friends who have experienced either arrest, police violence, or surveillance as a result of their activism who you think might be willing to talk to me about their experiences? If yes, can you please give them my contact information and encourage them to contact me? I want to talk to as many people as possible to better understand how activists can resist repression, and I would really appreciate if you can help me by telling your friends about the project.

Acknowledgments

From its beginning as a dissertation proposal several years ago, this project and the resulting book have benefited from the feedback, guidance, inspiration, and encouragement of many. First and foremost, I would like to thank my adviser, Jennifer Earl, who has been a steadfast source of knowledge, wisdom, encouragement, and friendship throughout graduate school and since. I am also grateful to my dissertation committee members, Robin Stryker and Jane Zavisca, as well as the School of Sociology at the University of Arizona for supporting me throughout my graduate studies. Thank you also to Colorado State University Pueblo and my colleagues in the Department of Sociology, Criminology, and Anthropology for providing a supportive environment to bring this book to fruition.

I am further indebted to many others who have provided feedback on this project at various stages, including but not limited to Luis Fernandez, Joseph West, Will Moore, Christian Davenport, David Cunningham, Pamela Oliver, Dana Moss, David Meyer, Rachel Einwohner, Mark Beissinger, Mike King, and Steve Barkan.

I would like to thank Kevin Sharp, Anne Reynolds, Ryan Tombleson, David Tolar, Adina Artzi, Olaide Adeniran, Samantha Coronado, Anthony Eulano, Jennica Schoppenhorst, Jamie Tugenberg, Andrew Wurzbach, and Natalie Montgomery for their assistance with transcription, coding, and copyediting.

I would also like to thank everyone at Rutgers University Press, especially Peter Mickulas, Luis Fernandez, and Ray Michalowski, for believing in me and this project and for their guidance through the revision and publishing process as well as Amron Gravett of Wildclover Books for her meticulous and thoughtful indexing.

I will also be forever grateful to my family, friends, and partner for their unwavering love, encouragement, and patience throughout this project and the rest of my life.

Finally, my deepest appreciation goes to the activists who shared their stories, passions, and lives with me. Without their generosity, openness, and inspiration, this project truly would not have been possible.

Notes

Chapter 1 Repression, Mobilization, and the Cultural Construction of Rationality

1 By "groups," I am referring not only to formal social movement organizations but also to looser collectivities, such as social movement communities (Buechler 1990; Taylor and Whittier 1992; Staggenborg 1998), networks (Diani 2004), and social milieus that develop within and out of social movements.

Chapter 2 A Brief History of the Policing of Dissent in the United States

1 These individuals were not identified until they came forward in 2014, after the statute of limitations for the break-in had expired (Pilkington 2014).

Chapter 3 Repression in the Eye of the Beholder

1 For more information on data collection and analysis, see the Appendix.
2 This (and all names used for activists studied) is a pseudonym.
3 All interviewees were classified as having persisted in or disengaged from activism following their experience(s) of repression, based on how they described their involvement after the experience, their trajectories over time, and their current levels of involvement as participants and/or organizers in various movements. As will become clear in the following chapters, just because an individual persisted does not mean these activists did not also take new precautions, adapt their tactics, or redefine their priorities and considerations about their participation in activism following these experiences. Therefore, those who changed, but did not cease, their participation were coded as having persisted in activism.
4 I considered someone to be disengaged from activism if they were no longer involved in working for political change through noninstitutional tactics such as public protests or direct action.
5 All respondents were asked about their experiences with four main types of state repression: arrest, police violence, surveillance, and infiltration. This allowed me to categorize interviewees by their experiences to understand how those with

different profiles of repressive experiences may think about repression differently or may have had different trajectories through activism since.

6 I inductively derived a scheme for coding the severity of repressive experiences based on how respondents, collectively, talked about the specific incidents, within each repression type, that impacted or worried them most. In the Appendix, I explain in depth how I made these distinctions. Using this coding scheme, all respondents were assigned a severity score for the total number of severe types of repression they had experienced, ranging from 0 to 4 (because they were all asked about four types of repression). For example, someone who had a severe experience of arrest and a severe experience of police violence but who either had no experiences with, or only mild experiences with, surveillance and infiltration would receive a severity score of 2. Someone who had only had mild experiences of repression would receive a 0. Measuring the severity of experiences, in addition to the types of experiences each interviewee had, enabled me to examine how both repression type and severity might explain subsequent participation.

Chapter 4 Shaping Experiences of Repression through Prevention, Preparation, and Support

1 However, some respondents explained that this tactic has become less common than it was a decade ago. This may be in part because modern (i.e., "smart") cell phones make removing the battery much more difficult.

Appendix

1 The fact that all interviewees were leftists is most likely a result of the fact that all those on the watch list used as a seed sample were leftists, and those suggested by these initial respondents were likely to share their political leanings. Furthermore, leftists have historically been targeted for state repression in the United States at a greater rate than right-wing groups. For example, Cunningham (2004) found that 98 percent of leaked COINTELRPRO files related to surveillance of leftist groups, although surveillance of right-wing groups like the Ku Klux Klan also occurred.

2 An additional form of repression, police harassment, came up in some of the initial interviews and was subsequently added to the interview schedule for the rest of the interviews.

References

Aaronson, Trevor and Katie Galloway. 2015. "Manufacturing Terror: An FBI Informant Seduced Eric McDavid into a Bomb Plot. Then the Government Lied about It." *The Intercept*, November 19.

Adam-Troïan, Jaïs, Elif Çelebi, and Yara Mahfud. 2020. "Return of the Repressed: Exposure to Police Violence Increases Protest and Self-Sacrifice Intentions for the Yellow Vests." *Group Processes & Intergroup Relations* 23(8):1171–1186.

Aho, James. 1994. *This Thing of Darkness: A Sociology of the Enemy*. Seattle: University of Washington Press.

Almeida, Paul D. 2003. "Opportunity Organizations and Threat-Induced Contention: Protest Waves in Authoritarian Settings." *American Journal of Sociology* 109(2):345–400.

Almeida, Paul D. 2008. *Waves of Protest: Popular Struggle in El Salvador, 1925–2005*. Minneapolis: University of Minnesota Press.

American Civil Liberties Union. 2002, "How the USA Patriot Act Redefines 'Domestic Terrorism.'" Retrieved March 31, 2021 (https://www.aclu.org/other/how-usa-patriot-act-redefines-domestic-terrorism).

Armstrong, Elizabeth and Mary Bernstein. 2007. "Culture, Power and Institutions: A Multi-Institutional Politics Approach to Social Movements." *Sociological Theory* 26:74–99.

Balko, Radley. 2013. *The Rise of the Warrior Cop*. New York: Public Affairs.

Barkan, Steven E. 1984. "Legal Control of the Southern Civil Rights Movement." *American Sociological Review* 49(4):552–565.

Barkan, Steven E., Steven F. Cohn, and William H. Whitaker. 1993. "Commitment across the Miles: Ideological and Microstructural Sources of Membership Support in a National Antihunger Organization." *Social Problems* 40(3):362–373.

Barkan, Steven E., Steven F. Cohn, and William H. Whitaker. 1995. "Beyond Recruitment: Predictors of Differential Participation in a National Antihunger Organization." *Sociological Forum* 10:113–134.

Becker, Howard S. 1953. "Becoming a Marijuana User." *American Journal of Sociology* 59(3):235–242.

Benford, Robert. 1993. "'You Could Be the Hundredth Monkey': Collective Action Frames and Vocabularies of Motive within the Nuclear Disarmament Movement." *Sociological Quarterly* 34(2):195–216.

Berger, Dan. 2006. *Outlaws of America: The Weather Underground and the Politics of Solidarity*. Oakland, CA: AK Press.

Blackstock, Nelson. 1988. *COINTELPRO: The FBI's Secret War on Political Freedom*. Atlanta: Pathfinder Press.

Blumer, Herbert. 1939. "Collective Behavior." In *Principles of Sociology*, edited by R. E. Park. New York: Barnes and Noble.

Blumer, Herbert. 1969. "Social Movements." In *Studies in Social Movements*, edited by B. McLaughlin, 8–29. New York: Free Press.

Blumstein, Philip. 2001. "The Production of Selves in Personal Relationships." In *Self in Society*, edited by J. A. Howard and P. L. Callero, 183–197. Cambridge: Cambridge University Press.

Boghosian, Heidi. 2013. *Spying on Democracy: Government Surveillance, Corporate Power, and Public Resistance*. San Francisco: City Lights Books.

Bond Graham, Darwin. 2015. "Counter-Terrorism Officials Helped Track Black Lives Matter Protesters." *East Bay Express*, April 15.

Bourdieu, Pierre and Loic Wacquant. 1992. *An Invitation to Reflexive Sociology*. Chicago: University of Chicago Press.

Boykoff, Jules. 2006. *The Suppression of Dissent: How the State and Mass Media Squelch USAmerican Social Movements*. New York: Routledge.

Brown, Alleen, Will Parrish, and Alice Speri. 2017. "Leaked Documents Reveal Counterterrorism Tactics Used at Standing Rock to 'Defeat Pipeline Insurgencies.'" *The Intercept*, May 27.

Brown, Pat. 2016. "Terrorism by Association: FBI Files on Food Not Bombs." *MuckRock*, March 25.

Brubaker, Rogers and Fred Cooper. 2000. "Beyond Identity." *Theory and Society* 29:1–47.

Buechler, Steven M. 1990. *Women's Movements in the United States*. New Brunswick, NJ: Rutgers University Press.

Buechler, Steven M. 2004. "The Strange Career of Strain and Breakdown Theories of Collective Action." In *The Blackwell Companion to Social Movements*, edited by D. A. Snow, S. A. Soule, and H. Kriesi, 47–66. Oxford: Blackwell Publishing.

Buechler, Steven M. 2011. *Understanding Social Movements: Theories from the Classical Era to the Present*. New York: Paradigm Publishers.

Burke, Peter. 1991. "An Identity Theory Approach to Commitment." *Social Psychology Quarterly* 54:239–251.

Burgess, John and Steven Pearlstein. 1999. "Protests Delay WTO Opening." *Washington Post*, December 1.

Callero, Peter L. 1985. "Role-Identity Salience." *Social Psychology Quarterly* 48:203–215.

Center for Constitutional Rights. 2011. "U.S. v. SHAC 7." Retrieved March 31, 2021 (https://ccrjustice.org/home/what-we-do/our-cases/us-v-shac-7).

Center for Constitutional Rights. 2013. "Blum v. Holder." Retrieved March 31, 2021 (https://ccrjustice.org/home/what-we-do/our-cases/blum-v-holder).

Center for Constitutional Rights. 2017. "Ag-Gag Litigation (Amicas)." Retrieved March 31, 2021 (https://ccrjustice.org/home/what-we-do/our-cases/ag-gag-litigation-amicus).

Chang, Nancy. 2002. *Silencing Political Dissent*. New York: Seven Stories Press.

Churchill, Ward. 1994. "The Bloody Wake of Alcatraz: Political Repression of the American Indian Movement during the 1970s." *American Indian Culture and Research Journal* 18(4):253–300.

Churchill, Ward and Jim Vander Wall. 1988. *Agents of Repression: The FBI's Secret Wars against the Black Panther Party and the American Indian Movement*. Boston: South End Press.

Churchill, Ward and Jim Vander Wall. 2001. *The COINTELPRO Papers: Documents from the FBI's Secret Wars against Dissent in the United States*. New York: South End Press.

Collins, Randall. 2004. *The Program of Interaction Ritual Theory*. Princeton, NJ: Princeton University Press.

Corrigall-Brown, Catherine. 2011. *Patterns of Protest: Trajectories of Participation in Social Movements*. Stanford, CA: Stanford University Press.

Coser, Lewis A. 1956. *The Functions of Social Conflict*. Glencoe, IL: Free Press.

Cosgrove, Ben. 2013. "Life and Civil Rights: Anatomy of a Protest, Virginia, 1960." *Life*, January 31.

Crossley, Nick. 2002. *Making Sense of Social Movements*. Philadelphia: Open University Press.

Crossley, Nick. 2003. "From Reproduction to Transformation: Social Movement Fields and the Radical Habitus." *Theory Culture Society* 20:43–68.

Cunningham, David. 2003. "Understanding State Responses to Left- versus Right-Wing Threats." *Social Science History* 27(3):327–370.

Cunningham, David. 2004. *There's Something Happening Here: The New Left, the Klan, and FBI Counterintelligence*. Berkeley: University of California Press.

Cunningham, David and John Noakes. 2008. "'What If She's from the FBI?' The Effects of Covert Social Control on Social Movements and Their Participants." In *Surveillance and Governance: Crime Control and Beyond*, edited by M. DeFlem, 175–197. New York: Elsevier.

Davenport, Christian. 2005. "Understanding Covert Repressive Action." *Journal of Conflict Resolution* 49(1):120–140.

Davenport, Christian. 2007. "State Repression and Political Order." *Annual Review of Political Science* 10:1–23.

Davenport, Christian. 2010. *Media Bias, Perspective, and State Repression*. New York: Cambridge University Press.

Davenport, Christian. 2014. *How Social Movements Die*. Cambridge: Cambridge University Press.

della Porta, Donatella and Herbert Reiter. 2006. "The Policing of the Global Protest: The G8 at Genoa and Its Aftermath." In *The Policing of Transnational Protest*, edited by D. della Porta, A. Peterson, and H. Reiter. Burlington, VT: Ashgate Press.

Diani, Mario. 2004. "Networks and Participation." In *The Blackwell Companion to Social Movements*, edited by D. A. Snow, S. A. Soule, and H. Kriesi, 339–359. Oxford: Blackwell Publishing.

Dixon, Chris. 2014. *Another Politics: Talking across Today's Transformative Movements*. Oakland: University of California Press.

Donner, Frank. 1990. *Protectors of Privilege: Red Squads and Police Repression in Urban America*. Berkeley: University of California Press.

Downton, James and Paul Wehr. 1997. *The Persistent Activist: How Peace Commitment Develops and Survives*. Boulder, CO: Westview Press.

Driscoll, Daniel. 2018. "Beyond Organizational Ties: Foundations of Persistent Commitment in Environmental Activism." *Social Movement Studies* 17(6):697–715.

Earl, Jennifer. 2003. "Tanks, Tear Gas and Taxes: Toward a Theory of Movement Repression." *Sociological Theory* 21(1):44–68.

Earl, Jennifer. 2005. "You Can Beat the Rap, but You Can't Beat the Ride." *Research in Social Movements, Conflict, and Change* 26:101–139.

Earl, Jennifer. 2011a. "Political Repression: Iron Fists, Velvet Gloves, and Diffuse Control." *Annual Review of Sociology* 37:261–284.

Earl, Jennifer. 2011b. "Protest Arrests and Future Protest Participation: The 2004 Republican National Convention Arrestees and the Effects of Repression." *Studies in Law, Politics, and Society* 45:141–173.

Earl, Jennifer and Jessica Beyer. 2014. "The Dynamics of Backlash Online: Anonymous and the Battle for Wikileaks." *Research in Social Movements, Conflict and Change* 37:207–233.

Earl, Jennifer and Heidi Reynolds-Stenson. 2018. "Innovations in Policing: Rethinking Changes in Protest Policing Protocols in the US." Presented at the American Bar Foundation, January 2018, Chicago, IL.

Earl, Jennifer and Sarah A. Soule. 2006. "Seeing Blue: A Police-Centered Explanation of Protest Policing." *Mobilization: An International Journal* 11(2):145–164.

Earl, Jennifer and Sarah A. Soule. 2010. "The Impacts of Repression: The Effect of Police Presence and Action on Subsequent Protest Rates." *Research in Social Movements, Conflicts, and Change* 30:75–113.

Einwohner, Rachel L. 2002. "Motivational Framing and Efficacy Maintenance: Animal Rights Activists' Use of Four Fortifying Strategies." *Sociological Quarterly* 43(4):509–526.

Einwohner, Rachel L. 2003. "Opportunity, Honor, and Action in the Warsaw Ghetto Uprising of 1943." *American Journal of Sociology* 109(3):650–675.

Einwohner, Rachel L. and Thomas V. Maher. 2011. "Threat Assessment and Collective-Action Emergence: Death-Camp and Ghetto Resistance during the Holocaust." *Mobilization: An International Journal* 16(2):127–146.

Elliot, Thomas, Jennifer Earl, Thomas V. Maher, and Heidi Reynolds-Stenson. 2022. "Softer Policing or the Institutionalization of Protest? Decomposing Changes in Observed Protest Policing Over Time." *American Journal of Sociology* 127(4):1311–1365.

Ennis, James G. and Richard Schreuer. 1987. "Mobilizing Weak Support for Social Movements: The Role of Grievance, Efficacy, and Cost." *Social Forces* 66(2):390–409.

Esquivel, Jenny. 2013. "Building Conspiracy: Informants in the Case of Eric McDavid." In *Life during Wartime*, edited by K. Williams, W. Munger, and L. Messersmith-Glavin, 315–348. Oakland, CA: AK Press.

Eyerman, Ron. 2005. "How Social Movements Move: Emotions and Social Movements." In *Emotions and Social Movements*, edited by H. Flam and D. King, 41–56. New York: Routledge.

Eyerman, Ron and Andrew Jamison. 1991. *Social Movements: A Cognitive Approach*. University Park: Pennsylvania State University Press.

Fang, Lee. 2015. "Why Was an FBI Joint Terrorism Task Force Tracking a Black Lives Matter Protest?" *The Intercept*, March 12.

Fang, Lee and Steve Horn. 2016. "Federal Agents Went Undercover to Spy on Anti-Fracking Movement, Emails Reveal." *The Intercept*, July 19.
Fantasia, Rick. 1988. *Cultures of Solidarity: Consciousness, Action and Contemporary American Workers*. Berkeley: University of California Press.
Farzan, Antonia Noori. 2017. "'Plan a Protest, Lose Your House' Bill, SB 1142, Killed by Arizona House." *Phoenix New Times*, February 27. Retrieved March 31, 2021 (http://www.phoenixnewtimes.com/news/plan-a-protest-lose-your-house-bill-sb-1142-killed-by-arizona-house-9121181).
Federman, Adam. 2015. "Keystone Protesters Tracked at Border after FBI Spied on 'Extremists.'" *The Guardian*, June 8.
Feeley, Malcolm M. 1992. *The Process Is the Punishment: Handling Cases in a Lower Criminal Court*. New York: Russell Sage Foundation.
Fernandez, Luis A. 2008. *Policing Dissent: Social Control and the Anti-Globalization Movement*. New Brunswick, NJ: Rutgers University Press.
Ferree, Myra Marx. 1992. "The Political Context of Rationality: Rational Choice Theory and Resource Mobilization." In *Frontiers in Social Movement Theory*, edited by A. D. Morris and C. M. Mueller, 29–52. New Haven, CT: Yale University Press.
Festinare, Leon, Henry E. Reiken, and Stanley Schachter. 1956. *When Prophecy Fails: A Social and Psychological Study of a Modern Group That Predicted the Destruction of the World*. Minneapolis: University of Minnesota Press.
Fireman, Bruce and William Gamson. 1977. *Utilitarian Logic in the Resource Mobilization Perspective*. Ann Arbor: University of Michigan.
Flanagan, Constance and Peter Levine. 2010. "Civic Engagement and the Transition to Adulthood." *Future of Children* 20(1):159–179.
Francisco, Ronald A. 1995. "The Relationship between Coercion and Protest." *Journal of Conflict Resolution* 39(2):263–282.
Francisco, Ronald A. 2004. "After the Massacre: Mobilization in the Wake of Harsh Repression." *Mobilization: An International Journal* 9(2):107–126.
Francisco, Ronald A. 2005. "The Dictator's Dilemma." In *Repression and Mobilization*, edited by C. Davenport, H. Johnston, and C. Mueller, 58–81. Minneapolis: University of Minnesota Press.
Friedland, Roger and Robert R. Alford. 1991. "Bringing Society Back In: Symbols, Practices, and Institutional Contradictions." In *The New Institutionalism in Organizational Analysis*, edited by W. W. Powell and P. J. DiMaggio, 232–263. Chicago: University of Chicago Press.
Friedland, Roger and John Mohr. 2004. "The Cultural Turn in American Sociology." In *Matters of Culture: Cultural Sociology in Practice*, edited by R. Friedland and J. Mohr. New York: Cambridge University Press.
Friedman, Debra and Doug McAdam. 1992. "Collective Identity and Activism: Networks, Choices, and the Life of a Social Movement." In *Frontiers in Social Movement Theory*, edited by A. D. Morris and C. M. Mueller, 156–173. New Haven, CT: Yale University Press.
Gamson, William A. 1990 [1975]. *The Strategy of Social Protest*. Homewood, IL: Dorsey.
Gamson, William A. 1992. *Talking Politics*. Cambridge: Cambridge University Press.
Garvin, Cosmo. 2006. "Conspiracy of Dunces." *Sacramento News and Review*, July 27. Retrieved March 31, 2021 (https://www.newsreview.com/sacramento/content/conspiracy-of-dunces/80311/).

Gelbspan, Ross. 1991. *Break-Ins, Death Threats and the FBI: The Covert War against the Central America Movement*. Boston: South End Press.
Gillham, Patrick F. 2011. "Securitizing America: Strategic Incapacitation and the Policing of Protest since the 11 September 2001 Terrorist Attacks." *Sociology Compass* 5(7):636–652.
Gillham, Patrick, Bob Edwards, and John Noakes. 2013. "Strategic Incapacitation and the Policing of Occupy Wall Street Protests in New York City, 2011." *Policing and Society* 23(1):81–102.
Gillham, Patrick and John Noakes. 2007. "More Than Marching in a Circle: Transgressive Protest and the Limits of Negotiated Management." *Mobilization: An International Journal* 12(4):341–357.
Glick, Brian. 1989. *War at Home: Covert Action against Activists and What We Can Do about It*. Boston: South End Press.
Goldberg, Chad Alan. 2003. "Haunted by the Specter of Communism: Collective Identity and Resource Mobilization in the Demise of the Workers Alliance of America." *Theory and Society* 32(5/6):725–773.
Goodwin, Jeff and James M. Jasper. 1999. "Caught in a Winding, Snarling Vine: The Structural Bias of Political Process Theory." *Sociological Forum* 14(1):27–54.
Goodwin, Jeff, James M. Jasper, and Francesca Polletta. 2000. "The Return of the Repressed: The Fall and the Rise of Emotions in Social Movement Theory." *Mobilization: An International Journal* 5(1):65–83.
Goodwin, Jeff and Steven Pfaff. 2001. "Emotion Work in High-Risk Social Movements: Managing Fear in the U.S. and East German Civil Rights Movements." In *Passionate Politics: Emotions and Social Movements*, edited by J. Goodwin, J. M. Jasper, and F. Polletta, 282–302. Chicago: University of Chicago Press.
Gordon, Ed. 2006. "COINTELPRO and the History of Domestic Spying." *News & Notes*, January 18 (https://www.npr.org/templates/story/story.php?storyId=5161811).
Grecas, Viktor. 2000. "Value Identities, Self-Motives, and Social Movements." In *Self, Identity, and Social Movements*, edited by S. Stryker, T. J. Owens, and R. W. White, 93–109. Minneapolis: University of Minnesota Press.
Grigoriadis, Vanessa. 2011. "The Rise and Fall of the Eco-Radical Underground." *Rolling Stone*, June 21.
Gross, Neil. 2009. "A Pragmatist Theory of Social Mechanisms." *American Sociological Review* 74:358–379.
Gupta, Devashree. 2017. *Protest Politics Today*. Medford, MA: Polity Press.
Hackett, Colleen. 2015. "Justice through Defiance: Political Prisoner Support Work and Infrastructures of Resistance." *Contemporary Justice Review* 18(1):68–75.
Hahn, Harlan and Judson L. Jeffries. 2003. *Urban America and Its Police*. Boulder: University Press of Colorado.
Haldeman, H. R. and Joseph Dimona. 1978. *The Ends of Power*. New York: Dell Publishing.
Hardt, Michael and Antonio Negri. 2004. *Multitude: War and Democracy in the Age of Empire*. London: Penguin Books.
Harring, Sidney. 1983. *Policing in a Class Society: The Experience of American Cities, 1865–1915*. New Brunswick, NJ: Rutgers University Press.
Hermes, Kris. 2015. *Crashing the Party*. Oakland, CA: PM Press.
Hess, David and Brian Martin. 2006. "Backfire, Repression, and the Theory of Transformative Events." *Mobilization: An International Journal* 11(1):249–267.

Hirsch, Eric L. 1990. "Sacrifice for the Cause: Group Processes, Recruitment, and Commitment in a Student Social Movement." *American Sociological Review* 55(2):243–254.

Hirschman, Albert O. 1986. *Rival View of Market Society and Other Recent Essays.* Cambridge, MA: Harvard University Press.

Hochschild, Arlie Russell. 2003. *The Commercialization of Intimate Life: Notes from Home and Work.* Berkeley: University of California Press.

Hodai, Beau. 2013. *Dissent or Terror: How the Nation's Counter Terrorism Apparatus, in Partnership with Corporate America, Turned on Occupy Wall Street.* Madison, WI: Center for Media and Democracy/DBA Press.

Hoffer, Eric. 1951. *The True Believer.* New York: Harper and Row.

Hunt, Scott A. and Robert D. Benford. 1994. "Identity Talk in the Peace and Justice Movement." *Journal of Contemporary Ethnography* 22(4):488–517.

Hunt, Scott A. and Robert D. Benford. 2004. "Collective Identity, Solidarity, and Commitment." In *The Blackwell Companion to Social Movements,* edited by D. A. Snow, S. A. Soule, and H. Kriesi, 433–457. Oxford: Blackwell Publishing.

International Center for Not-for-Profit Law. 2022. "U.S. Protest Law Tracker." Retrieved March 13, 2022 (http://www.icnl.org/usprotestlawtracker/).

Jagger, Alison. 1989. "Love and Knowledge: Emotion in Feminist Epistemology." *Inquiry* 32:151–176.

Jasper, James M. 2010. "Social Movement Theory Today: Toward a Theory of Action?" *Sociology Compass* 4(11):965–976.

Jasper, James M. 2011. "Emotions and Social Movements: Twenty Years of Theory and Research." *Annual Review of Sociology* 37:285–303.

Jasper, James M. and Jane D. Poulsen. 1995. "Recruiting Strangers and Friends: Moral Shocks and Social Networks in Animal Rights and Anti-Nuclear Protests." *Social Problems* 42(4):493–512.

Jenkins, J. Craig and Charles Perrow. 1977. "Insurgency of the Powerless: Farm Worker Movements (1946–1972)." *American Sociological Review* 42:249–268.

Jenkins, J. Craig and Kurt Schock. 2004. "Political Process, International Dependence, and Mass Political Conflict: A Global Analysis of Protest and Rebellion, 1973–1978." *International Journal of Sociology* 33(4):41–63.

Kaplan, Howard B. and Xiaoru Liu. 2000. "Social Movements as Collective Coping with Spoiled Personal Identities: Intimations from a Panel Study of Changes in the Life Course between Adolescence and Adulthood." In *Self, Identity, and Social Movements,* edited by S. Stryker, T. J. Owens, and R. W. White, 215–238. Minneapolis: University of Minnesota Press.

Khawaja, Marwan. 1993. "Repression and Popular Collective Action: Evidence from the West Bank." *Sociological Forum* 8(1):47–71.

Kiecolt, K. Jill. 2000. "Self-Change in Social Movements." In *Self, Identity, and Social Movements,* edited by S. Stryker, T. J. Owens, and R. W. White, 110–131. Minneapolis: University of Minnesota Press.

King, Mike. 2017. *When Riot Cops Are Not Enough: The Police and Repression of Occupy Oakland.* New Brunswick, NJ: Rutgers University Press.

King, Mike and David Waddington. 2006. "The Policing of Transnational Protest in Canada." In *The Policing of Transnational Protest,* edited by D. della Porta, A. Peterson, and H. Reiter. London: Ashgate Press.

Kitschelt, Herbert P. 1986. "Political Opportunity Structures and Political Protest: Anti-Nuclear Movements in Four Democracies." *British Journal of Political Science* 16:57–85.
Klandermans, Bert. 1984. "Mobilization and Participation: Social-Psychological Expansions of Resource Mobilization Theory." *American Sociological Review* 49:583–600.
Klandermans, Bert. 1997. *The Social Psychology of Protest*. Cambridge, MA: Blackwell Publishing.
Klandermans, Bert. 2002. "How Group Identification Helps to Overcome the Dilemma of Collective Action." *American Behavioral Scientist* 45:887–900.
Klandermans, Bert. 2004. "The Demand and Supply of Participation: Social-Psychological Correlates of Participation in Social Movements." In *The Blackwell Companion to Social Movements*, edited by D. A. Snow, S. A. Soule, and H. Kriesi, 360–379. Oxford: Blackwell Publishing.
Klapp, Orrin E. 1969. *Collective Search for Identity*. New York: Holt, Rinehart, & Winston.
Knoke, David. 1988. "Incentives in Collective Action Organizations." *American Sociological Review* 53(3):311–329.
Koopmans, Ruud. 1997. "The Dynamics of Repression and Mobilization: The German Extreme Right in the 1990s." *Mobilization: An International Journal* 2(2):149–165.
Kornhauser, William. 1959. *The Politics of Mass Society*. New York: Free Press.
Kraska, Peter B. and Victor E. Kappeler. 1997. "Militarizing American Police: The Rise and Normalization of Paramilitary Units." *Social Problems* 44(1):1–17.
Kraska, Peter B. and Derek J. Paulsen. 1997. "Grounded Research into U.S. Paramilitary Policing: Forging the Iron Fist inside the Velvet Glove." *Policing and Society* 7(4):253–270.
Leach, Darcy. 2013. "Prefigurative Politics." In *The Wiley-Blackwell Encyclopedia of Social and Political Movements*, edited by D. A. Snow, D. della Porta, B. Klandermans, and D. McAdam. Malden, MA: Wiley-Blackwell.
Le Bon, Gustave. 1960 [1895]. *The Crowd: A Study of the Popular Mind*. New York: Viking Press.
Levin, Sam. 2017. "Revealed: FBI Terrorism Taskforce Investigating Standing Rock Activists." *The Guardian*, February 10.
Lewis, Paul and Adam Federman. 2015. "Revealed: FBI Violated Its Own Rules While Spying on Keystone XL Opponents." *The Guardian*, May 12.
Lichbach, Mark Irving. 1987. "Deterrence or Escalation? The Puzzle of Aggregate Studies of Repression and Dissent." *Journal of Conflict Resolution* 31(2):266–297.
Lichbach, Mark Irving. 1998. *The Rebel's Dilemma*. Ann Arbor: University of Michigan Press.
Linden, Annette and Bert Klandermans. 2006. "Stigmatization and Repression of Extreme Right Activism in the Netherlands." *Mobilization: An International Journal* 11(2):213–228.
Lofland, John. 1996. *Social Movement Organizations: Guided to Research on Insurgent Realities*. New York: Transaction.
Loveman, Mara. 1998. "High-Risk Collective Action: Defending Human Rights in Chile, Uruguay, and Argentina." *American Journal of Sociology* 104(2):477–525.
Lusher, Adam. 2017. "At Least 10,000 People Died in Tiananmen Square Massacre, Secret British Cable from the Time Alleged." *The Independent*, December 23.
Macaskill, Ewen and Gabriel Dance. 2013. "NSA Files: Decoded." *The Guardian*, November 1.

Macy, Michael. 1991. "Chains of Cooperation: Threshold Effects in Collective Action." *American Sociological Review* 56:730–747.
Maguire, Edward. 2015. "New Directions in Protest Policing." *St. Louis University Law Review* 35:67–108.
Marwell, Gerald and Pamela Oliver. 1993. *The Critical Mass in Collective Action: A Micro-Social Theory*. New York: Cambridge University Press.
Matsakis, Louise. 2017. "AI Will Soon Identify Protesters with Their Faces Partly Concealed." *Vice*, September 6.
McAdam, Doug. 1983. "Tactical Innovation and the Pace of Insurgency." *American Sociological Review* 48(6):735–754.
McAdam, Doug. 1986. "Recruitment to High-Risk Activism: The Case of Freedom Summer." *American Journal of Sociology* 92:64–90.
McAdam, Doug. 1988. *Freedom Summer*. New York: Oxford University Press.
McAdam, Doug. 1994. "Culture and Social Movements." In *New Social Movements: From Ideology to Identity*, edited by E. Laraña, H. Johnston, and J. Gusfield, 36–57. Philadelphia: Temple University Press.
McAdam, Doug. 1999. *Political Process and the Development of Black Insurgency, 1930–1970*. Chicago: University of Chicago Press.
McAdam, Doug and Ronnelle Paulsen. 1993. "Specifying the Relationship between Social Ties and Activism." *American Journal of Sociology* 92:54–90.
McCarthy, John D. and Clark McPhail. 1998. "The Institutionalization of Protest in the United States." In *The Social Movement Society: Contentious Politics for the New Century*, edited by D. S. Meyer and S. Tarrow, 83–110. Lanham, MD: Rowman & Littlefield.
McCarthy, John D. and Clark McPhail. 1999. "Policing Protest: The Evolving Dynamics of Encounters between Collective Actors and Police in the United States." In *Eigenwilligkeit und Rationalität sozialer Prozesse*, edited by J. Gerhards and R. Hitzler, 336–351. Wiesbaden, Germany: Westdeutscher Verlag.
McCarthy, John D., Clark McPhail, and John Crist. 1999. "The Diffusion and Adoption of Public Order Management Systems." In *Social Movements in a Globalizing World*, edited by H. Kriesi, D. della Porta, and D. Rucht, 71–93. New York: St. Martin's Press.
McCarthy, John D. and Mayer N. Zald. 1977. "Resource Mobilization and Social Movements: A Partial Theory." *American Journal of Sociology* 82:1212–1241.
McCarthy, John D. and Mayer N. Zald. 2002. "The Enduring Vitality of the Resource Mobilization Theory of Social Movements." In *Handbook of Sociological Theory*, edited by J. H. Turner, 533–565. New York: Kluwer Academic/Plenum Publishers.
Medsger, Betty. 2014. *The Burglary: The Discovery of J. Edgar Hoover's Secret FBI*. New York: Alfred A. Knopf.
Melucci, Alberto. 1980. "The New Social Movements: A Theoretical Approach." *Social Science Information* 19(2):199–226.
Melucci, Alberto. 1995. "The Process of Collective Identity." In *Social Movements and Culture*, edited by H. Johnston and B. Klandermans, 41–63. Minneapolis: University of Minnesota.
Melucci, Alberto. 1996. *Challenging Codes: Collective Action in the Information Age*. Cambridge: Cambridge University Press.
Meyer, David S. 2004. "Protest and Political Opportunities." *Annual Review of Sociology*. 30:125–145.

Mitchell, Don and Don Stacheli. 2005. "Permitting Protest: Parsing the Fine Geography of Dissent in America." *International Journal of Urban and Regional Research* 29(4):796–813.

Monahan, Torin and Neal A. Palmer. 2009. "The Emerging Politics of DHS Fusion Centers." *Security Dialogue* 40(6):617–636.

Montgomery, Nick and Carla Bergman. 2017. *Joyful Militancy: Building Thriving Resistance in Toxic Times*. Oakland, CA: AK Press.

Morris, Aldon. 1981. "Black Southern Student Sit-In Movement: An Analysis of Internal Organization." *American Sociological Review* 46:744–767.

Morrison, Aaron. 2017. "Activists Win Access to NYPD's Black Lives Matter Surveillance Files." *Mic*, February 8.

Moynihan, Colin. 2009. "Activist Unmasks Himself as Federal Informant in G.O.P. Convention Case." *New York Times*, January 4.

Moynihan, Colin. 2014. "Officials Cast Wide Net in Monitoring Occupy Protests." *New York Times*, May 22.

Muller, Edward N. 1985. "Income Inequality, Regime Repressiveness, and Political Violence." *American Sociological Review* 50(1):47–61.

Muller, Edward N. and Erich Weede. 1990. "Cross-National Variation in Political Violence: A Rational Action Approach." *Journal of Conflict Resolution* 34(4):624–651.

Murdock, Sebastian. 2017. "NYPD Infiltrated Black Lives Matter Protests and Obtained Text Messages, Emails Show." *Huffington Post*, April 4.

National Lawyers Guild. 1982. *Counterintelligence: A Documentary Look at America's Secret Police*. (https://t.co/grhJHFv3us).

Neidhardt, Friedhelm. 1989. "Gewalt und Gegengewalt, Steigt die Bereitschaft zu Gewaltaktionen mit zunehmender staatlicher Kontrolle und Repression?" In *Jugend, Staat, Gewalt: Politische Sozialisation von Jugendlichen, Jugendpolitik und politische Bildung*, edited by W. Heitmeier, K. Möller, and H. Sünker, 233–243. Weinheim, Germany: Juventa Verlag.

Nepsted, Sharon Erickson. 2008. *Religion and War Resistance in the Plowshares Movement*. Cambridge: Cambridge University Press.

Noakes, John and Patrick F. Gillham. 2006. "Aspects of the New Penology in the Policing of Recent Mass Protests in the US." In *The Policing of Transnational Protest*, edited by D. della Porta, A. Peterson, and H. Reiter, 97–116. New York: Ashgate Press.

Noakes, John and Patrick F. Gillham. 2007. "Police and Protester Innovation since Seattle." *Mobilization: An International Journal* 12(4):335–340.

Oberschall, Anthony. 1973. *Social Conflict and Social Movements*. Englewood Cliffs, NJ: Prentice-Hall.

Odabaş, Meltem and Heidi Reynolds-Stenson. 2017. "Tweeting from Gezi Park: Social Media and Repression Backfire." *Social Currents* 5(4):386–406.

Olson, Mancur. 1965. *The Logic of Collective Action*. Cambridge, MA: Harvard University Press.

Ondetti, Gabriel. 2006. "Repression, Opportunity, and Protest: Explaining the Takeoff of Brazil's Landless Movement." *Latin American Politics and Society* 48(2):61–94.

Opp, Karl-Dieter. 1986. "Soft Incentives and Collective Action: Participation in the Anti-Nuclear Movement." *British Journal of Political Science* 16(1):87–112.

Opp, Karl-Dieter. 1989. *The Rationality of Political Protest: A Comparative Analysis of Rational Choice Theory*. New York: Routledge.

Opp, Karl-Dieter. 2009. *Theories of Political Protest and Social Movements*. London: Routledge.

Opp, Karl-Dieter and Wolfgang Roehl. 1990. "Repression, Micromobilization, and Political Protest." *Social Forces* 69(2):521–547.

Ortiz, David G. 2007. "Confronting Oppression with Violence: Inequality, Military Infrastructure and Dissident Repression." *Mobilization: An International Journal* 12(3):219–238.

Passavant, Paul. 2021. *Policing Protest: The Post-Democratic State and the Figure of Black Insurrection*. Durham, NC: Duke University Press.

Perez, Marcos Emilio. 2018. "Becoming a Piquetero: Working-Class Routines and the Development of Activist Dispositions." *Mobilization: An International Journal* 23(2):237–253.

Pilkington, Ed. 2014. "Burglars in 1971 FBI Office Break-In Come Forward after 43 Years." *The Guardian*, January 7.

Pilkington, Ed. 2015. "Role of FBI Informant in Eco-Terrorism Case Probed after Documents Hint at Entrapment." *The Guardian*, January 13.

Pinel, Elizabeth C. and William B. Swann, Jr. 2000. "Finding the Self through Others: Self-Verification and Social Movement Participation." In *Self, Identity, and Social Movements*, edited by S. Stryker, T. J. Owens, and R. W. White, 93–109. Minneapolis: University of Minnesota Press.

Piven, Frances Fox and Richard A. Cloward. 1977. *Poor People's Movements: Why They Succeed, How They Fail*. New York: Vintage Books.

Polletta, Francesca. 1997. "Culture and Its Discontents: Recent Theorizing on the Cultural Dimensions of Protest." *Sociological Inquiry* 67(4):431–450.

Polletta, Francesca. 1998. "'It Was Like a Fever . . .': Narrative and Identity in Social Protest." *Social Problems* 45(2):137–160.

Polletta, Francesca. 1999. "Snarls, Quacks, and Quarrels: Culture and Structure in Political Process Theory." *Sociological Forum* 14(1):63–70.

Polletta, Francesca. 2004. *Freedom Is an Endless Meeting: Democracy in American Social Movements*. Chicago: University of Chicago Press.

Polletta, Francesca and James M. Jasper. 2001. "Collective Identity and Social Movements." *Annual Review of Sociology* 27:283–305.

Potter, Will. 2011. *Green Is the New Red*. San Francisco: City Lights Publishers.

Pugh, Allison J. 2013. "What Good Are Interviews for Thinking about Culture? Demystifying Interpretive Analysis." *American Journal of Cultural Sociology* 1(1):42–68.

Rasler, Karen. 1996. "Concessions, Repression, and Political Protest in the Iranian Revolution." *American Sociological Review* 61(1):132–152.

Reger, Jo. 2004. "Organizational 'Emotion Work' through Consciousness-Raising: An Analysis of a Feminist Organization." *Qualitative Sociology* 27(2):205–222.

Reynolds-Stenson, Heidi and Jennifer Earl. 2020. "Towards a Repertoire of Protest Control." Presented at the Law and Society Association Annual Meeting, May 2020, Virtual.

Reynolds-Stenson, Heidi and Jennifer Earl. 2021. "The Puzzle of Protest Policing Over Time: Historicizing Repression Research Using Temporal Moving Regressions." *American Behavioral Scientist*.

Risen, James and Eric Lichtblau. 2005. "Bush Lets U.S. Spy on Callers without Courts." *New York Times*, December 16.

Rittgers, David. 2011. "We're All Terrorists Now." *Cato Institute*, February 2.

Roberts, Rebecca. 2010. "Kent State Shooting Divided Campus and Country." *Talk of the Nation*, May 3.

Russo, Chandra. 2018. *Solidarity in Practice: Moral Protest and the US Security State.* New York: Cambridge University Press.

Santa Cruz, Nicole. 2010. "Arizona Bill Targeting Ethnic Studies Signed into Law." *Los Angeles Times*, May 12.

Santoro, Wayne A. and Marian Azab. 2015. "Arab American Protest in the Terror Decade: Macro- and Micro-Level Response to Post-9/11 Repression." *Social Problems* 62(2):219–240.

Schwartz, Michael. 1976. *Radical Protest and Social Structure: The Southern Farmers Alliance and Cotton Tenancy, 1880–1890*. Chicago: University of Chicago Press.

Shadmehr, Mehdi. 2014. "Mobilization, Repression, and Revolution: Grievances and Opportunities in Contentious Politics." *Journal of Politics* 76(3):621–635.

Shantz, Jeff. 2012. *Protest and Punishment: The Repression of Resistance in the Era of Neoliberal Globalization*. Durham, NC: Carolina Academic Press.

Simmel, Georg. 1955. *Conflict and the Web of Group Affiliations.* Translated by K. H. Wolff and R. Bendix. New York: Free Press.

Singer, Natasha. 2014. "Never Forgetting a Face." *New York Times*, May 17.

Smith, R. Jeffrey. 2012. "Senate Report Says National Intelligence Fusion Centers Have Been Useless." *Foreign Policy*, October 3.

Snow, David A. 2004a. "Framing Processes, Ideology, and Discursive Fields." In *The Blackwell Companion to Social Movements*, edited by D. A. Snow, S. A. Soule, and H. Kriesi, 380–412. Oxford: Blackwell Publishing.

Snow, David A. 2004b. "Social Movements as Challenges to Authority: Resistance to an Emergence Conceptual Hegemony." *Research in Social Movements, Conflict and Change* 25:3–25.

Snow, David A. and Leon Anderson. 1987. "Identity Work among the Homeless: The Verbal Construction and Avowal of Personal Identities." *American Journal of Sociology* 92:133–171.

Snow, David A. and Robert D. Benford. 1992. "Master Frames and Cycles of Protest." In *Frontiers of Social Movement Theory*, edited by A. Morris and C. Mueller, 133–155. New Haven, CT: Yale University Press.

Snow, David A. and Richard Machalek. 1984. "The Sociology of Conversion." *Annual Review of Sociology* 10:167–190.

Snow, David A. and Doug McAdam. 1997. "Identity Work Processes in the Context of Social Movements: Clarifying the Identity/Movement Nexus." In *Self, Identity, and Social Movements*, edited by S. Stryker, T. Owens, and R. White, 41–67. Minneapolis: University of Minnesota Press

Snow, David A. and Pamela E. Oliver. 1994. "Social Movements and Collective Behavior: Social Psychological Dimensions and Considerations." In *Sociological Perspectives on Social Psychology*, edited by K. Cook, G. Fine, and J. House, 571–599. New York: Allyn and Bacon.

Snow, David A., E. Burke Rochford, Steven K. Worden, and Robert D. Benford. 1986. "Frame Alignment Processes, Micromobilization, and Movement Participation." *American Sociological Review* 51:464–481.

Snow, David A., Louise A. Zurcher, and Sheldon Ekland-Olson. 1980. "Social Networks and Social Movements: A Microstructural Approach to Differential Recruitment." *American Sociological Review* 45:787–801.

Soule, Sarah A. and Christian Davenport. 2009. "Velvet Glove, Iron Fist or Even Hand? Protest Policing in the United States, 1960–1990." *Mobilization: An International Journal* 14(1):1–22.

Staggenborg, Suzanne. 1998. "Social Movement Communities and Cycles of Protest: The Emergence and Maintenance of a Local Women's Movement." *Social Problems* 45(2):180–204.

Starr, Amory and Luis Fernandez. 2009. "Legal Control and Resistance Post-Seattle." *Social Justice* 36(1):41–60.

Starr, Amory, Luis A. Fernandez, Randall Amster, Lesley J. Wood, and Manuel J. Caro. 2008. "The Impacts of State Surveillance on Political Assembly and Association: A Socio-Legal Analysis." *Qualitative Sociology* 31(3):251–270.

Starr, Amory, Luis Fernandez, and Christian Scholl. 2011. *Shutting Down the Streets: Political Violence and Social Control in the Global Era*. New York: New York University Press.

Stryker, Sheldon. 1968. "Identity Salience and Role Performance: The Relevance of Symbolic Interaction Theory for Family Research." *Journal of Marriage and Family* 30:558–564.

Stryker, Sheldon. 2000. "Identity Competition: Key to Differential Social Movement Participation?" In *Self, Identity, and Social Movements*, edited by S. Stryker, T. J. Owens, and R. W. White. Minneapolis: University of Minnesota Press.

Stryker, Sheldon, Timothy J. Owens, and Robert W. White, eds. 2000. *Self, Identity, and Social Movements*. Minneapolis: University of Minnesota Press.

Sullivan, Christopher M., Cyanne E. Loyle, and Christian Davenport. 2012. "The Coercive Weight of the Past: Temporal Dependence and the Conflict-Repression Nexus in the Northern Ireland 'Troubles.'" *International Interactions* 38(4):426–442.

Swidler, Ann. 1986. "Culture in Action: Symbols and Strategies." *American Sociological Review* 51(2):273–286.

Swidler, Ann. 1995. "Cultural Power and Social Movements." In *Social Movements and Culture*, edited by H. Johnston and B. Klandersmans, 25–40. Minneapolis: University of Minnesota Press.

Tarrow, Sidney. 1994. *Power in Movement: Social Movements, Collective Action and Politics*. New York: Cambridge University Press.

Taylor, Michael. 1988. "Rationality and Revolutionary Collective Action." In *Rationality and Revolution*, edited by M. Taylor, 63–97. Cambridge: Cambridge University Press.

Taylor, Michael. 1989. "Social Movement Continuity: The Women's Movement in Abeyance." *American Sociological Review* 54:761–775.

Taylor, Verta and Nancy Whittier. 1992. "Collective Identity in Social Movement Communities." In *Frontiers in Social Movement Theory*, edited by A. Morris and C. Mueller, 104–129. New Haven, CT: Yale University Press.

Thien, Madeleine. 2017. "Tiananmen Square: The Silences Left by the Massacre." *The Guardian*, June 9.

Tilly, Charles. 1978. *From Mobilization to Revolution*. Reading, MA: Addison-Wesley Publishing.

Tucker, Evan. 2013. "Who Needs the NSA When We Have Facebook?" In *Life during Wartime: Resisting Counterinsurgency*, edited by K. Williams, W. Munger, and L. Messersmith-Glavin, 289–312. Oakland, CA: AK Press.

Turley, Jonathan. 2012. "The NDAA's Historic Assault on American Liberty." *The Guardian*, January 2.

Vitale, Alex S. 2007. "The Command and Control and Miami Models at the 2004 Republican National Convention: New Forms of Policing Protests." *Mobilization: An International Quarterly* 12(4):403–415.

Voss, Kim. 1998. "Claim Making and the Framing of Defeats: The Interpretation of Losses by American and British Labor Activists, 1886–1895." In *Challenging Authority: The Historical Study of Contentious Politics*, edited by M. P. Hanagan, L. P. Moch, and Wayne Ph Te Brake. Minneapolis: University of Minnesota Press.

Walker, Samuel. 1977. *A Critical History of Police Reform: The Emergence of Professionalism*. Lexington, MA: Lexington Books.

Weinstein, Jeremy M. 2006. *Inside Rebellion: The Politics of Insurgent Violence*. New York: Cambridge University Press.

White, Robert. 1989. "From Peaceful Protest to Guerilla War: Micromobilization of the Provisional Irish Republican Army." *American Journal of Sociology* 94(6):1277–1302.

White, Robert. 1993. "On Measuring Political Violence: Northern Ireland, 1969–1980." *American Sociological Review* 58:575–585.

Williams, Kristian. 2013. "Introduction." In *Life during Wartime: Resisting Counterinsurgency*, edited by K. Williams, W. Munger, and L. Messersmith-Glavin, 5–25. Oakland, CA: AK Press.

Williams, Kristian. 2014. "The Other Side of the COIN: Counterinsurgency and Community Policing." In *Life during Wartime: Resisting Counterinsurgency*, edited by K. Williams, W. Munger, and L. Messersmith-Glavin. Oakland, CA: AK Press.

Wiltfang, Gregory L. and Doug McAdam. 1991. "The Costs and Risks of Social Activism: A Study of Sanctuary Movement Activism." *Social Forces* 69(4):987–1010.

Wood, Elisabeth Jean. 2001. "The Emotional Benefits of Insurgency in El Salvador." In *Passionate Politics: Emotions and Social Movements*, edited by J. Goodwin, J. M. Jasper, and F. Polletta, 267–281. Chicago: University of Chicago Press.

Wood, Lesley J. 2014. *Crisis and Control: The Militarization of Protest Policing*. Chicago: Pluto Press.

Woodhouse, Leighton. 2012. "How the Pursuit of Animal Liberation Activists Became among the FBI's 'Highest Domestic Terrorism Priorities.'" *Huffington Post*, October 5.

Yoder, Traci. 2018. "Conservative-Led Anti-Protest Legislation Already Doubled since Last Year." Retrieved March 31, 2021 (https://www.nlg.org/conservative-led-anti-protest-legislation-already-doubled-since-last-year/).

Zwerman, Gilda and Patricia Steinhoff. 2005. "When Activists Ask for Trouble: State-Dissident Interactions and the New Left Cycle of Resistance in the United States and Japan." In *Repression and Mobilization*, edited by C. Davenport, H. Johnston, and C. Mueller, 85–107. Minneapolis: University of Minnesota Press.

Zwerman, Gilda and Patricia Steinhoff. 2012. "The Remains of the Movement: The Role of Legal Support Networks in Leaving Violence while Sustaining Movement Identity." *Mobilization: An International Journal* 17(1):67–84.

Index

About the Author

HEIDI REYNOLDS-STENSON is an assistant professor of sociology and criminology at Colorado State University Pueblo. Her research focuses on social movements, repression, and policing. Her academic work has appeared in the *American Journal of Sociology*, *Mobilization*, *Social Movement Studies*, *American Behavioral Scientist*, *Social Currents*, and *Social Science Quarterly*.

Available titles in the Critical Issues in Crime and Society series:

Laura S. Abrams and Ben Anderson-Nathe, *Compassionate Confinement: A Year in the Life of Unit C*

Laura S. Abrams and Diane J. Terry, *Everyday Desistance: The Transition to Adulthood among Formerly Incarcerated Youth*

Tammy L. Anderson, ed., *Neither Villain nor Victim: Empowerment and Agency among Women Substance Abusers*

Miriam Boeri, *Women on Ice: Methamphetamine Use among Suburban Women*

Christian L. Bolden, *Out of the Red: My Life of Gangs, Prison, and Redemption*

Scott A. Bonn, *Mass Deception: Moral Panic and the U.S. War on Iraq*

Mary Bosworth and Jeanne Flavin, eds., *Race, Gender, and Punishment: From Colonialism to the War on Terror*

Henry H. Brownstein, Timothy M. Mulcahy, and Johannes Huessy, *The Methamphetamine Industry in America: Transnational Cartels and Local Entrepreneurs*

Loretta Capeheart and Dragan Milovanovic, *Social Justice: Theories, Issues, and Movements*, revised and expanded edition

Alexandra Cox, *Trapped in a Vice: The Consequences of Confinement for Young People*

Anna Curtis, *Dangerous Masculinity: Fatherhood, Race, and Security inside America's Prisons*

Walter S. DeKeseredy and Martin D. Schwartz, *Dangerous Exits: Escaping Abusive Relationships in Rural America*

Patricia E. Erickson and Steven K. Erickson, *Crime, Punishment, and Mental Illness: Law and the Behavioral Sciences in Conflict*

Jamie J. Fader, *Falling Back: Incarceration and Transitions to Adulthood among Urban Youth*

Luis A. Fernandez, *Policing Dissent: Social Control and the Anti-Globalization Movement*

Mike King, *When Riot Cops Are Not Enough: The Policing and Repression of Occupy Oakland*

Ronald C. Kramer, *Carbon Criminals, Climate Crimes*

Timothy R. Lauger, *Real Gangstas: Legitimacy, Reputation, and Violence in the Intergang Environment*

Margaret Leigey, *The Forgotten Men: Serving a Life without Parole Sentence*

Andrea Leverentz, *The Ex-Prisoner's Dilemma: How Women Negotiate Competing Narratives of Reentry and Desistance*

Ethan Czuy Levine, *Rape by the Numbers: Producing and Contesting Scientific Knowledge about Sexual Violence*

Clara S. Lewis, *Tough on Hate? The Cultural Politics of Hate Crimes*

Michael J. Lynch, *Big Prisons, Big Dreams: Crime and the Failure of America's Penal System*

Liam Martin, *The Social Logic of Recidivism: Cultural Capital from Prisons to the Streets*

Allison McKim, *Addicted to Rehab: Race, Gender, and Drugs in the Era of Mass Incarceration*

Raymond J. Michalowski and Ronald C. Kramer, eds., *State-Corporate Crime: Wrongdoing at the Intersection of Business and Government*

Susan L. Miller, *Victims as Offenders: The Paradox of Women's Violence in Relationships*

Torin Monahan, *Surveillance in the Time of Insecurity*

Torin Monahan and Rodolfo D. Torres, eds., *Schools under Surveillance: Cultures of Control in Public Education*

Ana Muñiz, *Police, Power, and the Production of Racial Boundaries*

Marianne O. Nielsen and Linda M. Robyn, *Colonialism Is Crime*

Leslie Paik, *Discretionary Justice: Looking inside a Juvenile Drug Court*

Anthony M. Platt, *The Child Savers: The Invention of Delinquency*, 40th anniversary edition, with an introduction and critical commentaries compiled by Miroslava Chávez-García

Lois Presser, *Why We Harm*

Joshua M. Price, *Prison and Social Death*

Heidi Reynolds-Stenson, *Cultures of Resistance: Collective Action and Rationality in the Anti-Terror Age*

Diana Rickard, *Sex Offenders, Stigma, and Social Control*

Jeffrey Ian Ross, ed., *The Globalization of Supermax Prisons*

Dawn L. Rothe and Christopher W. Mullins, eds., *State Crime: Current Perspectives*

Jodi Schorb, *Reading Prisoners: Literature, Literacy, and the Transformation of American Punishment, 1700–1845*

Susan F. Sharp, *Hidden Victims: The Effects of the Death Penalty on Families of the Accused*

Susan F. Sharp, *Mean Lives, Mean Laws: Oklahoma's Women Prisoners*

Robert H. Tillman and Michael L. Indergaard, *Pump and Dump: The Rancid Rules of the New Economy*

Mariana Valverde, *Law and Order: Images, Meanings, Myths*

Michael Welch, *Crimes of Power and States of Impunity: The U.S. Response to Terror*

Michael Welch, *Scapegoats of September 11th: Hate Crimes and State Crimes in the War on Terror*

Saundra D. Westervelt and Kimberly J. Cook, *Life after Death Row: Exonerees' Search for Community and Identity*